CONCEPTUAL ISSUES IN PSYCHOANALYSIS

CONCEPTUAL ISSUES IN PSYCHOANALYSIS

Essays in History and Method

John E. Gedo

THE ANALYTIC PRESS

The Analytic Press

Distributed solely by

Lawrence Erlbaum Associates, Inc., Publishers
365 Broadway
Hillsdale, New Jersey 07642

Library of Congress Cataloging-in-Publication Data

Gedo, John E.
   Conceptual issues in psychoanalysis.

   Bibliography: p.
   Includes index.
   1. Psychoanalysis—History.   2. Psychoanalysis.
I. Title. [DNLM: 1. Psychoanalysis—history.
2. Psychoanalytic Theory.   WM 460 G296c]
RC503.G43   1986   150.19′5′09   86-1245
ISBN 0-88163-050-0

I dedicate this book to the coming generation of psychoanalytic theorists, in the hope that they will be able to look upon our travails with pity and forebearance.

Contents

Epilogue

Acknowledgments

Historical and methodological studies in psychoanalysis present the scholar with daunting obstacles. The challenge of mastering the skills of the intellectual historian and of the epistemologist, in addition to the subject matter of our own discipline, has discouraged activity in this important aspect of our field. My own hesitant efforts, which were to culminate in the present volume, began with the encouragement of various colleagues who entrusted me with special assignments to assess one or another significant development of the psychoanalytic past or present. For this book, I have made a fresh start on most of these topics, and I offer versions revised in important respects in the few instances that reuse portions of previously published work. It seems fitting, nonetheless, to acknowledge the manner in which my interest in the specific topics covered in this volume was initially aroused.

My first commission to study the intellectual history of psychoanalysis came from Germany. The journal *Psyche* asked me for a review of Ferenczi's contributions when, in the late 1960s, his collected works were reissued in German. That task occupied me for the better part of a year and taught me how difficult it is to place the work of an individual author into the context of his own time. Around 1970, *The Psychoanalytic Quarterly* asked me to assess the psychoanalytic writings of David Rapaport. It is noteworthy that the editor, Jacob Arlow, felt the need for such a special article because the *Quarterly* had not been able to procure an acceptable review of the 1967 edition of Rapaport's *Collected Papers*. When I immersed myself in the study of his immense *oeuvre*, I could well understand the general reluctance to undertake such time-consuming labors requiring perfectionistic attention to detail.

My awareness of the importance of the responses of Lou Andreas-Salomé to the psychoanalytic controversies of her day was one result of preparing a review of her correspondence with Sigmund Freud for the *Journal of the American Psychoanalytic Association*. In contrast, my first attempt to make a historical judgment concerning the contributions of Heinz Kohut came about when I acceded to Kohut's personal request to provide such a commentary when the Chicago psychoanalytic community honored him on the occasion of his 60th birthday.

Emboldened by the favorable reception of my early forays into intellectual history, in the mid-1970s I succumbed to the blandishments of George Pollock to collaborate in editing a volume of papers, all produced by faculty members of the Chicago Institute, on Freud's intellectual background, the scientific methodology of his work, and the problems of his relations with followers. In preparing extensive editorial comments on the materials included in the book (some of which were studies of my own, others written in collaboration with a variety of colleagues), I gained the experience needed to prepare me for the present work. And in a more restricted sense, that exposure to the Freudian universe, "the fusion of science and humanism," as Pollock and I called it, enabled me to accept the invitation of Paul Stepansky to contribute an essay to *Freud: Appraisals and Reappraisals*, which he has edited. That paper formed the backbone of the Freud chapter in this book.

On the methodological side, I have based much of my discussion on two recent projects undertaken at the invitation of the editors of *Psychoanalytic Inquiry*. Both papers were topical essays in response to books about observational research on infancy: Henri Parens's 1979 monograph on aggression and Joseph Lichtenberg's 1983 survey of the entire field. The chapter dealing with the limitations of the hermeneutic approach to psychoanalytic data was prepared for a conference entitled "Transformations in Psychoanalysis," organized by the California Graduate Institute (Valencia, CA, March 1985). My general introduction has also been published in a book edited by Reed Brockbank and Calvin Settlage, who invited me to provide this historical commentary on intractable differences of opinion among psychoanalysts in response to a discordant meeting of the Psychoanalytic Societies of the West Coast.

I am indebted to a number of professional organizations for opportunities to try out portions of my manuscript in friendly but challenging settings. Chapters 1 and 7 were presented to the Department of Psychiatry at the University of California at San Francisco (December 1984). Chapter 8 was given as the William Menaker Lecture for the New York University Postgraduate Program in Psychoanalysis (May

1985); it was also presented to the North Carolina Psychoanalytic Society (March 1985). Chapter 12 was read at the University of Utah (September 1985) as the Anderson Award Lecture.

The courage to undertake this effort to weld my prior studies into a cohesive whole was stimulated by my editor, Paul E. Stepansky, whose invaluable services in the preparation of three of my previous books I have acknowledged in the past. It was his dedication to the highest standards of scholarship that overcame my reluctance to produce substantially new versions of my preparatory studies, and his superior judgment deleted from this book some cherished old essays I had proposed to inflict on my readers for unworthy reasons of sentiment. I also wish to acknowledge the assistance of my copy editor, Eleanor Starke Kobrin, and that of the most intelligent of moonlighters, my typist, Eva Sandberg.

Chicago
Fall 1985

INTRODUCTION

1

Fluctuat nec Mergitur*

THE TWENTY YEARS SINCE PUBLICATION of Maxwell Gitelson's essay (1964) on the state of psychoanalysis have produced astonishing changes in every aspect of the field. This internal evolution has undoubtedly been hastened by the markedly unfavorable shift of the societal matrix of the profession: loss of public favor and insurance support, competition from a host of aggressively promoted therapies promising easier and quicker results, slippage in the economic status of some of our clientele, and the general turn of American intellectual life away from introspection and humanism (see Gedo, 1983, chapter 16; 1984a, chapter 12). Faced once again with an inhospitable reception reminiscent in many ways of its difficult origins, psychoanalysis has met the challenge through salutary scientific ferment—or, if you will, a bewildering loss of the consensus Gitelson always strove to embody.

In 1964, when he was President of the International Association and spokesman for our establishment, Gitelson's chief concern was the potential absorption of psychoanalysis by an eclectic "dynamic psychiatry" in which our hard-won insights would be misused in arbitrary ways as apotropaic formulae—the sophisticated tools of a contemporary suggestive technique. His fears in this regard have proved to be groundless: far from incorporating psychoanalysis, American psychiatry has all but abandoned psychological methods; its retreat from introspection and empathy did not stop at the tech-

---

*Motto quoted by Freud to predict the survival of psychoanalysis despite dissension. From the seal of the city of Paris, it means: It may waver, but will not sink.

niques of the era of Weir Mitchell, Charcot, and Bernheim, but pursued the age-old expectations of alchemists and exorcists before the Enlightenment to alter human nature through *force majeure*. Psychoanalysts are no longer threatened with the loss of their identity as explorers of the human depths; by the same token, they are no longer in command of the privileges—or subject to the temptations—of being ordained ministers of 20th century mass culture.

Of course, most of us did not share Gitelson's preference for emulating Diogenes: we coveted the rewards of public favor and have reacted to its loss with a decided sense of defeat. I believe this to be true of my generation of analysts, at any rate—those of us trained during the 1950s and currently serving as senior faculty members in psychoanalytic institutes. Our natural reactions have run the gamut, from the impulse to compel the attention of our colleagues (and a wider audience, if possible) through creative iconoclasm, to the opposite extreme, the tendency to enshrine existing theories and procedures as if they were sacred texts and liturgies. It cannot be coincidental that the resultant loss of cohesion within the psychoanalytic community has occurred at one of those junctures in the history of psychoanalysis—times of revolutionary change that seem to recur about once in every generation—when the scientific consensus that has long prevailed would tend to break down in any case. In other words, our loss of public favor probably reflects, at the same time, our diminishing clinical and scientific self-confidence.

Of course, it is something of a paradox to believe that clinical psychoanalysts have lost faith in their effectiveness while the profession has been proclaiming that the scope of its therapeutic tools has steadily widened (cf. Panel, 1954). Yet the dwindling proportion of analytic work (in the strict definition of the term) in the professional activities of members of the American Psychoanalytic Association attests to this disenchantment: whatever the claims of optimistic expansionists may be about their favorable results with the analytic method (e.g., Gedo, 1981a, 1984a), the routine technique practiced throughout the country has led to disappointing outcomes. These setbacks have ranged from the relatively low proportion of analyses found to have culminated in mutually agreed upon termination (see Erle, 1979; Erle & Goldberg, 1984); through the unsatisfactory results obtained with patients treated at the Menninger Clinic via psychoanalysis, when compared with matched groups of patients who received analytically informed psychotherapy there (Wallerstein, 1983); to the sobering yield of a variety of follow-up investigations (e.g., Firestein, 1978; Schlessinger & Robbins, 1983). It seems that collectively we have failed to teach the graduates of our training programs to carry out our difficult therapeutic prescriptions with the requisite skill. Little wonder that as a group they shy away from attempting what is beyónd their reach and prefer to offer their patients psychotherapeutic alternatives.

At the same time, there is good reason to believe that our contemporary technical armamentarium is capable of achieving more than analysis could aim for when our teachers began their careers (cf. Freud, 1937a). I can certainly assert this on the basis of personal experience, as I have extensively reported elsewhere (Gedo, 1979; 1981b; 1984a, chapter 2). It is self-evident that our better clinicians have always obtained results superior to the prevailing standards, of course; but as our clinical understanding has expanded, so have our expectations. Analysts can always apply the clinical theories they have learned to the therapeutic contingencies they currently encounter in practice, often with striking therapeutic benefit—but these results do not demonstrate the validity and relevance of the interpretations offered. Good results may flow from the use of appropriate analytic methods, or those results may merely reflect the charisma of the therapist. In order to benefit from the suggestive effects of such a pseudoanalytic encounter, however, the analysand needs to experience the magic of an omniscient healer. In other words, we tend to profit most from these unintended nonanalytic transactions whenever we have full confidence in our theories and technical methods.

When American psychoanalysis reached the peak of its popular success in the years following World War II, our collective approach had scarcely departed from the positions of the aged Freud. The cutting edge of progress was the ego psychology promulgated by Heinz Hartmann and his co-workers (see chapter 5, this volume) or, for the devil's advocates among us, the Kleinian doctrines emanating from the British Society (chapter 6, this volume). We had a virtual monopoly on psychological medicine and could fill our analytic schedules while selecting patients in accord with the most stringent criteria of analyzability. More recently, in extensive travels around the Continent as lecturer, site visitor for the Association, or private person, I have found no colleague able to pursue such a policy. Individuals seeking analysis for neurotic problems confined to oedipal issues are scarcely to be found.

Most observers seem to agree with Kohut (1977), who held that new forms of psychopathology have become prevalent among our clientele, albeit few would concur with Kohut's nosological suggestion that the typical sickness of our time is the incapacity to fulfill one's destiny. Although we lack the evidence to resolve this question definitively, I am convinced that our diagnostic impressions have changed not because the people who consult us are significantly different from their predecessors 25 or 50 years ago, but because the preconscious schemata we use to process our observations have gradually evolved in startling ways. Thus the apparent changes in potential analysands merely reflect the general progress of psychoanalysis in the past generation.

Perhaps the clearest example of one step in this evolution was the initial impact of Kohut's own work (1966a, 1971). Although he was at first careful to point out that he was focusing on observations widely reported for some time by many colleagues—he subtitled his 1971 book on these matters an *attempt* to be systematic—the very fact that Kohut brought these observations into the central position they occupied in his mature work and thereby captured the attention of a wide segment of the analytic community soon led him and a set of followers "more Catholic than the Pope" to assume that a novel group of nosological entities had been "discovered." A subjective report of the great impact of this "discovery" on an analytic novice troubled by her ineffectiveness exemplifies the problems in our training I have already outlined (see Goldberg, 1978, p. 203).

It did not take long for those whose analytic perplexities were relieved by replacing the schemata they had employed with the new ones proferred in Kohut's writings to stop using the old conceptual categories altogether. Their observations, sometimes valid, were no longer thought of as examples of the universally expectable emergence of one or another "narcissistic" transference constellation. In the first stage of their shift to a new clinical theory, they would diagnose the particular analysand under observation as a sufferer from a "narcissistic personality disturbance." A new illness had appeared on the social scene! Around 1970, in our extensive personal discussions, Kohut estimated that about four patients out of ten in his practice properly belonged to this new nosological category.

But expanding public interest in his exciting innovations soon led Kohut, and a growing band of students, continually to revise these estimates upward. At the present time, the Kohutians I most respect continue to believe, on reflection, that the concepts of traditional Freudian psychoanalysis are fully adequate in a small handful of cases. In other words, they adhere to the distinction between Guilty Man and Tragic Man that Kohut proposed in 1977, but they feel that Guilty Man is a dying breed, no longer produced in late 20th century industrial societies. Hence they use Kohut's clinical concepts as the (all-but-) universal explanatory framework for their analytic activities; they have become "self-psychologists." It is predictable that those who accept this framework will never again encounter a live patient of the kind who populated our consulting rooms before we read Kohut's revolutionary message, and the observations of those analysts who continue to do so will be explained by the adherents of "self psychology" as iatrogenic artifacts.

I have summarized the historical evolution of Kohut's impact on our community not because its progression has been exceptional; on the contrary, I regard it as entirely typical. Let me review the steps I have outlined in terms of generalizations applicable across a broad range of examples. First, a set of clinical observations is highlighted as a previously neglected aspect of clinical theory. Next, those instances in which the novel observations seem to be significant are defined as a nosological entity that was hitherto overlooked. Third, the mode of functioning characteristic of the new class of pathology is detected in ever wider circles of patients in analysis. As a logical consequence of this realization, the patterns in question lose their relevance for differential diagnosis and are elevated into the cardinal feature of a new theoretical framework intended to replace a previous psychoanalytic paradigm. Skeptics will then collect clinical observations poorly explained within this latest clinical theory, and the process of revision begins anew.

Our difficulties as a scientific community stem from the fact that our consensus inevitably breaks down at each stage of this normal progression. To return to the illustrative case of Kohut's impact on American psychoanalysis: even the preliminary announcement of his basic clinical findings (Kohut, 1968), initially delivered under the impeccable auspices of the New York Psychoanalytic Society as a Brill Lecture and published in that most traditional forum, *The Psychoanalytic Study of the Child*, failed to carry universal conviction. Every clinician had, of course, encountered the phenomena of idealization and subject-centered grandiosity Kohut was calling to our attention with such emphasis, but only a minority were prepared to accept his main conclusion, that the appearance of certain varieties of these behaviors within the analytic transference constitutes the repetition of essentially expectable childhood attitudes of cardinal developmental significance.

In his 1971 book, Kohut clarified his position. He stated that the transference patterns in question are evoked in a more definite manner if the analyst conducts himself in certain ways than if other technical procedures are followed. Depending on individual inclinations, based on emotional preference or pre-existing theoretical commitments, clinicians tried either to promote or to discourage the emergence of those transference patterns Kohut then believed to be pathognomonic of "narcissistic personality disturbance." It should be kept in mind that both choices could, in the hands of skillful analysts, lead to useful therapeutic results. But, as fascinating follow-up studies (Schlessinger & Robbins, 1983) have begun to document, the improvements achieved by following these alternative treatment programs, not to speak of the difficulties left in their wake, are distinct enough to be difficult to compare (see Firestein, 1978; Goldberg, 1978; and the discussion of the results they report in Gedo, 1980).

Some observers, myself included, predicted that the assumption of polemical positions about Kohut's hypotheses would inevitably lead to a split in the analytic community. Partly in an effort to forestall such polarization into extremist factions, I tried, in Models of the Mind (Gedo & Goldberg, 1973), to map out a framework for clinical theory potentially broad enough to accommodate the findings of analysts of every persuasion. Despite the favorable reception of that hierarchical schema, it had little effect on the evolution of psychoanalytic opinion about Kohut's work. Commentaries rejecting his proposals in toto (e.g., Stein, in Panel, 1974) began to appear in tandem with early announcements (e.g., Terman, 1976) about the possibility of developing "Self Psychology"—as Kohut's ideas were now called by his adherents—into a system of purportedly universal applicability. Ecumenicism was now repudiated by both camps, a tendency that gained momentum when Kohut, in his 1977 book, endorsed the most radical claims for his views: the transferences he had originally seen as characteristic of narcissistic pathology were now regarded as ubiquitous. Renamed "self-object transferences," for Kohut these patterns of human relationship now assumed decisive significance in health and disease.

The majority of those who had welcomed Kohut's delineation of so-called idealizing and mirror transferences as promising first approximations in an unfamiliar observational field could not accept his new position, which was widely regarded as reductionistic and therefore scientifically regressive. At the same time, this group of skeptical clinicians continued to disagree with hard-line conservatives who insisted that neurosegenesis is more or less exclusively determined by oedipal issues. Unlike these *retardataires*, or the "self psychologists," the "middle group"—*vide* the earlier controversies within the British Society!—lacked consensus, for it consisted of analysts of heterogeneous views, agreeing only in their "a plague on both their houses" attitude toward the warring camps.

Despite this heterogeneity, it is possible to discern two dominant trends within the uncommitted faction. A large segment of this group, perhaps the majority, is resigned to the theoretical disarray implicit in espousing bits of clinical theory derived from a variety of uncoordinated viewpoints. Sometimes this attitude might better be described as complacent rather than resigned; many colleagues seem to feel no discomfort about switching in an ad hoc manner among Freudian, Mahlerian, Winnicottian, Kohutian, and even Kleinian propositions if these possess some degree of heuristic usefulness. Others try to paper over the underlying incoherence of this procedure by stressing that the work of each author they cite centers on a developmental perspective—as if alternating without apology between incompatible schemata of development were scientifically justified. (Needless to say, I am unwilling to accept such thinking, even if apologies were offered!) Some contributors are keenly aware of the epistemological problems posed by the lack of integration of their clinical concepts. Modell (1983), for one, regards this state of affairs as inevitable and invokes the example of modern physics to justify the need to use complementary theoretical fragments for psychoanalysis.

If the authors I have just described follow the epistemological example of Niels Bohr, there are others within psychoanalysis—George Klein (1976), Roy Schafer (1976), and Hans Loewald (1980) might be cited as the most prominent—who have chosen Albert Einstein as their model in seeking to create a single theory for psychoanalysis based on consistent premises. Thus far, none of these proposals has captured the imagination of any large segment of the analytic community. On one hand, theories that profess to dispense altogether with any metapsychological framework, like those of Klein or Schafer (see also Gill & Holzman, 1976), seem to leave out of account the behavioral phenomena formerly included within the Freudian rubric of the repetition compulsion. To put this differently, psychoanalytic theories that focus exclusively on matters that can be deciphered in terms of their significance within a system of symbolic meanings can scarcely hope to encompass the legacy of the earliest phases of childhood, those preceding the acquisition of symbolic thought.

On the other hand, theorists like Loewald (or Kohut, for that matter), who attempt to ascribe the fundamental patterning of personality to the vicissitudes of early object relations, do not seem to give sufficient emphasis to the importance of inborn capacities in molding the individual's personal destiny. In both cases, I have stressed the *apparent* crux of the authors' theorizing, without necessarily making a judgment about their actual intentions here, because I am at this time only trying to indicate why these various proposals are not likely to win the allegiance of the majority of analysts.

From the point of view of theoretical inclusiveness and coherence, in other words, none of the revisionist systems can rival the structure erected by Freud around the armature of drive theory. Drive theory has continued to serve as the organizing framework used by most analysts, despite repeated demonstrations of its epistemological failings (e.g., Basch, 1976c, 1977; Swanson, 1977) because of the shortcomings of alternative proposals. Those of us who insist on building psychoanalytic theory on epistemologically sound foundations are, for the moment, forced to make do with *developmental* concepts derived from the greatest variety of observable phenomena—a veritable mosaic of evolving capacities in transaction with the infant's milieu (cp. A. Freud, 1965; Gedo & Goldberg, 1973). Although such conceptual schemata can be built on the basis of internally consistent criteria—in other words, they could potentially avoid the use of complementary but mutually inconsistent assumptions—the resulting outline of the progressive acquisition of functional capacities will be useful only in direct proportion to its complexity.

The particular version of such a schema of personality organization that I have advocated (Gedo, 1979, 1981b, 1981c) was intended to serve only as a skeletal suggestion of how the self-organization should be mapped out. Apparently, however, even this simplified hierarchical model has impressed many analysts as too unwieldy for practical purposes. Those who have applied my concepts clinically have rightly pointed out that the schema needs further elaboration (e.g., Gustafson, 1984; Robbins, 1983; Whitehead, 1983).

If efforts to integrate the varied clinical experiences of a hetero-geneous psychoanalytic community are, for the moment, unlikely to result in consensus, this disquieting state of affairs does reflect the stunning expansion of our psychology in the past decade into hither-to unplumbed depths of the human condition. Controversy may con-tinue to rage about the extent to which psychoanalytic technique may legitimately be stretched to accommodate patients whose archaic transferences require various measures "beyond interpretation," to echo the title of my 1979 book. Whatever we may decide to call the analytic therapies through which we succeed in modifying profound disturbances in character that originate within the vicissitudes of the first two or three years of life (see Gedo, 1984a), the clinical observa-tions made in the course of such treatments have profoundly altered our data base. These new findings from the analyses of children and adults are also congruent with the results of psychoanalytically in-formed observational studies of infants—a field recently surveyed by Lichtenberg (1983) and one I discuss in some detail in chapters 10 through 12.

In view of the volume of new information that must be incorporat-ed into our clinical theory, there is no reason to be discouraged about the relative disarray concerning theoretical matters in our ranks. Probably every generation of analysts will abide by one of the concep-tual alternatives available while that cohort is finding its professional identity; it is not reasonable to expect practitioners with decades of experience to adopt radically novel theories. The dominant psycho-analytic paradigm of the decades to come will turn out to be one that appeals to the intellectual elite of the current group of analysts-in-formation; these are the individuals who commit themselves whole-heartedly to the exercise of their demanding analytic craft and gain sufficient technical mastery to obtain better results than those re-ported in the disheartening follow-up studies I have already cited.

In every generation there have been analysts who do better treat-ment than the best we can expect if the model technique of contempo-rary psychoanalysis is optimally performed: without conscious in-tent, they operate in accord with necessary technical precepts that have not as yet been codified in the literature. As Bergin and Lambert

(1978) have shown, such covert aspects of the clinical transaction must account for the effectiveness of a whole variety of therapies poorly grounded in theory. Progress in the theory of psychoanalytic technique takes place when we succeed in formulating explicit therapeutic principles based on consistently successful ad hoc interventions. One illustration from my own work is the recommendation (Gedo, 1984a, chapter 8) to communicate with certain patients suffering from developmental deficits in language skills through affectively charged messages. This is one measure "beyond interpretation" that may be necessitated by the presence of psychopathology referable to the vicissitudes of very early developmental phases—in this instance, language acquisition.

Before such measures are incorporated into the analyst's regular armamentarium,—with an explicit rationale—they are employed more or less preconsciously as part of the analyst's therapeutic art. It is very likely that superior therapists will espouse those clinical theories that offer them convincing rationales for the greatest number of successful technical innovations. By the same token, I suspect that theories will fall into disuse when they can no longer generate successful corollaries in technique. I have the impression that this is the current fate of "ego psychology," the school of thought almost universally accepted in this country in Gitelson's day. Its propositions have never been repudiated, as such, but one hears less and less of them as the focus of psychoanalytic interest shifts away from the realm of intersystemic conflicts, in the direction of the behaviors under the sway of the compulsion to repeat.

Some 65 years ago, Freud, insisting that anyone who took proper account of the phenomena of transference and resistance in psychological treatment qualifies as an analyst, encouraged the maverick therapist, Georg Groddeck to make a commitment to psychoanalysis (Groddeck, 1977, p. 36). In the current atmosphere of sectarian rancor, we can only feel nostalgia for the tolerance of diversity implicit in Freud's attitude. It is true that the integration of important new ideas into the fabric of psychoanalysis was to take place almost entirely in Freud's mind for another twenty years, so that the Founding Father could well afford to be generous toward his professional progeny. By comparison, contemporary psychoanalysis resembles the electorate of a democratic society: those who would gain popular favor must woo the voters by promising them bread and circuses. This social situation may encourage the acceptance of ideas characterized by simplicity rather than rigor, and the creation of analytic superstars distinguished by charisma instead of rationality. No doubt Freud's marked distaste for the New World was based on his understanding that its ethos would subject psychoanalysis to such populist pressures. Let us hope that the voice of the intellect will prevail nonetheless, as he predicted.

HISTORICAL
SECTION

2

Sigmund Freud's Character and the Definition of Psychoanalysis*

CHILDHOOD IN CORINTH

NOT LONG AGO, AT ONE OF OUR national meetings, I was asked to discuss an impressive paper (Abraham, 1982) dealing with the influence of Sigmund Freud's inner life on the intellectual history of psychoanalysis. Informed by the latest results of archival research, the author convincingly argued that Freud's personal difficulties centered on the legacies of his troubled relationship in earliest childhood to his self-centered and volcanic young mother. The paper in question explored the possibility that Freud's clinical theories paid little attention to the pregenital era and *pari passu* to maternal influences stemming from that period of development, because of his defensive need to deny the relevance of those emotional vicissitudes he was unable personally to overcome. Only in his 1931 essay, "Female Sexuality," did Freud acknowledge the primal influence of the pregenital mother on human destiny.

---

*In homage to Freud, I have chosen subtitles that summarize my theses by allusion to the Oedipus myth. I have used foreign phrases in the chapter in the same spirit.

One can hardly dismiss the prima facie plausibility of this straight-forward psychobiographical thesis. To be sure, its proponent seemingly overlooked the self-analytic insight Freud communicated to Fliess in 1899 (Bonaparte, Freud, & Kris, 1954, pp. 218–221) to the effect that the availability of a nursemaid during the second year of his life, when his next sibling was born—and died—had conferred lifesaving benefits on him. In other words, Freud was aware, before he constructed his initial psychoanalytic theory in 1900, that in his own life experience events decisive for character development went back to the preverbal era. Did he then repress this vital piece of insight for the next three decades?

Our answer to this question will depend on our assessment of Freud's character in adult life. As I read her thesis, Abraham (1982) viewed the middle-aged Freud, in the process of erecting his psychoanalytic edifice, as a rather pathetic person, unable to obtain psychological assistance for the archaic problems besetting him. Thus she understood as an evasion Freud's 1931 statement that a boy's ambivalence toward his mother is diminished during their oedipal love affair because of the opportunity to displace its negative component onto his male rivals: In her judgment, such an evolution of the child's relationship with his mother is primarily a defensive maneuver. To complete this picture, she implied that in Freud's own case developments of this kind would have lacked authenticity because the boy's father, far from being a threatening rival, was (in her view) a mild little man. Evaluations of the character of the protagonist thus may turn out to rely on dubious character diagnoses about other actors who have roles in the drama![1]

My own conception of the interplay between Freud's personality and his scientific contributions has changed little since I wrote my first piece of Freudiana (Gedo, 1968) almost twenty years ago. In my opinion, Freud used introspective insights to validate and advance

---

[1]It is also pertinent to note that Abraham's contention is based on a profound misunderstanding of Freud's developmental theory: he did not presuppose that the oedipal child's fantasies about the father-as-potential-castrator are grounded in realistic appraisals of the parent's character. On the contrary, such fantasies are assumed to be the result of the projection of the child's oedipal hostility. Such hostility may be unusually intense whenever the father behaves in a hateful manner (cf. the imago of Claudius in Shakespeare's *Hamlet*), but it is equally likely to be provoked if the parent behaves in a manner that traumatically disappoints the child. As I describe later, Sigmund Freud may have had ample reason to be disillusioned by his father.

the findings of his clinical work with neurotic patients; in other words, his attention was generally focused on the same issues in his own life that he was encountering as matters of central concern in his therapeutic activities. As Gardner (1983) recently showed, analytic discoveries are unlikely to be made in any other way! And Freud himself was clearly testifying to this constraint when he wrote (Bonaparte et al., 1954, pp. 234–235) that self-analysis is basically the application to one's own instance of what one has learned from and about patients: Oedipus does not recapture memories of his infancy; he learns about it from witnesses.

In point of fact, whatever the subjective roots of his intellectual work may have been, Freud's delineation of the Oedipus complex in the late 1890s has stood the test of time. The psychoanalytic consensus today still views oedipal vicissitudes as nuclear for the neurotic conflicts of adults. If many of us are equally interested in studying a number of other psychological issues as they relate to personality organization, that expansion of concern to preoedipal transactions has been necessitated by the broadening scope of our investigations, beyond the boundaries of neurosis as such, to questions relating to character, as well as creativity. Hence a significant *historical* inquiry must first address itself to Freud's intellectual agenda around the turn of the century, instead of looking for reasons, in his subjective world or elsewhere, for his putative failure to tackle certain problems that interest us today.

During the period most relevant for the thesis we are considering, Freud was seeking a solution for the *general* problem of the psychological influence of the past on the present. We should recall that in *Studies on Hysteria* (Breuer & Freud, 1895) only the pathogenic effects of traumatic events in *adult* life were looked upon as relevant aspects of the past. In the next decade, as Freud gained experience with nonhypnotic methods of exploratory therapy, the etiologically significant traumata he uncovered were invariably infantile-sexual. Consequently, he gradually realized that in the neuroses it is the shadow of the *childhood* past that falls upon the present. By 1900, he understood that his own neurotic conflicts, like those of his hysterical and obsessional patients, were linked to a nexus of repressed childhood fantasies that echoed the manifest themes of Sophocles' *Oedipus Rex*. To gain understanding of these cardinal issues of psychoanalytic psychology—insights that were to insure him a unique place in the history of science—Freud did not need to investigate his troublesome preoedipal transactions with his mother (or with his nursemaid, or his living and dead siblings, or his bewildering extended family).

To put the matter more briefly, I have begun my exposition by citing as a cautionary tale an assessment of Freud's character that miscarried because its author failed to understand that the evolution of his scientific ideas was a logical outcome of certain historical necessities. To be precise, she imagined that Freud should have asked questions of maximal interest to contemporary psychoanalysts, such as the effects of transactions in the second year of life on the organization of personality. But answers about such archaic issues are barely becoming available today as a result of refinements in psychoanalytic technique that permit the management, without untoward consequences, of profound therapeutic regressions that involve largely nonverbal transference enactments (see Gedo, 1981b, 1984a). There was absolutely no way of arriving at valid insights about su h matters before 1900, when Freud's therapeutic technique did not as yet make use of free associative material. To the contrary, Freud's genius showed itself in very large measure in his uncanny ability to pick fruitful problems to investigate, that is, those for which heuristically useful answers could be proposed.

Perhaps, after all, I have merely stated the obvious in stressing that our psychological tools must be used with discretion in weaving the complex web of explanations necessary in historical studies. Yet I feel that it has not been generally appreciated that the relation between psychological conclusions and historical insights is fully reciprocal: We are just as likely to misdiagnose Freud's character if we fail to understand the history of his ideas as we are prone to distort history through psychological reductionism (see Gay, 1976).

OEDIPUS REX

I last considered the problem of Freud's character about a decade ago, when I was putting together a collection of essays (Gedo & Pollock, 1976) intended to present a portrait of our great predecessor. That volume was entitled *Freud: The Fusion of Science and Humanism*—a phrase designed to sum up the man's complexity by means of synecdoche; I shall return to that characterization of Freud later. Despite his well-deserved reputation as a peer of Rousseau and St. Augustine in candid self-exposure, Freud was at the same time an intensely private man, and his family have guarded that privacy with a zeal that borders on secretiveness. Predictably, this policy has led to the very results it was intended to forestall: a spate of recent commentators (e.g., Swales, 1983a) express dissatisfaction with the limited extent of Freud's public candor.

At any rate, on the basis of information in the public domain, it is scarcely possible to fathom the Freudian depths. Consequently, like many other Freud scholars, I have for some time confined my activities in the biographical realm to matters that do not call for intrusion into his private life (see Gedo, 1983, chapters 11–13). I would note, however, that Pollock and I decided to cap our 1976 volume of Freudiana with a specially commissioned essay about the difficulties inherent in writing about a genius of Freud's stature.

The task was entrusted to Heinz Kohut (Gedo & Pollock, 1976, chapter 16), whose then recent clinical hypotheses about idealizing transferences (Kohut, 1971) seemed particularly germane to this theme. When Kohut undertook this assignment, the Freud biographies of prominence were the semiofficial works of such worshipful Freud intimates as Ernest Jones (1953–57) and Max Schur (1972). Consequently, Kohut rightly focused on the distorting influence of psychoanalytic training as such on the work of Freud biographers. He astutely pointed out that the process of steeping themselves in Freud's writings inevitably pulls psychoanalysts into an attitude of placing the Founding Father of their discipline in the position of an ideal object. Kohut also noted a tendency on the part of certain apostates to react to the temptation to overidealize Freud with compensatory efforts to debunk him. At the time he wrote his essay, Kohut had no major example of this genre to offer; the cogency of his formulation has been demonstrated only very recently in such a production as Masson's (1984) thesis that Freud's scientific views were shaped by their advantages or disadvantages for marketing his clinical services!

Be that as it may, the era of Freud studies undertaken only by individuals trained as psychoanalytic clinicians has come to an end. The author of the paper in which Freud was faulted for overlooking the significance of mother-child transactions (Abraham, 1982) is a young psychologist whose doctoral dissertation was a lengthier biographical study—of Sigmund Freud. Her ill-considered judgment about her subject is not likely to be a reaction against idealizing his person in the manner Kohut attributed to psychoanalysts, for she is not a student of psychoanalysis as such but a trained psychologist-biographer whose interest in Freud appears to be secondary to a passionate commitment to women's issues. *Sic transit gloria patris!*

Although persons trained in disciplines other than psychoanalysis are not likely to have mastered the intellectual history of our discipline—unless they happen to be intellectual historians with a specialization in psychoanalysis, a very rare breed, indeed—the entry of a wide spectrum of individuals into the field of Freud studies may well prove to be salutary for the very reasons highlighted by Kohut's pessimistic assessment of the capacity of analysts to avoid severe distortions in their characterization of Freud. I do not mean to imply that nonanalysts will necessarily be free of the need to idealize or to debunk Freud; in point of fact, however, to date most of them do not seem to have fallen into these particular methodological errors. At the same time, in contrast to Abraham's (1982) study, their work often fails to address explicitly the issue of Freud's personality, however germane questions about his character might be for specific scholarly purposes.

Probably the most important effort illustrating such an approach is Frank Sulloway's (1979) major attempt to demonstrate the place of Freud's contributions within the biological thought of his time. Sulloway is a historian of science, and his study is ostensibly confined to intellectual issues for which personality factors should have little or no bearing. Yet his argument that Freud's development as a psychological theorist is better understood in the context of Darwinian evolutionary biology than it is on the basis of the need to order the data he collected in the course of his therapeutic work (and his self-analysis) depends on an unstated assumption about the psychology of Sulloway's subject: Whether a scientist's ideas are more likely to emerge from the matrix of a preexisting theoretical system, from fantasies stimulated by patterns perceived within his observational field, or from one of a variety of ways to combine inductive and deductive modes of inference is very much a matter of character.

In my judgment, Sulloway's thesis presupposes that Freud was a man for whom ideas were more important than personal experiences of other kinds. To examine this view in the detail it deserves would take me too far afield from the confines of this volume; suffice it to say that along with the vast majority of psychoanalytic readers, I found the thesis incredible. Needless to say, Sulloway was prepared for this reception. Indeed, a chapter of his book (see Sulloway, 1979, pp. 445–495) is taken up with a discussion of the "myths" psychoanalysts have, in his view, constructed about Freud and the latter's scientific efforts, prominent among which (according to Sulloway) is their consensus that the decisive factor affecting Freud's ideas was the outcome of his introspective self-inquiry. Here I have no wish to assert that Sulloway is mistaken whereas our fraternity has grasped the truth—I wish only to point out that these respective opinions are the all but inevitable consequences of our commitments: to intellectual history on Sulloway's part and to introspection on ours.[2]

The implications of the foregoing example are, I hope, transparent: Not only do biographers form transferences to Freud (Baron & Pletsch, 1985); many of them choose to study him because he can serve as an externalized alter ego for some aspect of themselves. For Frank Sulloway, he is a fellow Darwinian; for John Gedo, he embodies a fusion of science and humanism. For the elderly Jones, he was the sage Methuselah; to the fortyish Masson, he looks like an ambitious careerist.

THE RIDDLE OF THE SPHINX

For me, the most intriguing, if least believable, Freud portrayal of the recent past is the one Peter Swales (1982a, b, c; 1983a, b, c) has communicated to a select readership in a series of private *feuilletons*. The media have relayed to a wide public one conclusion growing out of his investigations: based on carefully researched circumstantial evidence, Swales argues that Freud impregnated his sister-in-law, Minna Bernays, and then arranged an abortion for her. This inference is only one of a number of similar biographical inferences in which Swales portrays Freud, evidently only on the basis of his overall

---

[2]I have encountered an illuminating example of an identical divergence of opinion, one in which the subject of the biography gave unequivocal testimony about his own view in the matter. At a colloquium at the San Francisco Psychoanalytic Institute (partly available in *Dialogue*, fall 1981), some historians of art flatly contradicted Picasso's own statements about the *personal* meaning of his entire oeuvre. These highly intellectual scholars asserted, with an extraordinary degree of certitude, that the artist's remarks were not to be taken at face value; allegedly, they were (deliberately) intended to conceal an elaborate program of (nonpsychological) intellectual messages encoded within Picasso's work. The psychoanalysts present found this thesis as unbelievable as Sulloway's.

conception of the latter's character, as the embodiment of hidden evil. In comparison, Masson's image of Freud as a "commercial Jew" with dubious ethics is almost endearing.[3]

Although I believe Swales to be grotesquely mistaken in his conception, I should note that unlike Freud's *detractors*, he at least acknowledges his subject's greatness, albeit as a Faustian figure. In light of Swales' complete dismissal of psychoanalysis both as a psychology and as a method of treatment, it may be fruitful to ponder why he has chosen to devote a major portion of his own life to Freud studies. Whatever his reasons, they can only testify to Freud's stature as one of the truly significant figures of the recent past. It is particularly striking that today, almost a century after he began to develop his central ideas, Freud is still seen as one of the architects of our civilization. For psychoanalysts, of course, this longevity gives him the aura of *vir heroicus sublimis;* Swales, for his part, characterizes him as a veritable Prince of Darkness. I suspect that Freud (1917a) himself may have had such images in mind when he bracketed his work with those of Copernicus and Darwin as turning points in Western cosmology.

It is fruitless to engage in arguments about matters of faith and morals, and I do not discuss the fascinating work of Peter Swales in order to refute it. I cite him, instead, because his view exemplifies what I believe to be true of almost every Freud biographer: We all tend to experience our subject as a contemporaneous presence rather than as a figure from a specific historical period no longer familiar to us. Bruno Bettelheim (1983) called attention to the pitfall of misreading Freud in modern English translation: His oeuvre is in fact encoded in a German no longer spoken by our contemporaries. Bettelheim's *caveat lector* is well taken, but the issue should not be construed narrowly as a matter of language. Much as we Freudians

---

[3]For my purposes here, the validity of the "charge" that Freud seduced Minna Bernays is not a matter of importance, for I cannot view the possibility of such an affair as a mark of evil. On the contrary, had Freud been capable of setting up such a ménage-à-trois, my estimation of his human qualities would be raised. It was Carl Jung, the earliest propagator of the sexual fantasy about Freud and Minna, who used this allegation as a rationale for his disillusionment with his mentor (Billinsky, 1969). As I have tried to show elsewhere (Gedo, 1983, chapter 13), Jung never overcame a certain confusion between himself and Freud; it was he who more than once insisted on living in a ménage-à-trois. Hence I give *his* testimony little credence in this matter. Alas, I cannot believe that Freud was capable of seducing anyone. His lifelong inhibition vis-à-vis women stood in the way, as Abraham (1982) convincingly argues.

may dislike it, the West has gradually slipped into the postmodern era, one that is no longer the age of Freud (cf. Gedo, 1972a).

There is some flavor of paradox about the contemporary upsurge of interest in Freud as a person, for his intellectual heritage finds less and less favor with the public in an age of mass culture (see Gedo, 1983, Epilogue; 1984a, chapter 12). Yet this apparent discrepancy between acceptance of a man's contribution and interest in his person may well be characteristic of our era—witness the emergence of literary or artistic superstars whose main activities are confined to self-promotion. Hence, awesome personalities of past centuries, like Michelangelo, elicit an unceasing stream of biographical attention, although nothing could be less congenial to the spirit of the late 20th century than Michelangelo's undeviating commitment to the human figure or his fervent religiosity. Pablo Picasso is a more recent example of a genius who attracts more attention than does his work; in contrast, his great peer and contemporary Henri Matisse enjoys the benefits of biographical neglect.

I have taken a roundabout way to say that Sigmund Freud, like Picasso and Michelangelo, seems to be one of those historical figures whose life is destined to become an ideal for a significant part of the public. Culture heroes are continually reinvented by new devotees in the image the latter require; to make this process possible, the actual historical context of their activities must be disavowed. An author like Swales, for example, dazzles his readers with his detective work as an archivist and collector of testimonies, but with this mass of material he creates a gestalt that impresses me as brilliant science fiction—a portrait of Freud as if he were a member of the contemporary drug scene electing to spend his life under the yoke of clinical responsibility for the afflicted.[4]

THE LOVE OF JOCASTA

When, on the eve of the second World War, Freud died, I was eleven years old; just ahead of *dies irae*, my family had left Central Europe.

---

[4]I suspect that no one can imagine how burdensome psychoanalytic work as Freud practiced it is unless he or she has performed it on a continuous and full-time basis. If most American psychoanalysts devote less than a third of their professional time to the task, the explanation for this choice must lie, in large measure, in the fact that their alternative activities—research, teaching, administration, or even doing other forms of therapy—are experienced as much less difficult.

The decade of my adolescence, arguably the most catastrophic period in the history of the West, I spent (*fato profugis*, as Freud would have said) on three other continents. When I began my psychoanalytic apprenticeship at the age of 26, the discipline had barely absorbed the shock of losing its founder. I believe I was propelled into the field not only by the usual need to unravel the tangles of my personal history, otherwise banal enough, but also by a wish to sort out the influence of a succession of civilizations on my inner world. If family tradition made me into a *médicin malgré lui*, I have been an amateur historian from inner necessities even more pressing. Insofar as I know, this set of commitments is not to be found any more in the psychoanalytic community.

I mention these personal matters only to underscore my own emotional bias about the problem of Freud's character, not to lay claim to professional credentials as a historian. For me, he stands for the world of my grandfather—an exact contemporary who was, like Freud, educated at the University of Vienna. I cannot assert that such a perspective is more *cogent* than those of Sulloway, Swales, or Masson, only that it can illuminate certain aspects of Freud's thought and his behavior that may appear to be based on personal idiosyncrasies *if* we fail to distinguish the late 19th century from the end of the 20th. Even the best educated segments of the American public have been so caught up in the popular demand for current "relevance" that their knowledge of Freud's early milieu is unlikely to go beyond the information contained in Carl Schorske's (1980) provocative book, or that of Peter Gay (1978).

But works of that kind, excellent as they are, do not speak to the point of the cultural context within which an *homme moyen cultivé*, such as the youthful Freud, operates—they are focused, and properly so, on the summits of civilized achievement, like Freud's mature oeuvre. Nor do we possess Central European counterparts to the great French, Russian, or English novels of manners of the 19th century to help us to get our bearings in that archaic world, the *Kaiserliches und Königliches Reich* of Franz Josef. Freud did not emerge from the milieu of *Die Fledermaus* or *Der Rosenkavalier*—but neither are we likely to capture his spirit by falsely assigning him to the ambiance of the East European *shtetl*, even if his forebears did migrate to the Habsburg Empire from the east.

How does the point of view I espouse alter our perception of Freud's activities? Let us take as an initial illustration the current feminist critique of Freud, a good (and relatively muted) example of which is provided by the paper (Abraham, 1982) with which I began this chapter. It requires no expertise about Central Europe or the 19th century to recognize that its author commits a solecism in expecting Freud to possess late 20th century insights about the role of mothers in the emotional development of their children. But the critique of psychoanalysis (i.e., the product of Freud's intellect) implicit in this and similar feminist statements accuses its inventor of a contemptuous bias against women, presumably because of the patriarchal nature of the "Victorian" bourgeoisie.

In my judgment, nothing could be further from the truth: Freud impresses me as a man whose admiration and respect for women was quite out of the ordinary—not only for the Victorian age, but in an absolute sense.[5] The evidence for this conclusion is ubiquitous; hence, I shall here confine myself to citing the fact that as a result of Freud's attitude women found a welcome within psychoanalytic practice with full equality earlier than in any other profession. I had always assumed that it was the unusual qualities of some of the early female recruits to his cause, such as Lou Andreas-Salomé, that helped Freud to do better than his contemporaries in this regard. From the unexpurgated edition of the Fliess correspondence (Masson, 1985) we may conclude, however, that in the late 1890s Freud helped his patient Emma Eckstein to establish a "psychoanalytic" practice—in

---

[5]The psychological roots of this propensity are not strictly germane for my thesis, but they are easy to state: I assume that they stemmed from Freud's hope to reestablish the qualities of his trusting relationship to his nursemaid before her dismissal for petty theft (see Jones, 1953, pp. 5–6). Hypotheses about Freud's relations with women that assume that these might repeat aspects of the disappointment with his mother overlook the efficient operation of characterological defenses against such potential calamities. Insofar as I can judge, Freud was threatened by setbacks of that kind only once or twice in his lifetime, when he fell into relationships characterized by aspects of an archaic transference.

As I have described elsewhere (Gedo, 1968), this conception best fits Freud's excessively trusting attitude toward Wilhelm Fliess. Masson (1984) has correctly pointed out that on the occasion of the surgery Fliess performed on Freud's patient "Irma," this unwarranted confidence led Freud to condone an act of malpractice on the part of Fliess. Unlike Masson, I do not understand this as an act of evil-doing; I see it, instead, as a repetition of Freud's childhood involvement with the criminality of his nursemaid. In his overly empathic response to Carl Jung's confession of a sexual involvement with the latter's patient, Sabina Spielrein (see Carotenuto, 1982; Gedo, 1983, chapter 12; McGuire, 1974), Freud may once again have repeated the same pattern. In neither case did the transference, if such it was, involve negative aspects of Freud's infantile relations with women.

other words, he promoted the talents and careers of women even if they did not happen to be Princesses,[6] or the presumed *inamorata* of Nietzsche and Rilke, or the daughters of Louis Tiffany and Sigmund Freud . . . .

All of which leads me to the conclusion that Freud's feminist critics confuse the Central European *bourgeoise* of 1900 with her American greatgranddaughters of today. They cannot even imagine how devastating are the effects of the actual oppression of women in a backward society—they do not seem to be familiar with the heroines of Chekhov, to cite a parallel from the same era, if not exactly the right milieu or social class. Girls raised in such circumstances are not simply victims (or transvestite rebels, as Isaac Bashevis Singer would impishly have us believe)—they typically develop complex disturbances of character, like those of my grandmothers, or the protagonist of *The Seagull!* It is true that Freud believed this fate to be essentially unavoidable and therefore assigned universality to psychological developments that *can* be avoided by the happy few. But is this a valid reason for drawing inferences about his character based on his alleged misogyny?

THE CRIMES OF LAIUS

Not to overburden this chapter with examples, I shall take up only one other issue I deem to be incomprehensible without historical perspective: that of Freud's integrity, so insistently challenged by Swales and Masson. I cannot here examine the very convoluted particulars of each specific charge leveled against Freud by accusers— that task would require a monograph after years of detailed study. I wish to focus instead on the very definition of "integrity," a concept I believe to be tightly culture bound.

I would like to approach this problem by considering one of the matters Swales (1982b) has stressed in his evolving indictment of Freud—the charge I have already alluded to, that Freud had an affair with his sister-in-law. As I stated earlier, it is difficult for me to grasp

---

[6]In addition to Marie Bonaparte, Lou Salomé could also perhaps claim this title: her husband, "Professor Andreas," is said to have been a member of the famous Georgian family of the Princes Bagraton. I am unable to furnish a scholarly reference for this assertion; I found it some years ago in the memoirs of a Hungarian journalist related to Ferenczi, who claimed she was a friend of the family (Dénes, 1970).

why the possibility of such an action should be evaluated in moral terms.[7] Such moral judgments were hardly uncommon in the 19th century: Freud's well-known distaste for America was based in part on his opinion that our Puritan heritage would ensure moralizing about sexuality for a long time to come. The old attitudes, which have largely disappeared from public view, seem to have made a startling reappearance in the writings of Swales.

At any rate, Freud's *integrity* in the sexual sphere should be evaluated in accord with his own moral standards, rather than those of later observers. In this regard, he is hardly likely to have been greatly different from his peers; no Central European gentleman was expected to be monogamous. I do not think it is an exaggeration to propose that the philandering heroes of Viennese operetta truly represented a cultural *ideal*. The concept has reached our day in the form of the celebrated joke about the courtesan and the Hussar: When the morning after, she gently reminds him about money, he responds, his spurs clicking, "But Madame, a Hungarian officer *never* takes money!"[8]

Although I do not think that Freud had the personal freedom to console himself with his sister-in-law for the miseries of his sour marriage, I also doubt that he was *semper fidelis*—only a plaster saint would have been faithful under the circumstances. The whole matter is, of course, intimately connected with the oppression of women and their resultant, inevitable hostility to males. The point was best made by Lampedusa, in *The Leopard*, his elegy for the *ancien régime*. When his confessor reproves him for frequenting prostitutes, the Prince angrily rejoins that the sin is upon the head of his wife, who in decades of marriage had never permitted him to view her navel! Bruno Bettelheim (personal communication) quotes one of his uncles,

---

[7]As a matter of fact, I have always believed that one of Freud's greatest (and probably most enduring) contributions to our civilization has been his persuasive recategorization of private behaviors, taking them out of the sphere of absolute morality and permitting their assessment in pragmatic terms, in accord with the moral principle of *nihil nocere*.

[8]The aspect of the Sabina Spielrein-Carl Jung story that still has the power to shock is Jung's response to the protest of Spielrein's mother about the seduction of her daughter, who was Jung's patient at the Burghölzli, a public institution (see Carotenuto, 1982, pp. 93–95). Jung is said to have replied that the family would have grounds for complaint if he had continued (!) to receive payment for his professional services. And he offered to break off the affair if the family resumed tipping him! By then, Switzerland had clearly suffered a great decline in public morality as a consequence of centuries of democratization . . .

who claimed to have gone to the brothels with Sigmund Freud. *Honi soit qui mal y pense.*

Masson's charge that Freud changed his scientific views to conform with the desiderata of establishing a lucrative practice would, if true, cast very serious doubts on Freud's integrity. Masson has put the accusation badly, for the seduction theory Freud abandoned would, on purely prudential grounds, have served him much better than did that of the Oedipus complex. But we should not dismiss this challenge simply because it is made maladroitly, for Freud's covetous attitude toward money was rather unusual in a Central European intellectual, as he himself recognized. The prevalent cultural *mores* demanded a prudish distaste for gold.

In his elementary instructions to psychoanalysts about setting conditions for beginning treatment, Freud (1913) advocated maximally rational attitudes about money matters, but he often fell short of this ideal. Thus in 1918 he took up a collection on behalf of his destitute ex-patient, the Wolf Man, largely because prior to 1914 he had charged him extraordinary fees. During the postwar inflation, he did not hesitate to confine his practice to patients who could pay him in foreign currency (see Jones, 1957, p. 29). I believe these behaviors of Freud betray a conflict of some intensity about the possibility of exploiting (or being exploited) for financial gain. The rules of thumb he recommended to his colleagues to avoid such difficulties with patients are effective; how extraordinary they must have seemed in the Vienna of 75 years ago can be gleaned from the fact that until the second World War, Central European professionals often rendered their accounts on a yearly basis! *Pecunia olet . . .*

Freud's difficulties about money should not surprise us, for it is reasonably clear that during his childhood members of his family were engaged in felonious "financial" activities. As Freud (1900, pp. 136–145) reported in his Dreambook, his uncle "with the yellow beard" was sentenced to prison for such a crime. Maria Török (1979) has shown that this offense involved the passing of counterfeit [Russian] currency. Note the similarity to Freud's screen memory about his Czech nursemaid's petty thefts! Török (personal communication) has unearthed the records of the trial and discovered that the counterfeit rubles were produced in Manchester. She has inferred, undoubtedly correctly, that Freud's half-brothers, who were Manchester residents, must have been implicated.

Moreover, Swales (1983a), who is apparently unaware of the fore-going information, reports that Freud's future wife and her mother came to Vienna from Hamburg in the early 1880s, decades after the imprisonment of Freud's uncle, because her father, Herr Bernays, was then in prison—on a charge of counterfeiting! It begins to sound as if the secretiveness of the Freuds is designed to hide something truly shameful about Jacob, Sigmund's father.

The manner in which Jacob Freud earned a living in Vienna is an unsolved mystery. If the criminal activities of other members of the family are any indication, we may now have an answer. Should Jacob have, in fact, been criminally engaged, as I fully expect, Freud's con-flict about financial ethics would hardly be surprising. Nor would the patricidal wishes revealed by Freud's dreams, even following Jacob's death! Masson (1984), reading the unconscious as if it determined every man's behavior *in toto*, looks upon Freud as the legendary *Galizianer*—a scoundrel. But it was Freud (1908) who first stated that every man unconsciously craves glory, gold, and the love of women. And if one actually wishes to be a mafioso, it is hardly necessary to make a detour through the laboratory of Ernst Brücke and the semi-nars of von Brentano.

All this is to say that Freud, whose adolescent ideal was Don Quijote (see Gedo & Wolf, 1973), who took the role of Shakespeare's Brutus in family theatricals at the age of 14 (see Freud, 1900, p. 483), was trying to *repudiate* a heritage of corruption. If occasionally an element of identification with his devalued father broke through, this fact in itself should serve to remind us that Freud achieved his stature in the face of great handicaps. And this is the point that brings me back to the historical dimension of my argument: Masson overlooks the emotional position of the young genius whose father is a despised Jewish immigrant and probably a chronic scofflaw.

Why did Sigmund Freud become a *German* nationalist at the Uni-versity? Why did he call attention to the probable origins of his family in the Rhineland of the Middle Ages? (see Freud, 1925, p. 8). I believe these attitudes betrayed the insecurity of the second generation in a land of opportunity[9]—the effort to disavow origins perceived as un-acceptable in many ways. If Freud's references to Jewishness were

---

[9]In the 1870s, Germany had a greater claim to this title than any other country, and Freud was an advocate of the *Anschluss* that was to drive him from Austria in 1938!

nonetheless generally positive, they invariably alluded to the higher values implicit in that culture. As for the stereotypes of Eastern Jewry, let me quote the earliest Freud letters we have on the subject, written when he was 16 and 17: "Oh Emil," he wrote his friend Fluss on June 16, 1873, "Why are you a prosaic Jew?" A year earlier (September 18, 1872) he had fulminated about a "Madame Jewess and family" whose behavior displeased him (Freud, 1969, p. 42; see also Gedo & Wolf, 1970).

OEDIPUS AT COLONUS

Was Freud the "commercial Jew" of Masson's imagination? That identification was probably the grain of sand around which the pearl of his genius formed. As I have discussed elsewhere (Gedo, 1984a, chapter 6), Freud was incapable of dealing with patients who had problems of "integrity"; he advocated their exile to underdeveloped regions, a proposal not far removed from early Hitlerian schemes to resettle Jews in Africa. But the cultural issue is even more decisive, for the Freuds did not try to make good in contemporary America, where money suffices if one wishes to climb the social ladder. In the semi-feudal Habsburg empire, money was neither sufficient nor necessary for the purpose. *Only* aristocratic credentials would do, and the aim of every bourgeois was to obtain a patent of nobility—as did the father of Hugo von Hoffmansthal, who immortalized those ambitions in the figure of his Sophie, bride of the Cavalier of the Rose.

One could become a baron if one made as much money as the Rothschilds, but scarcely by counterfeiting. The best way, of course, was to enter the *noblesse de robe*, people who received their titles for accomplishments in professional spheres. The collapse of the Habsburg empire deprived Freud of the pleasure of becoming a *Freiherr*, but his daughter finally achieved equivalent status in the England of Elizabeth II.[10]

Freud's ambition thus became focused on achievement through intellectual eminence—a goal he could gently mock by calling himself a would-be *conquistador* (e.g., Jones, 1955, p. 415). As I have previously noted (Gedo & Wolf, 1970), he seems to have taken for his

---

[10]For the most overt expression of these ambitions within the family, see the memoirs of Freud's son Martin (1957).

own the claim of the Latin poet Horace: "In this human race/ Where position and wealth and physical strength and good looks/ And talent and mental accomplishments all have their place,/ I come in last of the first and first of the last." In his adolescence, Freud was particularly involved with the ideals articulated by Cervantes in *Don Quijote* and the *Novelas Ejemplares* (see Gedo & Wolf, 1973), presumably in identification with that great author's need to transcend a legacy of parental corruption. As many commentators have noted, Freud's passionate commitment to truth, rationality, independence, and honor have profoundly stamped his intellectual work.

The obverse of the same coin was Freud's preoccupation with the psychological issues that troubled him and his definition of psychoanalysis as the tool designed to master these issues. If he tended to overemphasize the importance of ambivalence about the father in neurosogenesis, this propensity was but a natural side-effect of his principal reliance on introspection for arriving at his conclusions about human nature. It will be recalled that in his most candid self-revelation, the 1899 paper on "Screen Memories," the focal conflict of Freud's adolescence is flatly presented as a choice between higher aspirations and those of the "commercial Jew."

Without a doubt, Sigmund Freud stamped psychoanalysis most indelibly with his subjectivity. Freud's intellectual course followed the needs of self-inquiry and was specifically focused on questions for which he could find some answer with the means available to him: introspection and the crude therapeutic technique of early psychoanalysis. It is preposterous to criticize Freud for achieving success in those psychological realms that his life experience particularly equipped him to master. However, we must note that in his lifetime his early followers could hardly expand the boundaries of psychoanalytic investigation into areas Freud was unable to enter without separating themselves from the analytic community.

Had I undertaken to write the intellectual history of psychoanalysis *in toto*, it would be necessary to begin my accounts of dissidence with the secessions of Adler and Jung. These initial ruptures of the Freudian circle took place about twenty years before the climax of Ferenczi's dissidence, the first major unresolved disagreement I examine in detail in this book. The activities of Adler and Jung fall into place as the response of a still earlier generation of students to the limits imposed on the discipline by the individuality of its founder. As Stepansky (1983) has shown in convincing detail, Adler never did accept Freud's presuppositions, so that his temporary adherence to psychoanalysis and Freud's cordial reception of this promising disciple were grounded in mutual misunderstanding. I do not consider Adler's work in this study, partly because I have nothing to add to Stepansky's masterful account, but principally because it makes better sense to exclude it from the province of psychoanalysis altogether. In making this choice, I am but following in the footsteps of Lou Salomé, who dismissed Adler because he was uninterested in the purport of Freud's stunning empirical discoveries (see chapter 4, this volume).

The case of Carl Jung is more complex and more interesting; I have already devoted considerable attention to it (Gedo, 1983, chapters 12–14) and will barely summarize my findings and conclusions here. Propelled by a sincere admiration for Freud's intellectual achievements and a personal need to find an idealized mentor, Jung made a valiant effort to become a Freudian. At the same time, he was a discriminating critic of Freud's theoretical efforts; it was in response to his cogent queries that the great innovator amended the libido theory by devising the concept of narcissism (Freud, 1914a) and, a few years after their rupture, included the phenomena of the repetition compulsion within the purview of psychoanalysis (Freud, 1920). Jung provoked the disruption of this fruitful partnership precisely because of his anxiety about the overwhelming influence of Freud's genius, for he was ultimately forced to acknowledge that his basic cosmological commitments were completely at variance with the older man's scientific humanism.

Initially, Jung tried to justify his disaffection through a series of paranoid accusations about Freud's alleged intolerance of his pupil's original ideas. The Freud-Jung correspondence (McGuire, 1974) discloses a different picture: Freud rightly regarded these ideas as unscientific, and it was Jung who could not tolerate this disagreement with his mentor. The actual dissolution of their relationship appeared to take place on purely personal grounds—in a treatment setting, one would explain the imbroglio as a transference/countertransference impasse. As I have tried to show on the basis of Jung's (1963) memoirs, these painful transactions resulted from the participants' characteristic reactions to the shared realization that they disagreed on the most fundamental issues about human existence. Jung was keenly aware of the social context that made his religious approach to these matters unacceptable within the scientific arena; consequently, he called his convictions an "arrheton," a thing not to be named, and cloaked his mysticism with an empirical veneer. Nor did he ever abandon his insistence that Freud unconsciously shared his point of view but was unable to acknowledge his true convictions.

Delusional as this viewpoint appears to be, Jung, with his customary intellectual brilliance, was able to pinpoint the fact that Freud's scientific edifice was founded on an unwarranted assumption, the linkage of the duality of mind and matter through the hypothetical construct of "libido." As Lou Salomé conceded, this invention failed to establish the sought-for bridge between Freud's clinical findings and neurobiology. Of course, Jung was far from *objecting* to such a state of theoretical cloudiness—he ferreted it out triumphantly to drag the would-be rationalist, Freud, into his world of occultism. He mocked Freud for having a hidden god within his system, the *deus absconditus* of libido. However misguided this appellation, Jung correctly identified the beginnings of subsequent fissures within the psychoanalytic community.

3

Sándor Ferenczi

The First Psychoanalytic Dissident

WHEN THE COMPREHENSIVE German edition of Sándor Ferenczi's psychoanalytic writings was reissued in the 1960s, *Psyche* (Frankfurt) commissioned me to prepare a review article on the life work of Freud's "paladin and grand vizier." Writing in 1967, I concluded that with respect to scientific content, psychoanalysis had caught up with those aspects of Ferenczi's work that were initially neglected because in Freud's lifetime their author was regarded as a dissident. Almost two decades later, I see no reason to revise my estimate. Ferenczi's writings deserve careful scrutiny in the context of the *intellectual history* of psychoanalysis rather than as a quarry for overlooked ideas.

Intellectual historians have become interested in Freud's thought from various perspectives (see Ricoeur, 1970; Rieff, 1959, 1966; Sulloway, 1979), but deviations from the psychoanalytic mainstream have seldom received dispassionate scrutiny. (For an outstanding exception, see Stepansky's 1983 study of Adler; Homans, 1979, also came close to this ideal in his work on Jung.) In recent years, Ferenczi has received scant attention, although Grünberger (1980) attempted to explain the dynamics of Ferenczi's "dissidence" on the basis of his personal psychopathology. These speculations do throw some light on the difficulties of the Freud-Ferenczi friendship, at least on those that developed following the intermittent efforts during the years 1914–1918 to establish an analytic relationship between the two men while they continued to be intimates. However, it cannot be legitimate to assume, as does Grünberger, that in all their subsequent disagreements Freud was substantively correct and that Ferenczi fell into error because of his unresolved transference.

Brome (1983) has summarized the historical evidence made public about these transactions; but that essential details are still unknown becomes apparent as snippets of Ferenczi's correspondence gradually come to light. Although publication of the extant documents may alter our understanding of these matters, we already know enough to be reasonably certain that these personal difficulties were caused by unacknowledged attitudes on the part of both participants. The most satisfactory discussion of these complexities has been presented by Török (1984), who has had the opportunity to study both the Freud-Ferenczi correspondence and Ferenczi's entire scientific diary.

Török brings to light the astonishing story that Freud prohibited Ferenczi's marriage to the woman he loved (see also Ferenczi's 1922 letter to Groddeck, quoted in Covello, 1984, p. 75). This nonanalytic intervention inevitably led to irredeemable bitterness on the part of the analysand and guilt impossible to expiate on that of the analyst. Freud's need to view Ferenczi as a traitor to psychoanalysis would seem to be the logical consequence of such an impasse—the best avenue available to Freud to punish himself for his error of therapeutic judgment. In his scientific diary (B. 308)[1] Ferenczi was the first to claim that many of his most radical proposals grew out of introspective insights; in other words, he felt that he had made creative use of his own psychology in outlining a syndrome of archaic character pathology he called that of "the wise baby" (in English). As I stated in my previous discussion of Ferenczi's career (Gedo, 1967, p. 378), the discovery of new insights about man's psychological depths seems to

---

[1]Numbers in parentheses preceded by the letter B. are those assigned to Ferenczi's publications in the *Verzeichnis der Wissenschaftlichen Veröffentlichungen von Dr. Sandor Ferenczi* (Ferenczi, 1908–1933a, Vol. 4, pp. 295–327). This system has been adopted for the English edition of his psychological works (see Ferenczi, 1908–1933c, pp. 377–386). Of the works mentioned in this chapter, English translations of numbers B. 67, 80, 85, 92, 100, and 111 appear in *Contributions to Psychoanalysis* (Ferenczi, 1908–1914); numbers B. 195, 210, 211, 215, 216, 217, 232, 234, 243, 265, 269, and 271, in *Further Contributions to the Theory and Technique of Psychoanalysis* (Ferenczi, 1908–1926) and numbers B. 86, 235, 239, 244, 281, 283, 287, 291, 292, 294, 301, and 308 in *Final Contributions to the Problems and Methods of Psychoanalysis* (Ferenczi, 1908–1933b). Number B. 218 has been translated as *Psychoanalysis and the War Neuroses* (Abraham, Ferenczi, Simmel, and Jones, 1919), B. 264 as *The Development of Psychoanalysis* (Ferenczi and Rank, 1924), and B. 268 as *Thalassa: A Theory of Genitality* (Ferenczi, 1924). A translation of B. 277 appeared in *The International Journal of Psycho-Analysis* (Ferenczi, 1927).

depend on the capacity to make new discoveries about oneself—as Ferenczi thought he had done. It is generally believed that Freud's most enduring contributions, notably those about the meaningfulness of dreams and methods for their interpretation, as well as the centrality of the Oedipus complex in neurosogenesis, were similarly derived from systematic self-inquiry (see Schlessinger et al., 1967, p. 204). Obviously, the source of a psychoanalytic hypothesis in the inner world of its proponent has no bearing on the validity or relevance of that proposition.

If we approach Ferenczi's work from the perspective of the history of ideas, it may conveniently be subdivided chronologically into several distinct periods. His psychoanalytic publications began within a year of his clinical debut in 1907, with a short series of expository papers. By the time this brilliant recruit to Freud's banner consolidated his relationship to his mentor on their joint trip to America in 1909 (for the notable lecture series at Clark University), his own writings were already making original contributions; by 1911 at the latest, Ferenczi had achieved autonomous status as a psychoanalytic researcher. This phase of his career was interrupted by military duty in World War I, a circumstance that forced him to abandon his psychoanalytic practice. Yet Ferenczi's reputation as the outstanding contributor among Freud's early disciples is based on the work of the years preceding 1914 (see B. 67, 85, 111).

The disruption of his career, as well as certain personal difficulties that impelled him to seek analysis with Freud, created a hiatus in Ferenczi's productivity at this time. He continued to write reviews, brief clinical notes, articles for the popular press; he translated Freud's "Three Essays on Sexuality" into Hungarian; but his major contribution during the war years was a joint monograph with Abraham, Simmel and Jones on the war neuroses (B. 218). He also devoted himself to a speculative effort to integrate the libido theory with Lamarck's biology; he discussed these ideas extensively with Freud, who eventually prevailed on him to publish them (B. 268).

His resumption of analytic practice in 1919 inaugurated a new phase of Ferenczi's scientific life. The limitations of analytic technique in the era preceding Freud's revision of psychoanalytic theory in 1923 impelled Ferenczi to assay a series of experiments with what came to be known as an "active technique." These efforts culminated in 1924 with a monograph coauthored with Rank in which Ferenczi attempted to put the psychoanalytic theory of technique on a novel footing. Freud's partial disagreement with his conclusions marked the beginning of Ferenczi's departure from psychoanalytic "orthodoxy," although his work through 1926 continued to struggle with the issues of the day from a Freudian vantage point.

An American lecture tour in the winter of 1926–27 marked another turning point in Ferenczi's intellectual course. In his eulogy for the lost prodigal, Freud (1933) conjectured that in his last years Ferenczi had set himself therapeutic goals unattainable through contemporary methods. The radical technical experiments of this period actually constitute the "deviation" Ferenczi led within psychoanalysis; their results were reported in another series of important papers.

Before attempting to examine the substantive issues about which Ferenczi held dissident opinions, we should point out that his "deviation" did not lead to a secession from psychoanalysis, like those of Adler or Jung; his activities amounted to the formation of one of the psychoanalytic schools of his day—analogous to those of Melanie Klein and Heinz Kohut more recently. Adherents of those schools believe themselves to be the true inheritors of the Freudian tradition, albeit each school may define the essence of that tradition in a different manner (see Gedo, 1984a, chapter 10). In contrast, former members of the psychoanalytic community who initiate antipsychoanalytic movements, like Individual Psychology or Jungian Analysis, explicitly disavow sharing any premises with the Freudian heritage. Unlike such secessionists, Ferenczi continued to follow prevailing psychoanalytic observations and theories, except for matters about which he indicated explicitly that he disagreed with accepted views.

Perhaps we might best approach the nature of the psychological universe Ferenczi attempted to explore by summarizing the description of his own personality disorder—the "wise baby"—contained in his late papers. It should be kept in mind that in these publications he defined this syndrome without connecting it with his own person; ostensibly, he was communicating his findings about a sizable group of analytic patients. The patients whom he was describing had been traumatized by parental failures in helping the child with the tasks of weaning, habit training, and renouncing the status of childhood in favor of more mature adaptive modes. In the course of these patients' development, excessive strictness or deficient external controls had led to the formation of a harsh superego. Children brought up in these ways tend to have difficulty in differentiating fantasy from real-

ity (B. 281). These patients cannot trust the analyst's dependability
and will test him repeatedly, so that the negative transference must
be analyzed before a positive transference can blossom. Consequently, the analyst must not be authoritarian, his formulations must
be presented tentatively, and he must engage in constant self-scru-
tiny of his countertransference (B. 283). These traumatized patients
have psychological handicaps that render them unable to observe the
basic rule of free association. Moreover, they need unlimited time for
working through. Termination in these cases cannot be initiated by
the analyst; it should occur because mourning for the lost gratifications of childhood has been completed (B. 282).

Many of these patients are suicidal, with self-destructiveness so
intense that it could serve its supporters to illustrate Freud's concept
of a death instinct. Their oedipal problems are unresolved, and they
are preoccupied with what we have come to call existential concerns.
Their early traumatization acts like a constitutional adaptive defect, as
if a solid "life force" had failed to come into being because of the
deficiency of "good care" (B. 287). The personality is fragmented by
multiple splits defending against the affective recognition of the infantile traumata, so that Ferenczi saw the pathology as quite similar to
that of the psychoses (B. 291). The most sensitive issue for these
patients is abandonment, against which they defend themselves
through narcissistic withdrawal (B. 292).[2] Often, however, a pre-
cocious maturity develops: some of these patients assume a protec-
tive role toward their parents during childhood (B. 294). This al-
truistic surrender amounts to identification with the opponent,
screening unconscious fantasies of devouring the aggressor. (This
theme will find elaboration in the work of Melanie Klein, surveyed in
chapter 6, this volume) Any failure of these pathological defenses
leads to profound hopelessness and helplessness. The reality of the
traumatic events of childhood is ultimately defended against by pervasive doubts or depersonalization (B. 308).

The similarity of my synoptic account of Ferenczi's description of
his patients to recent psychoanalytic views of the "borderline states,"
such as those of Winnicott (1931–1956, 1957–1963), is apparent. The
emphasis on the failure of "good-enough mothering," on the development of a "false self," on narcissistic withdrawal and deper-

---

[2]Kohut (1971) believes that such schizoid defenses should forewarn the analyst
that there are serious doubts concerning analyzability.

sonalization, and on the difficulties of establishing a therapeutic al-
liance because of the patient's latent mistrust were at least 25 years
ahead of their time. The most astonishing conceptual achievement of
this work may have been Ferenczi's explicit formulation of *transitional
objects* (B. 281).

It is because of the repressed helplessness behind these patients'
accomplished facades that Ferenczi termed their syndrome "the wise
baby." He was keenly aware that he had arrived at these prodigious
insights through introspection. He wrote in his scientific diary (B.
308): "The idea of a wise baby could be discovered only by a wise
baby." At any rate, although he was not successful in conveying the
import of his work, Ferenczi, propelled by his own emotional crisis
and his self-analytic attempts, was actually engaged in a pioneering
study of so-called borderline patients and their treatment by psychoanalysis.

I think we may legitimately conclude that Ferenczi's dissident
views did not emerge solely as a consequence of unanalyzed negative
transference to Freud, as Grünberger (1980) believes: archaic pathology of the kind he had found could not have been conceptualized
by means of the theoretical tools available prior to 1933. Witness
Winnicott's resort to a theory of object relations to explicate cases of
this type, or, more recently, the analogous work of Kernberg (1975),
who has managed to remain in the psychoanalytic mainstream only
by means of the rhetorical device of declaring "borderline" patients
not to be analyzable, so that the phenomenology encountered in their
quasianalytic treatment allegedly need not be dealt with in our theory
of technique!

Ferenczi did attempt to treat the syndromes in question through
the psychoanalytic method, and he devised technical modifications
necessitated by the patients' unfavorable response to the traditional
technique of analysis. He thought he had discovered that these patients had to be analyzed in the same manner as children, that is, as
children were being analyzed by Anna Freud circa 1927.[3] He believed
that little active effort could be demanded of these people and even
that certain gratifications had to be given before the cautious intro-

---

[3]Melanie Klein's cogent objections to such modifications of analytic technique in
work with children are discussed in Chapter 6. It is not without irony that the Freudian
position was espoused by the future dissident, Mrs. Klein, while the experimental
techniques of Ferenczi resemble those of Freud's daughter in her first period of analytic
activity.

duction of analytic privations (B. 287). This method of indulgence had
the aim of "creating an atmosphere of confidence and securing fuller
freedom of affect," as one might hope for in a normal nursery (B.
291). At times Ferenczi entered into the reliving of certain recollec-
tions in the manner of present-day psychodrama and subsequently
worked through the resultant material analytically (B. 292). He became aware that his patients needed tenderness, not erotic gratification, and he was also cognizant of the dangers of the analyst's acting
out when he used a technique of such flexibility (B. 294).

Because great trust in the analyst has to develop before these patients dare to experience their profound dependency, Ferenczi concluded that he must really show himself to be a sympathetic helper,
strong enough to forestall the patient's destructiveness. Since it is
ultimately unavoidable to frustrate these fragile people, the realistic
limits of the analyst's availability must be clarified. Each new trauma
leads once more to splitting (i.e., primary repression), narcissistic
regression, and "self-care." Nonetheless, real growth can occur only
after the patients permit themselves to reexperience their infantile
helplessness and hopelessness, a process that entails real suicidal
risks. In such a situation, the analyst's "tenderness" gives the patient
courage to make a *new beginning* from the pretraumatic state (B. 308).

None of this sounds in any sense radical or unusual today. On the
contrary, it is becoming the orthodoxy of the day in the treatment of
"borderline" patients. Two generations ago, it may have seemed like
a naive attempt to cure through love. This impression was compounded by Ferenczi's imprudent remarks to the effect that Freud's
standard technique was invariably excessively frustrating. People did
not see this in the context of a transference neurosis, as the "wise
baby's" reproach to his analyst, who had wanted him to be "a companion on an equal footing." Jones (1933), for one, preferred to believe that Ferenczi's attitude about psychoanalysis had "regressed."
The "dissident's" failed experiments, such as the affectionate physical contact he tried with some patients, were held against him, even
when he reported their failure and abandoned their use. Unsubstanti-
ated derogatory rumors about his conduct with patients have been
reported as facts.

From the vantage point of the 1980s, the disagreements between
Freud and Ferenczi seem more like a "confusion of tongues" (to echo
the title of the latter's celebrated paper [B. 294] of 1933) than a scientific rupture. The protagonists began to talk past each other, both

seeming to have forgotten that in the course of time, as the renown of Ferenczi as a technical innovator grew, his clinical focus narrowed to the special problems of unusually difficult cases. Moreover, he neglected to clarify the difference between special modifications and an improved classical technique. This difficulty was perhaps unavoidable in an era of rapid evolution in the standard technique of psychoanalysis, such as the work of W. Reich (1933) and somewhat later that of Anna Freud (1936). At such a time, even the subtlest of technical suggestions, such as Ferenczi's methods of encouraging the verbalizations of fantasies in patients whose fantasy life is impoverished (B. 265), is likely to be mistaken for a general formula.

With the passage of half a century, we are in a position to say that each man was espousing a point of view valid for that group of selected analysands who gravitated into his orbit. Neither man was able to use the other's experience to expand the general theory of technique into one applicable for the entire spectrum of individuals seeking analytic assistance. Ferenczi was seen as the dissident because in Freud's lifetime the accepted point of view within psychoanalysis was inevitably that of the founder of the discipline.

Whatever the effects of unresolved transferences on Ferenczi's conceptual work might have been (if any!), there is no doubt that his feelings about Freud interfered with the communication of his views to the psychoanalytic audience. Jones reports (1957, p. 57) that Freud's partial disagreement with Ferenczi's contribution to the 1924 book he coauthored with Rank "shattered" the younger man—prima facie evidence for the kind of transference bond Kohut (1971) called a need for a "mirroring" relationship (specifically, the need for an alter ego). Freud appears to have been quite aware of these issues; in his eulogy of Ferenczi (Freud, 1933), he explained the latter's withdrawal from contacts in the psychoanalytic community as a need to remain aloof until he found a way to integrate his work into the mainstream of psychoanalysis. In January 1928, in a letter to Freud, Ferenczi (1908–1933b) explicitly spelled out his erroneous conviction that his views did not depart from those of his analyst; this preposterous claim could mean only that at the age of 55 he was still unable to maintain his self-esteem without feeling at one with Freud.

Until the unfavorable reception of *The Development of Psychoanalysis* (B. 264), it had apparently never occurred to Ferenczi that his work could be regarded as dissident. While he was writing this book, in 1923, his 50th birthday was celebrated with a *Festschrift* that included

a tribute from Freud. Freud (1923b) praised Ferenczi's most significant contributions and the mastery of his sibling rivalries that had
enabled him to become "an irreproachable elder brother, a kindly
teacher and promoter of young talent" (p. 268). What Freud overlooked at the time was the capacity of his "grand vizier" to unearth
unsolved problems in the psychoanalytic field that had escaped his
own attention. This point was convincingly demonstrated by Covello
(1984) in her cogent review of the evidence about the last encounter
between Freud and Ferenczi, in the fall of 1932.

Ferenczi's major contribution in this monograph on technique was
his novel stress on the crucial importance of affective experience in
the here and now of the analytic transference. The theory of psychoanalytic technique had previously laid exclusive emphasis on the effects of genetic interpretations. In proposing his modification, Ferenczi demonstrated his understanding of the revolutionary
significance of the new model of the mind Freud had proposed in
"The Ego and the Id" (1923a). He also understood that the next task
consisted in the translation of this general theory into specific improvements in technique. He gave a beautiful exposition of the reciprocal influence of analytic theory and practice—the improvement
of technique that follows advances in theory and simultaneously re-
tests them. He was the first to enunciate that if confusion resulting
from its manifold details is to be avoided, analysis must be understood as a *process*. Finally, he pointed out that both "symptom-analy-
sis" and "complex-analysis" had become outdated.

An adequate analytic process must promote affective reliving and
the working through of the infantile neurosis by means of repetition
as a transference neurosis. This aim, Ferenczi explained, can be at-
tained only by overcoming the resistance of the ego, certainly never
by the naive attempts to fill gaps in the patient's knowledge that
characterized psychoanalysis before 1920. Hence resistances, including the negative transference, must not be treated as undesirable or,
worse, sinful.

If this work is slightly disappointing in retrospect, the reason lies in
what it fails to accomplish rather than in any real flaw in its contents.
Ferenczi was never able to devise a detailed theory of technique based
on the new ego psychology. With the hindsight of fifty years, we can
state that valid genetic interpretations can be made only on the basis
of the specifics of affectively charged transference transactions, but
both Ferenczi and his opponents saw his proposals as alternatives to

the prevailing Freudian position. Ferenczi's point of view has once again gained prominence in the recent past, most notably in the work of Gill (1983; Gill & Hoffman, 1983). This resurgence demonstrates that unsolved problems in psychoanalysis cannot be overcome by the proscription of "heresies."

The technical experiments that constituted Ferenczi's departures from the analytic mainstream clearly were designed to bring about the development of maximally affect-laden transferences. It should be recalled that these innovations began to characterize Ferenczi's clinical work after the resumption of his analytic practice in 1919, following his demobilization from wartime army service. All these experiments were concerned with methods to deal with what today we call the defenses of the ego. They were modeled on Freud's recommendation that in the analysis of a phobia it is ultimately essential that the patient give up his avoidances. Ferenczi extended the principle by demonstrating that certain behaviors within the analytic setting may have to be overcome in order to break through a therapeutic stalemate. The method he first used was the prohibition of the activity concerned (B. 210). He did insist, however, that such an exploitation of the transference must be interpreted before the analysis can be terminated (B. 215).

Even such temporary departures from strict neutrality on the part of the analyst inevitably brought the problem of countertransference into sharper focus than it previously achieved. Ferenczi therefore started to emphasize that the observation and control of his countertransference was a necessary part of the analyst's task (B. 216). Evidently his technical advice had been seized upon in an indiscriminate manner, for at the Hague Congress of 1921 he felt obliged to reiterate that modifications of technique are justified only when an analysis is stagnant, and the "rule of abstinence" can be enforced via prohibitions only in the presence of a positive transference. In selected cases, however, he was now experimenting with setting patients certain unpleasant tasks so that resistance would be accentuated, to facilitate analysis of the ego (B. 234).

Ferenczi made strenuous efforts to define indications and contraindications for his "active technique," and he gradually shifted his position about it in response to unfavorable results in his actual practice. He clarified that the "activity" must never be that of the analyst but always that of the patient, an effort to achieve better tension tolerance, particularly with respect to pregenital impulses (B. 269). By

1926 he came out against giving the patient any kind of command, including the setting of arbitrary time limits for termination, a measure strongly advocated by Rank and one with which Ferenczi had also experimented. At this time he saw "activity" as a mere preliminary to interpretation (B. 271). He never did explain, however, what criteria he used to decide that interpretive efforts alone would not suffice. Apparently he abandoned the "active" technique proper as a failed experiment, the sole conceptual result of which was his discovery of a precursor of the superego, the "sphincter morality" of the child in the anal phase. This aspect of his career was closed by a brilliant critique of Rank (B. 277), from whom he now completely dissociated himself.

I have already alluded to the second set of technical innovations Ferenczi introduced in the last several years of his life—appropriate for patients burdened with primitive personality organizations but rightly rejected by the psychoanalytic community as a model technique applicable in all cases. Ferenczi failed to gain many advocates for his proposals not only because he placed himself in opposition to Freud, but because in his last years his personal behavior underwent unfavorable changes. The fact that these unfortunate developments accompanied the neurological complications of pernicious anemia made no difference in their inevitable consequences, a general loss of confidence in Ferenczi's judgment.

A loss of scientific rationality makes its first appearance in Ferenczi's writings in September 1932 (B. 308). He speaks of the possibility of an "ideal power" working magically, each telekinetic action subordinating externals to the will of "the ego." This regression of Ferenczi's sense of reality to belief in the omnipotence of thoughts must have been in the service of disavowing the dying man's helplessness. Moreover, this was merely an entry in a diary published posthumously, without the final revision every scientist must perform before he approves a product as a valid representation of his scientific reality testing. Ferenczi had never published anything prima facie irrational, although he *was* a believer in occultism, in periodic correspondence with Freud on the subject (see McGuire, 1974).

In Ferenczi's psychoanalytic works (the sole criteria by which his scientific contributions can be gauged), there are, however, few indications of magical thinking. In 1912 there was a respectful reference to Fliess's nasal theory of neurosis (B. 100) and an indication of belief in phylogenetic memories (B. 86); in 1924 there was the publication of

Thalassa: A Theory of Genitality (B. 268). This purely speculative essay in applying psychoanalysis to evolutionary biology had lain dormant since its wartime composition with Freud's quasicollaboration. The decision to publish followed Freud's urging (see Freud, 1933), and Ferenczi expressed his doubts in the monograph itself by specific discussion of his nonscientific methodology. Much of the argument leans on concepts that psychoanalysis and biology have since abandoned, although they were still respectable at the time: anxiety as transformed libido, the birth trauma, Lamarckian evolutionary theory, Haeckel's biogenetic law. Such obsolescence is, of course, a danger common to all efforts in applied analysis. However, the overt psychomorphism, the teleological argumentation and reasoning by analogy in this book simply cannot be overlooked, and occasional concepts of value (e.g., that of the unconscious fusion of coital partners via identification) do not redeem an embarrassing product of fantasy: to assert that sexuality serves to recapture man's prehistoric roots as a marine animal is to create science fiction.

Ferenczi's lapses from rationality are, however, less spectacular than those to be found in Freud's writings on telepathy or his speculative papers in applied analysis (see Freud, 1939). We cannot account on this basis for the general reputation of Ferenczi as the wild man of psychoanalysis. In fact, many people have written very favorable reviews of *Thalassa*, including Federn (1933), Radó (1933), and of course Freud himself (1933). In the aggregate, Ferenczi's psychoanalytic oeuvre is solid, broad, and deep. Reading it in sequence has convinced me that his contribution to the field before 1930 is second only to Freud's.

It is therefore no coincidence that it was Freud's "grand vizier" who detected certain shortcomings of his clinical procedures. We cannot guess about the probability of Ferenczi's succeeding in resolving the legitimate questions he had raised had he not been incapacitated by illness. His demise certainly prevented him from putting his objections to prevailing views into a rational framework. His exclusive emphasis on matters of technique in his late career also obscured his earlier achievements in developing the clinical theory of psychoanalysis.

To illustrate Ferenczi's evolving conceptualizations, some of his papers from 1919 already contain a workable ego psychology. For instance, he discussed the traumatization of the child's "inexperienced ego" by unexpected quantities of libido stimulated by adult exhibitionism (B. 217). The concept of a superego is implicit in his statement that "Sunday neuroses" are caused by a hypersensitive conscience spoiling the day of rest (B. 211). In some posthumously published notes of 1920 (B. 301) he was quite explicit about the need for psychoanalytic study of the ego. He foresaw that this conceptual advance would permit the understanding of various talents and their multiple determinants. This brief contribution prefigures Hartmann's work on the autonomous apparatuses of the personality twenty years later. In 1921, with his study on tics (B. 232), Ferenczi began to talk about *conflict inside the ego*—a concept implying that the ego is a coherent system lasting through time, that is, a structure. In an important 1922 monograph on general paresis (B. 239), he implied a principle of ego organization, with hierarchies, a tendency to unification, and the potential for dissolution into independent entities, a regression that is always accompanied by severe anxiety.[4] These components of the ego in turn consist of old identifications.

Elsewhere (B. 244), Ferenczi asserted that these identifications take place between the stages of narcissism and object love through the annexation of qualities of the object, that is, by way of introjection. He pointed out that ego psychology depends on data from novel sources, like the war neuroses he described in 1919; the transference neuroses do not provide pertinent information about ego pathology. Another important concept in ego psychology Ferenczi discussed (B. 243) is that of *relative autonomy* of derivatives split off from the unconscious. Finally, he defined the primary task of the psyche as the *inhibiting function*, or control of the paths of motility.

Perhaps I have now reviewed Ferenczi's conceptual work in sufficient detail to reassess the circumstances that led to his leadership of a "dissident" school within psychoanalysis. Need I repeat that intellectual distinction was the primary requirement for this role? Ferenczi could grasp the essence of his clinical experiences and draw from them the appropriate conclusions about the limitations of existing theories. For example, by 1913 he understood that although the nature of symptoms depends on the level of libidinal fixation, the *mechanisms* used in symptom formation depend on fixation points in

---

[4]In terms of more recent concepts, I question whether the dissolution of the cohesion of the personality Ferenczi was describing is referable to the system ego or, rather, whether it may be more pertinent to conceptualize it as the reversal of a more primitive structuralization, that of the self-organization (see Gedo and Goldberg, 1973; Gedo, 1979, 1981b, 1984a).

ego development (B. 111). He concluded that character traits are determined not by the fantasies of the Oedipus complex, but by the *outcome* of that developmental experience (B. 92). He discerned that the cause of the breakthrough of homosexuality in incipient paranoia was unknown and that therefore the ubiquitous homosexual material encountered in the fantasies of paranoid persons does not necessarily constitute a primary element of their psychopathology (B. 80). In other words, even as an analytic neophyte, Ferenczi was able to transcend the exclusive attention then devoted to unconscious mental contents in psychoanalytic discourse—to differentiate structural considerations from dynamic issues.

The most severe challenge to existing psychoanalytic conceptualizations was presented by the syndrome Ferenczi and his collaborators labeled "the war neuroses" (B. 218). Ferenczi tried to explicate this regressive illness as a response to traumatic narcissistic blows, a reaction characterized by a return to previously abandoned methods of adaptation. Because of the depth of the regression in these cases, he postulated that predisposed individuals must have suffered from narcissistic fixations. Ferenczi extended his conclusions about the war neuroses to syndromes arising as reactions to somatic illnesses of all kinds; he called these the "pathoneuroses" (B. 195). In the early 1920s, he also began to study other forms of primitive pathology, such as tics (B. 232, 235), as well as the devastating losses of functional capacity and the resultant (nonrepressive) defensive operations in general paresis (B. 239).

Thus the clinical data Ferenczi singled out for discussion came from sectors of the personality outside the realm of the transference neuroses. He was by no means the only member of the psychoanalytic community to bring such matters to public attention: C. G. Jung, for one, convinced Freud that his topographic theory and the theory of drives put forward in his early writings could not account for the phenomenology of the psychoses. The development of a theory of narcissim (Freud, 1914a) was a first attempt to meet these cogent objections to the universal applicability of propositions based on the phenomenology of the transference neuroses. The conceptualization of the repetition compulsion (Freud, 1920) and that of the structural theory (Freud, 1923a) were later and more radical efforts to meet this type of challenge.

Ferenczi was quick to embrace these new Freudian theories, for they promised to reconcile his novel observations with the conceptual framework of psychoanalysis as a whole. To be sure, this hope was disappointed. Not only did such a reconciliation fail to develop in Ferenczi's lifetime, but the same problems have continued to provoke the formation of dissident schools among psychoanalysts to this very day, as I shall try to describe in subsequent chapters. For the majority of psychoanalysts, the theoretical revolution Freud wrought in the 1920s was itself very difficult to accept: the first generation of Freud's adherents tended to remain "id psychologists" for the rest of their careers. Their conservatism was naturally impervious to Ferenczi's experimental efforts.

A new generation of analysts, the cohort of Hartmann, Waelder, Melanie Klein, and Anna Freud had to come into its own to reap the harvest of ego psychology; this perfusion of conceptual progress through the psychoanalytic community was the prerequisite for establishing criteria of analyzability by means of the classical techniques of Freud. By the time psychoanalysts generally accepted the sobering fact that these therapeutic measures suffice only in cases that present with optimal ego resources (cf. Eissler, 1953), the actual purport of Ferenczi's technical contributions, the solution of therapeutic impotence in less fortunate instances, was largely forgotten.

Was Ferenczi alone in the psychoanalytic community of the 1920s to realize that adults whose ego development led to maladaptation require departures from the standard technique of contemporary psychoanalysis if they are to profit from treatment? Clearly, we are in no position to answer this question. All that we can say about it is that other analysts who were dissatisfied with Freud's methods, such as Otto Rank and (somewhat later) Wilhelm Reich, left organized psychoanalysis, while Ferenczi persevered in trying to persuade his colleagues that technical modifications might enable them to broaden the therapeutic scope of their discipline.

Perhaps the most interesting of intellectual positions was occupied by still other analysts, who avoided the stigma of "dissidence" but managed to record cogent objections to prevalent views. One of these contributors, Lou Andreas-Salomé, is discussed in the following chapter.

4

The Loyal Opposition of Louise von Salomé

IT IS PROBABLY DIFFICULT for us today to grasp the significance of Louise von Salomé's adherence to psychoanalysis. We do not remember her for her scientific contributions. Indeed, her attempts to grapple with Freud's ideas were generally cloudy. Her letters elicited from Freud no more than polite refusals to go into specifics about psychoanalytic problems. In recent years, her name has been used in a tasteless effort to denigrate Freud in connection with the sad fate of their mutual problem child, Victor Tausk. Even rebuttals of those fantastic misconstructions have had to deal with her life in a way that cannot convey her stature. K. R. Eissler (1972) called her "the most distinguished woman in central Europe" at the time she joined the psychoanalytic community, and he has acutely pointed out that in 1912 she was much better known than Sigmund Freud. But it is impossible to recapture in the here and now the prestige of the ante-bellum intelligentsia on the Continent, and there is no woman in America today whose credentials are comparable. It may help to remember that Salomé has been the subject of three full-scale biographies (Peters, 1962; Binion, 1968; Livingstone, 1985) because of her accomplishments before becoming a psychoanalyst—a distinction unlikely to be matched in our ranks again.

Freud, in his 1937 eulogy of her, accented Salomé's modesty and discretion, the harmony of her personality, and her genuineness. The letters between them (Pfeiffer, 1972) are devoid of references to such private matters. To be sure, the editor made a very few deletions of personal material, presumably the written portions of a rudimentary analysis (which, according to his Notes [p. 211], may well have started in 1895). Historians of psychoanalysis can never be happy with truncated versions of Freud's correspondence; in that volume, at least, the reader is made aware that something is missing in every instance. The context makes it quite clear, however, that the deleted fragments had nothing to do with Salomé's celebrated relationships to Friedrich Neitzsche and Rainer Maria Rilke; in fact, in a letter to A. Zweig (11 May 1934) Freud stated "She never wanted to tell me about him" (E. Freud, 1970, p. 76).

I cannot forego noting the outstanding literary quality of the Freud-Salomé letters. Freud tended to be terse in this interchange, so that the most beautiful and moving of the letters are Salomé's toward the end of her life. She must have been a woman of grace and tact, in addition to her beauty and intelligence. From the beginning, she refrained from burdening Freud, by writing him less often than she might have wanted to. It was in the fall of 1914, during a period of renewed isolation caused by the loss of his followers and sons to the military, that Freud turned to her openly, asking for a word of comfort. Salomé responded by stepping up the pace of the correspondence. The steady stream of correspondence during the war years came to an end in August 1919, to be succeeded by very occasional contacts until the fall of 1921. At that time, Salomé came to Vienna at Freud's invitation and stayed at Berggasse 19 for almost six weeks. Much of this time was evidently devoted to continuous "analytic work" (whatever that may have meant) with the young Anna Freud, who subsequently made a number of visits to Salomé's home in Göttingen, presumably to continue this effort. An active correspondence then began between the two women, the letters to Freud henceforth serving only special functions not adequately taken care of by communicating through his daughter.

In spite of this change in the nature of the interaction, most readers will doubtless respond with greater appreciation to the postwar letters than to the earlier ones. The 1921 visit seems to have altered the entire relationship, from one involving a great man and his valued adherent to a more personal bond, a profound mutual appreciation. One outward sign of this change shows up in the salutation Freud's letters: until the 1921 visit, he had called her "Dear Frau Andreas"; thence she is "My dear Lou" or "Dearest Lou." On her part, Salomé always addressed him as "Dearest Professor"; her signature changed from "Lou Andreas" to "Lou" at this juncture.

During the disastrous postwar inflation in Germany, Freud found means to send Salomé financial help, and he continued to send paying patients to her in her isolated university town for many years. As late as 1930, when her husband died, he sent her a major part of the money he received as the Goethe Prize, with the doubtless sincere comment that, in his opinion, it was she who deserved the honor. Perhaps in the time of our fathers, people of a certain class simply behaved better than we do: Salomé kept Freud's subsidies not because she wanted anything for herself but to help her relatives, trapped in the Soviet Union by the Bolshevik Revolution. She was a genuine aristocrat, in every sense of the word.

One of the advantages Freud derived from her consistent high-mindedness was that he could rely on the judgment of one who had invariably proved herself to be fair in her assessment of his opponents. During her initial study trip to Vienna, she had given the theories of Adler a judicious hearing and had found them inadequate on scientific grounds. I shall return to Salomé's scientific views later. Here I should like to note only that she clearly did not share Freud's loathing for Adler as a human being. As for Jung, she was even capable of empathy for the personal illness that had necessitated his break with analysis. Her matter-of-fact response (Pfeiffer, 1972, p. 99) to Freud's announcement of Tausk's suicide is another example of objectivity in difficult circumstances. About Otto Rank, on the other hand, she had a lower opinion than Freud, and her condemnation of his book on birth trauma, especially because of its lack of philosophical underpinnings, apparently helped Freud to accept Rank's defection without rancor. Salomé had pointed out that the course of events actually constituted a misfortune for the unhappy Rank (pp. 139–40, 234).

The correspondence provides important evidence about Freud's attitude concerning the intellectual independence of his adherents. Salomé's responses to his theories never influenced the relationship in any way one can detect from these letters: there was never any danger of her being regarded as a dissident. Yet she disagreed with him on many issues, mostly on matters derived from archaic developmental stages—the same problems that had led Ferenczi into opposition.

Freud was explicitly aware that Salomé had accepted psycho-analysis because the concept of narcissism permitted her to fit into its general framework certain convictions and observations of her own about matters that did not interest him. He never discouraged her from pursuing these, although he did not respond to her attempts to explicate them; all he ever wrote in criticism was that she put her views in terms too close to the level of observation about matters in which metapsychological rigor is necessary. He also reassured her about the value of her efforts by acknowledging the possibility that her thoughts might anticipate the later evolution of his ideas. As Grünberger (1980) has pointed out, Freud's attitude about Ferenczi's disagreements with him were much less conciliatory. I would add that Salomé was able to avoid "dissidence" by using the rubric of narcissism as a catchall for the varied phenomena poorly understood by means of the Freudian concepts of the day. As I tried to show in chapter 3, Freud had devised this new concept precisely in response to the earliest challenge to his theoretical system by colleagues who studied syndromes other than the transference neuroses.

The scientific portion of Salomé's letters also contains periodic requests for Freud's comments about specific clinical problems. Very occasionally, she included a detail of her self-analysis; once she complained that she could not go as deep in this effort as in her analyses of others. In later years, Salomé described clinical problems not so much to seek Freud's advice but to give him progress reports on patients he had referred to her. She continued to perform analyses well into her old age, noting with gratification that ultimately she liked her patients as human beings more than she did people whom she encountered in other ways.

Although the psychoanalytic content of her correspondence is of interest in the context of the history of ideas, one must conclude that Freud sought Salomé's friendship for reasons more personal than because he valued her as a professional collaborator. It is true that she was the only one of his adherents who was a contemporary of Freud (being only some five years his junior) and could be regarded as a peer on the strength of her prior achievements. It could not have been without profound significance for a master of the German language such as Freud that she was able to introduce him to the greatest modern German poet, Rilke; indeed, he complained to Salomé about the poet's reluctance to keep in touch with him when the distraught Rilke was in Vienna during the war. From the start of the correspondence, he was able to share his deeper concerns with her in a way that presaged their later rapport. It was the cosmopolitan Salomé who reacted to the war in 1914 with appropriate distress about the shattering of the world they had known, while Freud still retained illusions about "our German people" at the time. She may have been the only person who could wholly share his conclusion that the madness of man's group behavior confirmed the pessimistic assumptions of psychoanalysis.

It is little wonder, then, that Freud was willing to overlook Salomé's deficiencies as a theoretician and to regard her as the possessor of the "brighter light and more spacious horizon." These qualities enabled her to see, in 1923, that "in these days one cannot be certain whether the German man-in-the-street will not go berserk" (Pfeiffer, 1972, p. 126). Freud valued the difference between her mind and his own: "I strike up a—mostly very simple—melody; you supply the higher octaves for it; I separate the one from the other, and you blend what has been separated into a higher unity . . ." (p. 185) He called hers an "exquisitely feminine intellectual approach." The letters demonstrate his sincerity in making these statements, his genuine belief in Salomé's superiority, "in accord with the heights from which you descended to us" (p. 195).

On her part, Salomé gave eloquent testimony to the revolution psychoanalysis had produced in her life. In 1915 she was already writing that Freud's works did not "merely advance my theoretical knowledge but help me in the widest human sense" (p. 34). In September, 1923, when she was past sixty, she wrote, "Recently I tried to think what things would have been like if I had grown old without ever having met you: I would have been thoroughly disgusted at this old woman, while as things are I am utterly contented with the life that I have, as long as it may last" (p. 127). This is not the place to go into detail about Salomé's personal difficulties before her adherence to psychoanalysis; I have addressed myself to that problem in a different context (Gedo, 1983, chapter 10). Suffice it to say here that she was clearly a very troubled person. Leavy (1964), in his Introduction to Salomé's "Freud Journal," describes her effort "to make a kind of ethical norm out of her life of serial polyandry"—a life that repeatedly left her dissatisfied "with that ennui that is always based on anxiety" (p. 8). Binion's (1968) evaluation of her character is downright unfavorable; he asserts that she falsified the historical record of her relations with men to conceal her misbehavior. Hence we have to take very seriously Salomé's statements about the revolutionary effect adherence to psychoanalysis produced in her life, for it seems to have helped her to achieve serenity.

To be sure, this reorganization of her personality could not have been the result of analytic insight alone, and Salomé was aware that having been chosen as Anna Freud's mentor must have had a great role in it: "I feel only too acutely how completely I am identified with you all, as though I were a fragment of some age-old Anna, and somehow inseparable from you all" (Pfeiffer, 1972, p. 154). Nonetheless, Salomé's self-analytic capacities were considerable (as shown, for example, by the account in May 1927 of her reaction to Rilke's premature death); she paid tribute to Freud for having helped her to acquire these abilities: "It forms the enormous bond which I have always had and always shall have with you" (p. 167). She insisted that she owed her gratitude not to psychoanalysis in general but to the human experience she had had with Freud, and she attributed her own continued productivity as a writer (as well as that of others who had come into his orbit) to his influence. When she became too ill to travel and the infrequent personal meetings with Freud that had occurred until 1929 had to cease, she wrote, "If only . . . I could look for just ten minutes into your face—into the father-face which has presided over my life" (p. 208).

The central concerns of both writers of the correspondence ultimately focused on the related problems of aging and creativity. Freud initiated this interchange in 1916, during one of his fallow periods, when he complained that he could never feel secure because his creativity depended on his mood, just as it does for the artist. Perceptively, Salomé replied that, on the contrary, it was his artistic disposition that had made Freud's achievement possible, that the subject matter of psychoanalysis demands an approach similar to that of creative art. She criticized theories of creativity based on a "specifically Anglo-American type of optimism" that assume it is a product of harmonious maturity (p. 55).

As Freud put it, the cumulative impact of the tragic war years had a demoralizing effect on him. He reacted to events with "impotent resentment" and cried, as if in despair, "What the human beast needs above all is restraint" (p. 75). By the time his daughter Sophie died in early 1919, however, he was able to refer to that blow matter-of-factly. Salomé's acute empathy is demonstrated by the fact that her tenderest response occurred neither to this loss nor to the news of

Freud's malignancy but to the death of his grandson, although his letters contain no hint of how traumatic this tragedy had been for him.

As Freud approached his 70th year, he declared that for him life was losing its value: "A crust of indifference is slowly creeping up around me." He attributed this development to a change in his instinctual economy, a predominance of death instinct over the life forces; "Some kind of resonance is lacking" (p. 154). Because at this same time he had just produced his major work on anxiety (Freud, 1926), Salomé replied, "We perhaps often owe to old age our finest products." She felt that aging produces great losses but may also swing the balance "in favor of the essential and vital" (p. 155). She found it natural that analysis, a "science for the young at heart," was being carried forward by its oldest member. Freud replied, not without a trace of malice, "It does no harm for people to realize that we have not yet earned the right to dogmatic rigidity and that we must be ready to till the vineyard again and again" (p. 163). At the age of 70, Freud saw himself as the eternal dissident!

Freud periodically repeated his expressions of displeasure about old age, particularly when Salomé reported that she was experiencing this phase of her life as sunny: ". . . with me crabbed age has arrived—a state of total disillusionment whose sterility is comparable to a lunar landscape, an inner ice age. But perhaps the central fire is not yet extinguished, the sterility only affects the peripheral layers and later perhaps, if there is time, another eruption may come" (p. 165). According to Salomé, old age requites the losses it imposes with deeper developments that may be difficult to record. The body grows troublesome, but the diminution of needs for object love provides a new freedom that may create wider relationships than ever before. She thought Freud might enjoy not having to act as the leader of psychoanalysis any longer and that his illness could spur his creativity in the way the frustrations caused by some of his pupils had done earlier. In 1933, she was still reporting her delight about the "internalizations" of old age and the new friendships she had been able to form.

Although Freud described his experience of growing old as one of "suppressed rage," as he was about to enter his ninth decade he struck a new note in his letters to Salomé: "My one source of satisfaction is Anna." It was particularly in his daughter's independence and mastery of psychoanalysis that he found pleasure. "What will she do when she has lost me? Will she lead a life of ascetic austerity?" (p. 204). He described his own situation in the words of Goethe's Mephistopheles: "In the end we all depend on creatures we ourselves have made," adding with touching simplicity, "In any case it was very wise to have made her" (p. 209). The correspondence thus approached its end in an elegiac manner; the remarkable beauty of the last letters is beyond description here. Salomé died in February 1937, more than two years before Sigmund Freud.

Have I contrasted the fate of Sándor Ferenczi with that of Andreas-Salomé because I disagree with the general verdict that she was "not a major theoretician, not a systematic thinker in psychoanalysis at all" (Leavy, 1964, p. 26)? Not so. Her psychoanalytic writings were few and of minor significance—I have nothing to add to Leavy's judicious account on this score (pp. 22–24). But Salomé's failure to propose a set of dissident theories or technical recommendations does not diminish the significance of her skepticism about certain Freudian propositions—reservations she noted both in her Journal and in her correspondence with Freud. Immediately following the academic year she spent "in Freud's school" (as she called her 1912–1913 stay in Vienna), Salomé went to Budapest to familiarize herself with Ferenczi's thinking. She concluded that Ferenczi's ideas contained the seeds of "defection" from psychoanalysis (p. 136) because of a fundamental philosophical divergence between him and Freud. She noted with a mixture of humor and amazement that Ferenczi himself looked upon his departures from Freud's premises as "craziness" (p. 137). As for her own attitude about these matters, it was summed up in the line, "Ferenczi's time *must* come" (p. 137; for Salomé's reservations about Ferenczi's positions of 1913, see Leavy, 1964, pp. 170–72).

To be sure, these prodissident remarks were written many years before Ferenczi proposed the modifications in technique that one of his later followers was to call "the leaven of love" (deForest, 1954). Salomé's literary executor reports (Pfeiffer, 1972, p. 238) that she continued to be "deeply concerned" about Ferenczi until his death, but no information is available about her reactions to his technical innovations. Neither her Journal nor the letters to Freud reveal any interest in such problems on her part; she was concerned, instead, with the philosophical underpinnings of psychoanalysis. Perhaps her disagreements with Freud never distressed him because of his dismissive attitude about the importance of such questions.

Yet Salomé's objections were by no means negligible. In 1912, she was already aware of those epistemological shortcomings of Freud's metapsychology that have gained general currency in the past decade. She discerned that the armature of Freud's theory, the concept of drives, "remains a mere crutch, an unwilled inconsistency in our knowledge of nature and mind" (Leavy, 1964, p. 39). She understood that Jung, whose defection from psychoanalysis was unfolding at that very moment, was attempting to escape the unacceptable dualism of Freud's theory. However, Salomé believed that his monism was achieved by reducing the term "libido," still used as an explanatory construct, to meaninglessness (p. 43). She thought that psychoanalysis needs an epistemology based on sound monistic premises and looked to the philosophy of Spinoza as a possible source for it (p. 75). And she protested against the misuse of the concept of a system *Ucs.* as a receptacle in which unsolved theoretical problems could be hidden (p. 109).

Salomé understood that the limits of what we can describe are those of consciousness—beyond this we are able only to note bodily correlates or fall into metaphysical statements (Leavy, 1964, p. 119). She conceived of psychoanalysis as a biological discipline, dealing with data reflecting the operational aspects of a physiological substrate (p. 127). Salomé made clear her lack of agreement with Freud's epistemology. In a letter to Adler (p. 158), she stated explicitly that for her this disagreement was outweighed in importance by Freud's empirical discoveries. She believed that these novel insights would in the future prove to be of prime importance to the philosophical enterprise of understanding humankind.

Yet Salomé's psychoanalytic convictions did not evolve out of empirical evidence from her consulting room; her views had already crystallized when she arrived in Vienna in the fall of 1912 to study with Freud. I assume that her convictions developed from introspective insights about her own creativity and her observations of such intimates as Nietzsche, Rilke, Beer-Hofmann—and Freud. From the first, she objected to Freud's concept of unavoidable conflict between instincts and culture (Leavy, 1964, p. 56); she felt that he neglected the fact that the creation of cultural values can take place only when the effort is nurtured in "the soil" of the Unconscious (p. 66). She believed that this area of mental life unites us with our past, both in the ontogenetic sense and in the broader one of a "primal order of existence" (p. 91). In other words, Salomé concluded that Freud had confused the primitive with what is "primary." She knew that various structured behaviors with an onset in early life prove to have permanent value; their renunciation would impoverish the personality (p. 101).

In the psychoanalytic discourse of the day, such primary behaviors were assigned to the narcissistic stage of development. Salomé believed that narcissism is not merely a stage to be transcended but that it refers to a "persistent" accompaniment of all our deeper experience (Leavy, 1964, p. 109). She refused to equate archaic roots with pathology. In her view, psychopathology grew out of some developmental *distortion;* in contrast, the primordial roots of our humanity give rise to the creative potentials within us (p. 115). It is only by means of the vitality furnished by "libido" (to use the vocabulary of Salomé's *Journal*) that "the ego" may rise to the level of art (p. 122). She puts this idea another way in her statement that in the normal state of unconsciousness, sexuality and the ego maintain a unity that may be called narcissistic (p. 68).

Salomé's (1921/1962) explicit effort to explicate her views on narcissism did not achieve a desirable level of clarity, but we can gain an adequate grasp of her thinking from her letters to Freud. She differentiated the self-love of secondary narcissism (the subject matter of Adler's psychological work) from a primary state that serves as *Anlage* to our creativity and our values (Pfeiffer, 1972, p. 23). She described the creative act as unselfconscious and lacking in vanity, as occuring in a state in which the "frontiers of the ego" are eliminated. She contrasted these conditions with those prevalent in hypochondriasis: in this pathological state, the hypercathexis of the body is experienced as *alien* to oneself. She concluded that one function of sexual experience is self-confirmation; hence sexual tension as such is both needed and desired (pp. 24–25).

As Heinz Kohut was to do two generations later (see chapter 7, this volume), Salomé explicitly concluded that "narcissistic libido develops on its own lines" (Pfeiffer, 1972, p. 226). In normal development our reservoir of narcissism contains the "elixirs of life" (p. 169). Elsewhere (p. 171), she called it the source of our "life faith," that sense of confidence that may find expression in religion—or in science. Our access to the primal experiences producing this state is by means of humor (p. 169) or creative activity (p. 227). Be it noted that in these statements Salomé was also challenging Freud's concept of sublimation; she kept reiterating that superior performances can arise only from the *Ucs.* (see Leavy, 1964, pp. 56–57, p. 65), that creativity is, in fact, a matter of self-realization (p. 146). She was equally insistent on the view that idealizations are not mere defenses but constitute actual eruptions from the depths (Pfeiffer, 1972, p. 220; see also Leavy, 1964, p. 59). Hence she regarded religious belief, wherein gods are anthropomorphized, and magic, through which man may naïvely feel godlike, as creative acts (Leavy, 1964, p. 78).

A corollary of these conclusions was Salomé's conviction that Freud's theories granted an unnecessarily large role to repression. For example, she stated that it is unwarranted to see all kindness as a product of reaction formation; only *excessive* kindness can be attributed to repressed sadism (Leavy, 1964, p. 103). Today, I would concur with her view by reference to our understanding, initiated by Hartmann's (1939) work on adaptation, that many psychic functions are conflict free (see also Gedo and Goldberg, 1973).

Louise von Salomé began to practice psychoanalysis during the first world war, when she was in her mid-50s. Her letters to Freud reveal that, appropriately enough, she continued to regard herself as a clinical neophyte well into her seventh decade. Unlike that master clinician, Ferenczi, she was never able to challenge Freud in the realm of his theory of technique; nor was she qualified to transpose her acute critique of the developmental propositions of psychoanalysis to the parallel problem of nosology. Hence she remained a loyal Freudian, however radical and perceptive her disagreements with accepted psychoanalytic hypotheses may have been. But the issues she raised with Freud, like those around which Ferenczi created his dissidence, have continued to bedevil psychoanalysis to this very day.

5

Kant's Way

The Epistemological Challenge of David Rapaport

DAVID RAPAPORT WAS ONE OF THE MOST learned persons ever to become involved with psychoanalysis. Aside from his encyclopedic grasp of psychology, he studied physics and mathematics, and his doctorate was obtained in epistemology. His expertise in scientific methodology was seldom matched among psychoanalysts. He was well qualified to review Kris's collection of papers on art, having thought deeply about matters of style and form. He gave evidence, in his only piece of published self-revelation, of significant immersion in poetry, and he was a writer of touching eulogies—capacities astonishing in a person whose work is characterized primarily by intellectual austerity. He was also a political activist deeply committed to Zionism, but one who was able to step back to view the causes he espoused with detachment when scientific questions arose about them.[1] He spent little more than two decades in the United States but gave to and took from this country in full measure without ceasing to be a typical Central European Jew. This array of qualities and achievements is so seldom found in one man that it is difficult to grasp that Rapaport died before the age of fifty. His intellectual brilliance and his prodigious scientific output had earned him the status of a senior theoretician at what is usually considered the age of a fledgling.

---

[1]Thus he wrote a reasoned article about the effects of the child-rearing practices of the Israeli kibbutz movement (1967, pp. 710–721). Along the same lines, one can cite his farsighted statements about public policy and research in the behavioral sciences (see Rapaport, 1967, pp. 237–244.)

Rapaport's work, as it impinges on psychoanalysis directly, is now available in four volumes: *Organization and Pathology of Thought* (1951), a book of readings he selected, translated, and supplemented with copious notes and commentaries; a synthesizing monograph, *The Structure of Psychoanalytic Theory* (1959); *The Collected Papers of David Rapaport* (1967), 65 papers written from 1938 to 1960, edited by his friend and collaborator, Merton Gill; and finally *The History of the Concept of Association of Ideas* (1974), the epistemological treatise Rapaport prepared as his dissertation for the University of Budapest in 1938.

A concentrated reading of Rapaport's contributions to psychoanalysis gives an overall impression of a superb intelligence at work with untiring zeal to master the entire system of the theory and its evidential base, to systematize it, to spotlight its inconsistencies and omissions, to make refinements, and to devise critical tests for some of its more crucial but controversial hypotheses.

Rapaport was a master teacher of psychoanalytic theory who influenced a whole generation of students at The Menninger Foundation, Topeka, Kansas, and The Austin Riggs Center, Stockbridge, Massachusetts. He acquired a distinguished following of analytic researchers such as George Klein, Merton Gill, Robert Holt, Philip Holzman, and Roy Schafer and became the one voice of psychoanalysis respectfully listened to by behavioral scientists without analytic training. The reverence and awe with which his students recall David Rapaport that has puzzled those who knew him only from his published writings may become understandable from the facts I have just cited. These qualities have also stamped his writings in a way that could not have been detected when they were originally published. Very little that he wrote seems to be dated. It is just as fruitful to study his papers today as it was when they were written; this is true even of his earliest efforts in the late 1930s.[2]

Perhaps one reason both for Rapaport's mastery of the field and for his ability to write with lasting value about it was his prevailing commitment to a historical approach. It was no accident that his dissertation dealt with the *history* of the association concept. His greatest

---

[2]This does not mean that Rapaport was invariably *right*. The question of validity is not to be confused with that of detecting important issues and dealing with them in a thoughtful and thorough manner.

talent may well have been his brilliance as an expositor, as a reviewer, and as a historian of ideas. Many of his contributions consisted in bringing to light certain historical developments. For instance, his translations of selected analytic works from German into English did much to further the triumph of ego psychology within American psychoanalysis. Because of this mode of exerting influence, Rapaport's originality may have been underestimated; it has been screened by his championship of others, mostly Hartmann and Erikson, or it has passed modestly as an echo of some prior discoverer. Yet it is a major accomplishment that Rapaport could uncover what is most vital and germane within the immense body of work of a genius such as Freud.

Rapaport did not begin to focus on analytic topics in any regular way until 1950. His great reputation as a theoretician actually rests on some 15 papers produced during the last ten years of his life. The progressive increase in quality and in depth in the works of the last decade sadly underscore the great loss psychoanalysis suffered from David Rapaport's premature death.

Rapaport's approach to his profession is clear from his statements defining the human condition. As early as 1947 he described what is uniquely human as the evolution of the function of thought (1967, pp. 276–284). The study of this developmental process was at the center of Rapaport's life work. In other words, he was not primarily a psychoanalyst. As a psychologist of thinking, he had found that he needed psychoanalytic theory as a tool—one he believed to be the most crucial—in order to make sense of his chosen subject matter.

Thus Rapaport's tremendous effort to become a polymath was wholly in the service of solving the age-old problems of epistemology. The annotated source book, *Organization and Pathology of Thought,* was his first major effort to bring psychoanalysis to bear on the psychology of thinking. There Rapaport (1951) stated:

> How can the mind form knowledge of the world of objects? The 2500 years of struggle of Western epistemology with the problem testify that the grasp of thinking on objective reality was most puzzling to man. The importance of this problem can be gauged from the fact that it stood in the center of the system of most great Western philosophers, from Parmenides and Heraclitus to Kant and Husserl. A study of the various solutions offered . . . might add an important chapter to the theory of thought-processes.

When at the end of the last and the beginning of the present century, attempts were made to wrest this epistemological problem from philosophy and offer a psychological solution . . . these attempts were discredited not so much by philosophical a priori criticism as by attacks upon their factual relevance. The growth of psychological knowledge brought us closer to the possibility of a more satisfactory answer . . . .

In his developmental studies, Piaget has demonstrated that the possibility of knowing is rooted in the organic adaptation-relationship of man to his environment. He has shown how, from this basic root, a hierarchic series of thought-organizations arises, in the course of maturation and development, culminating in reality-adequate thinking. The functional categories which he found to exist on all levels of this hierarchy led him to specific epistemological conclusions similar to Kant's. The relatedness of Kant's epistemology to the assumptions underlying dynamic psychology seems to be more than apparent or accidental [pp. 721–722].

The only area of knowledge relevant for the epistemologist in which Rapaport made no attempt to gain expertise was language. Because he had concluded that the strongest lever for the understanding of thinking processes is the study of motivation, he made psychoanalysis his principal conceptual tool. His relative lack of interest in the clinical aspects of analysis was probably due to their marginal relevance for the study of thinking processes. On this score, Rapaport (1951) wrote: "The clinical psychoanalytic method, though it yielded fundamental theoretical knowledge and observations concerning the intellectual functions and the thought-organization underlying them . . . is not the method of choice for a systematic investigation of this area" (p. 154, n. 2).

David Rapaport has sometimes been depreciated as a theoretician by intellectual opponents because his concepts were not based on clinical experience. He probably was somewhat handicapped by this limitation: his comments on the psychoses, which reflect his extensive clinical experience as a psychodiagnostician, are less schematic and rely more on acute observations than his papers on other topics. Only one of his papers contains a case illustration from a treatment he conducted, under supervision (cf., 1967, pp. 530–568); by contemporary standards, this vignette is uninspired. In his use of this clinical observation, Rapaport commits a rare scientific indiscretion: his inferences involve too great a leap into abstraction. As Waelder (1962) said nonclinicians regularly do, Rapaport leaves out the intermediate steps between observations and theory, the processes of interpretation and generalization. Perhaps his mode of operation—using the generalizations arrived at by the profession as a whole for his theory building—served as a needed constraint on a penchant for excessively speculative inferences.

It may be in matters of methodology, as exemplified by his procedures for his work, that Rapaport made his most valuable contributions to psychoanalysis. Even his *example*, of scholarly zeal, erudition and an untiring intellectual struggle with the issues, had a salutary influence through his numerous students. His lectures on the methodology of psychoanalysis are models of their kind and show a great teacher in action (cf., 1967, pp. 165–220). Gill's (pp. 165–166) report that in his lifetime Rapaport did not regard them as important enough or definitive enough to publish casts the strongest light on the standards he set for himself.[3]

Rapaport regarded *systematization* as the most urgent methodological requirement of psychoanalytic theory in the 1950s; he admired Otto Fenichel's previous efforts in this area. His own monograph, *The Structure of Psychoanalytic Theory* (1959), which was full of sophisticated methodological and historical material, he called a mere "systematizing attempt." In 1947 he wrote:

> It is the job of research, and research alone, to produce tested knowledge that can be used *with* the art of the clinician. The question should be raised: Is it possible that clinicians in their clinical work produce this tested knowledge? The atmosphere of the Hippocratic oath, the importance to the clinician to discharge his duties to the patients first, is inimical to research. Add to this the present-day never-ending stream of patients and there is no room left for clarification. We have seen a stream of ingenious, top-flight clinicians lecture in our institutions . . . . I believe that . . . systematizing ingenuity was not a part of these clinicians' equipment [Rapaport, 1967, p. 239].

Thus he stayed away from practice deliberately, in order to save himself for the more urgent investigative task: "Research is the fat of

---

[3]The informality and liveliness of his lecture style shows that Rapaport's dry and Talmudic manner in his published papers was deliberate. The sacrifice he made in restraining his pen is also demonstrated by his single published polemic, in which he demolished a critic of psychoanalysis by pointing out his inadequacies as a historian (1967, pp. 682–684). Clearly, Rapaport did not wish to seduce his readers through his rhetorical skills—only to inform them through reason.

the land on which practice and teaching live—we must act vigorously to replenish this fat of the land" (Rapaport, 1967, p. 244).

Rapaport took little for granted. He called for exploration of the methodological problems inherent in introspective observation—the very basis of psychoanalysis as science. He pointed out that the teleological nature of some analytic concepts had been justified only early in its history, in that phase of a science when causal explanations are not yet possible. He also noted that theory building in new areas may initially require the use of models and analogies. He also defended the legitimacy of verification by the observational method of psychoanalysis against the exponents of exclusively experimental methods. On the other hand, he made serious efforts toward making experimental verification of analytic propositions feasible, particularly by clarifying the formal organization of analytic theory and the problems of quantification and mensuration peculiar to it. About the method of clinical research, Rapaport (1951) wrote: "Its inherent postulate is the fundamental lawfulness of the biological individual; its inherent danger lies in the difficulty of knowing the realm of applicability of the inferences drawn from the sample chosen" (p. 584, n. 8). In other words, the integration of data from clinical psychoanalysis and the research laboratory presents a formidable problem.

Rapaport was emphatic in the belief that in order to accomplish this task of integration, the gap between the disciplines would have to be bridged at the conceptual level of metapsychology, that is, beyond the clinical theory of psychoanalysis. Hence he produced his monograph, *The Structure of Psychoanalytic Theory* (1959), and his justly celebrated collaborative paper with Gill (1967, pp. 795–811) to clarify the points of view and assumptions of metapsychology. Although he arrived at the conclusion that the five points of view used in metapsychology must be assumed independently, Rapaport's writings probably laid most stress, as a historian's should, on the genetic viewpoint as central to the study of behavior. He had already espoused this bias in a review of Heinz Werner's work on genetic psychology in 1941. One of Rapaport's last papers (1967, pp. 820–854) reiterated that psychoanalysis is in its core an epigenetic developmental psychology that gives due weight to the effects of experience and at the same time stresses the importance of intrinsic maturational factors. Rapaport defended the genetic constructs derived from clinical findings on the basis of the possibility of confirmation through the method of direct child observation. (I discuss the methodological complexities of contemporary efforts to carry out such a research program in chapters 10–12).

In his generation, Rapaport was, by virtue of his mastery of the whole system, the strictest critic of metapsychology, ever alert to its inconsistencies and shortcomings. In a 1953 paper on the development of analytic affect theory, for example, he noted that this aspect of metapsychology was unsatisfactory because in Freud's statements on the subject prior to the conceptualization of the structural theory, there was not yet a concept of discharge thresholds. In his later, "conflict theory" of affects, on the other hand, Freud had overlooked the fact that the "discharge" of drives is just as affectful as is their frustration—an error that originated with Spinoza (Rapaport, 1967, pp. 476–512).

Another objection Rapaport articulated about metapsychology was that the economic and dynamic points of view had not been sufficiently differentiated because the relation of energy concepts to force concepts had not been made explicit. One consequence of this vagueness was the unsatisfactory state of the prevailing theory of affects. Another is the neglect by psychoanalysis of the issue of volition: "will" has been regarded as an epiphenomenon, "an outcome of impulse dynamics" (Rapaport, 1951, p. 507, n. 49). Rapaport believed that psychoanalytic psychology would have to come to grips with this matter in a more illuminating way, a prediction subsequently borne out in theories centered on the self-organization and its relation to initiative (e.g., Kohut, 1971; Gedo, 1979, 1981b, 1984a).

Rapaport (1967, pp. 599, 750) also asserted that the prevailing complacency about simultaneously using a psychology of drives and one of object relations involving interpersonal communication was ill founded, that it involved disavowal of a gap in psychoanalytic theory where these divergent realms of discourse ought to be connected. He called for the construction of a new theoretical framework to bridge this gap. (In chapters 7 and 8 I discuss the manner in which Heinz Kohut attempted to respond to this challenge.) Here we should recall that at the time Rapaport was writing, the existentialists showed more interest in a holistic approach to behavior than did psychoanalysts; there was no satisfactory reply to their critiques prior to recent analytic hypotheses about basic motivations stemming from the earliest phases of development (e.g., Gedo & Goldberg, 1973).

Rapaport restated the problem of the psychoanalytic theory of object relations in 1956 (1967, pp. 594–623). He saw the contributions of

Hartmann and Erikson as the major efforts within psychoanalysis to supply the missing link between drive psychology and adaptation. In an unfinished draft from the same period (pp. 685–709), Rapaport went beyond their concepts, asserting that ego psychology had focused on certain issues while it neglected a number of conceptual problems, for example, issues involving the superego. This may be the paper in which Rapaport's lack of clinical experience as a psycho-analyst shows up most regrettably. Forced to accept traditional clinical theory, he falls short of the necessary breakout from the tri-partite framework applicable to the study of the differentiated psyche (Gedo and Goldberg, 1973). Thus, he could not tackle the unsolved problems substantively, despite his awareness that it is to be found in the realm of "narcissism" (see chapters 3, 4, and 7, this volume).

Rapaport's last statement on this theme was in a 1959 critique of Edward Bibring's theory of depression (1967, pp. 758–773). He con-curred with the latter's dissatisfaction with existing theories of de-pression, based on drive vicissitudes, and he also espoused Bibring's proposal to replace them with a theory postulating a return to a feeling state previously experienced in infancy. Such regressions are precipitated by a narcissistic trauma that shatters self-esteem. Rapa-port stated unequivocally that "Bibring's formulations seem to re-quire a more radical redefinition of narcissism" (p. 765). He also fore-saw that such a revision would bring in its wake a reformulation of the psychoanalytic theory of aggression (p. 679; for one such attempt see Kohut, 1972) and that these advances in psychoanalysis would successfully meet the challenge of existentialist critiques of its psychology.

With more insistence than on any other issue, Rapaport reiterated his view that psychoanalysis is in need of a viable learning theory. In a 1960 paper (1967, pp. 853–915), he commented that "psychoanalytic theory so far has no theory of learning, but it does have, in its theory of consciousness, a possible point of departure for such a theory" (p. 906). He pointed out that this lack makes it impossible effectively to rebut the claims of behaviorists. In *The Structure of Psychoanalytic Theory*, Rapaport wrote:

> This lack is not palliated by the demonstration that the condi-tioning theory of learning does not meet the empirical require-ments (e.g., automatization problems, structure formation, dis-tinction between primary and secondary processes) which a psychoanalytic learning theory will have to meet. Psycho-

analysis will be totally free of embarrassment from this quarter
only when it has a learning theory which not only fulfills its own
empirical and theoretical requirements, but is also broad enough
to account for conditioning phenomena—including the condi-
tioned analogues of "unconscious mechanisms"—as special
cases [1959, pp. 116–117].

Rapaport believed that the search for a psychoanalytic theory of
learning had failed because Freud's concept of the secondary process
arising from the primary process leads to contradictions. Leaning on
the findings of Piaget, he postulated:

> . . . the secondary process does not simply arise from the pri-
> mary process under the pressure of environmental necessity,
> but, like the primary process, arises from an undifferentiated
> matrix in which its intrinsic maturational restraining and inte-
> grating factors are already present . . . . animism, which is so
> striking a form of the primary process in pathological states,
> preliterates, children, etc., is a "theoretical" system and as such
> is organized in terms of a synthetic function alien to the primary
> processes . . . demonstrating that animistic thought and prac-
> tices involve secondary processes as well as primary. [1967, pp.
> 842–843].

He concluded

> that both the primary processes and the secondary processes
> involve intrinsic maturational factors. The intrinsic maturational
> factors involved in the primary process are related to the in-
> stinctual drives, and those involved in the secondary processes
> are related to instinctual-drive restraints and synthetic func-
> tions . . . . the ontogenetic course of these restraining factors,
> and their interaction with experience . . . have been given very
> little attention so far. It is probable that the study of these rela-
> tions of restraining factors will center on the problem of struc-
> ture development and will lead to a learning theory compatible
> with developmental psychology [p. 844].[4]

The work I have reviewed thus far suggests that it is grossly inaccurate to characterize Rapaport's theorizing, as is usually done, exclusively under the label of "ego psychology" (Loch, 1971; Zelmano-

---

[4]For Rapaport's impressive critique of existing learning theories, see 1967, pp.
435–436.

witz, 1968). It is true that he accepted the value of Hartmann's concepts, modifying Freud's structural theory of 1923—for instance the new emphasis on the role of inborn capacities as the basis of ego development, instead of viewing this as a consequence of conflict resolution. Rapaport's own refinement in this realm was the concept of inborn "thresholds" as built-in impediments to behavior governed exclusively by the influence of the drives. Despite this commitment to the importance of autonomous regulatory apparatuses, Rapaport cautiously defined the "quasi-stationary functions" of the personality, such as memory and attention, as having "much to do with the ego." In other words, he never lost sight of Freud's early conclusions that memory is also id-derived; hence he understood that studies of thinking cannot be subsumed in a direct way under "ego psychology" (1967, pp. 256, 405–431, 631–644).

Rapaport espoused the concept of ego autonomy to explain the relative contributions of the ego and the id to cognitive and perceptual achievements. This strategy made it possible to assume that thought processes, whatever their origin, are ordinarily removed from the sphere of intrapsychic conflicts. In line with this theoretical decision, Rapaport then conceived of ego development as a process in which there is progressive mastery over the drives. He apparently thought that his most original theoretical contribution was his stress on the importance of such ego mastery. The polar opposite of this achievement is a state of passivity vis-à-vis the drives. The conceptualization of an activity/passivity gradient permits the differentiation of passive regressions—collapse of the prevailing ego organization—from regressions in the service of the ego, which must be seen as evidence for ego activity.[5]

Rapaport accepted Erikson's epigenetic schema of psychosocial development as "the only consistent attempt to characterize the autonomous course of ego development" (1967, p. 592). Aware that Erikson had presented this without concern for systematization of theory, Rapaport attempted to integrate this contribution with that of Hartmann in a sequence of papers on psychoanalytic intellectual history (pp. 594–623, 745–757). In the process, Rapaport injected metapsychological content into Erikson's writings. In retrospect, however,

---

[5]Note Kohut's (1966b, p. 413) claim of originality about the concept of ego dominance—one of many examples of his tendency to forget the sources of his conceptual borrowings.

Rapaport was too optimistic about the possibility of integrating into metapsychology a body of work that does not refer to the intrapsychic world but finds its points of reference in the realm of social relations. Today one has to question whether Erikson's schema properly refers to ego development at all; it seems instead to focus on the whole person's adaptive fit with his milieu.

Rapaport seems to have misconstrued the purport of Erikson's contribution because of his awareness that psychoanalytic psychology needed expansion in the realms Hartmann included within the purview of the "adaptive viewpoint." Although Erikson's work was undoubtedly concerned with these issues, they were to be addressed explicitly by a later generation of theorists, among whom Rapaport's student George Klein (1976) was one of the most influential. The work of Heinz Kohut (discussed in detail in chapters 7 and 8) may also be seen as part of the same necessary expansion of analytic theory.

As Gill and Klein (in Rapaport, 1967, pp. 8–34) have pointed out, Rapaport's greatest contribution to ego psychology was his extension of the concept of ego autonomy (an idea Hartmann originally applied only to motivations independent of the drives). In a paper of 1957, Rapaport stated:

> Man can interpose delay and thought not only between in-stinctual promptings and action, modifying and even indefi-nitely postponing drive discharge, he can likewise modify and postpone his reaction to external stimulation. This indepen-dence of behavior from external stimulation we will refer to as *the autonomy of the ego from external reality* [1967, p. 723].

As the individual's relative freedom from the requirements of the drives is guaranteed by the development of inborn, autonomous ca-pacities, so freedom from the pressure of one's milieu is safeguarded by a set of constitutionally given drives. Rapaport successfully corre-lated these concepts with his other major contribution to ego psychol-ogy—the activity/passivity gradient of the ego (see p. 71 this chap-ter). Autonomy from the environment may be lost under certain conditions in which the required stimulus nutriment is no longer provided (e.g., perceptual deprivation, brainwashing, etc.), leading to ego regression analogous to those Rapaport postulated in condi-tions characterized by passivity vis-à-vis the drives.

In sum, Rapaport was more interested in the conflict-free sphere of the personality than in the ego proper. It is true that it has been customary to equate such interests with "ego psychology." As I have spelled out in detail elsewhere (Gedo and Goldberg, 1973), like Rapaport's disciple George Klein (1968) I believe that psychoanalysis has most to gain from restricting the definition of the ego to a set of functions activated in circumstances in which there is an ongoing intrapsychic conflict. Although Rapaport's position on these matters was more traditional, on occasion he made statements that fore-shadowed the revisionist argument, such as:

> . . . discovery, invention, and creation, in science as well as in art, will always be based on the creative impulse, which is unique, individual, and autistic. . . . Validity is provided for scientific invention by empirical and logical criteria, and in artis-tic inventions by concern for communication. The roots of in-vention will, however, always be autistic. The unique quality of the creative man is that he is both sufficiently free and strong to allow his impulses and their ideational representations to come to consciousness and sufficiently controlled to be able to delay and hold these in order to validate them by empirical or logical criteria (science) or communicability (art). Creation and in-vention are autistic products, but they are so constructed as to reveal a segment of nature or to communicate a segment of experience [1951, p. 439, n. 3].

Note that Rapaport characterized creative thinking as an activity that simultaneously possesses the characteristics of the ego (e.g., val-idation by means of rational criteria) and of the id (it is "autistic," its ideation represents the life of the impulses). Such a conception is incompatible with a definition of thinking as an ego function sec-ondarily freed of conflict over the drives: it simply does not conform with the conceptual categories available within the tripartite model of mental functioning. More frequently, however, Rapaport equated the hierarchic organization of various aspects of the personality with "the ego"; he called the intellect "the ego organization of thinking," de-spite the fact that he included the drive organization of memories within this hierarchy. In one of his last papers he discussed Freud's failure to conceptualize explicitly the development of the ego as a set of drive restraints (1967, pp. 820–854); yet, in this context, he reduced the "synthetic function" to an aspect of ego psychology, instead of realizing that this concept bursts the boundaries of the structural theory Freud proposed in 1923.

It seems most cogent to look upon Rapaport's research into the "quasi-stationary functions," which operate autonomously from conflict, as investigations of personality attributes that partake of the human depths, rather than studies of the realm of the ego alone (Kohut and Seitz, 1963). This point may be illustrated by Rapaport's first important contribution to psychoanalysis: a theory of thinking in which he lucidly discussed the need to examine states of altered consciousness, such as fugues, in order to understand the gamut of possibilities (1967, pp. 313–328). These archaic states of behavioral organization are regulated in large part by drive pressures and can by no means be understood as active ego functions exclusively. In practice, Rapaport understood these considerations perfectly: his succinct footnotes on thought disorders in obsessional neurosis stressed the drive cathexis of thinking in this condition (Rapaport, 1951, p. 589, n. 17; pp. 622–625, n. 107). His discussions of various schizophrenic symptoms show a similar awareness (pp. 602–603, n. 49; pp. 606–608, n. 60; pp. 612–613, n. 70, n. 71). Analogously, his concluding chapter in *Organization and Pathology of Thought* (1951) emphasizes the importance of memories of drive gratification for the development of thinking, and it noted that "the autonomy" of thought is never complete, despite the fact that thinking purportedly operates by means of capacities that develop autonomously.

In his paper "The Conceptual Model of Psychoanalysis" (1967, pp. 405–431), Rapaport stressed that the primary analytic model for all behavior is that of drive cathexis and tension discharge, albeit through implied threshold structures. In other words, Rapaport never lost sight of the archaic determinants of behavior. He took into account that the hierarchic organization of the more mature personality involves not only drive restraint through a layering of defenses but also the continuing discharge of drive derivatives, generally partially tamed, as well as the need to *maintain* an optimal degree of tension. Clearly, Rapaport's view of man was hardly a picture of disembodied intellect.

In his statement of a theory of affects, Rapaport once again proposed the concept of a complex hierarchy, the most archaic component of which involves affects as pure discharge phenomena (1967, pp. 505–508). The alteration of discharge thresholds, which permits the delay of such responses and the substitution of thinking and reality-oriented action, is accompanied by the progressive taming of affects, eventually leading to the capacity to utilize affect signals in the service of the ego. Yet the more archaic modes of affect discharge remain available at all times, and it is the richness and modulation of the range of potential affects that indicate that adaptation is adequate: "... enduring affective states ... come about as integrations of complex balances and conflicts of components from all three major structural divisions of the psyche" (p. 508). In my view, the persistence of "archaic discharge channels" indicates that the situation is even more complex and that prestructural conditions must be taken into account simultaneously in any comprehensive assessment of behavior.

In his paper "Cognitive Structures" (1967, pp. 631–664), Rapaport gives a similar account of the organization of complex hierarchies. In this context, consciousness is shown to have a wide variety of primitive and more developed alternative forms which remain at the disposal of a supra-ordinate integrative agency. Elsewhere Rapaport restated this as follows:

> ... the ego network includes as archaic levels of its structure the integrates which are passively regulated by drive tension. ... The differentiation of the ego and the id is not sharp but progressive. It reaches a definitive crystallization with those defense-identifications which arise as a solution of the oedipal conflicts. This point is a separating line between the integrates that are passive and those that are active in relation to the drive tension [1967, p. 706].

I think this quotation demonstrates that Rapaport overextended the applicability of ego concepts only in his more generalized statements and not in his detailed handling of specific psychological issues.

Rapaport's most ambitious attempt to outline a psychoanalytic theory of thinking, written in 1959, was organized around his concepts about attention cathexis (1967, pp. 778–794; see also Rapaport, 1951, pp. 689–699; 1967, pp. 405–431). However, as part of his emphasis on drive motivations as invariably playing a role in all thought formation, Rapaport also showed that one of their effects is to establish "a certain state of consciousness and a corresponding form of thought-organization: for example, hypnagogic state, sleep-dream state, fugue state" (1951, p. 224, n. 78). In other words, he did not reduce the problem of consciousness to a simple quantitative formula in terms of the distribution of attention.

Rapaport credited the phenomenologists (represented in psychiatry by Paul Schilder) with the realization that empirical investigation of the form-variants of consciousness is feasible. His discussion (1951, pp. 627–628, n. 115) of the hypermnesia frequently encountered in psychoses is an example of such a study; it deals with the vivid recall of previously forgotten life experiences after the psychotic break. In fact, Rapaport tried to develop a hypothesis to explain much of schizophrenic phenomenology on the basis of pathological alterations of consciousness (1951, p. 603, n. 49).

Rapaport conceived of variant forms of consciousness such as dreaming or fugue states as returns to differing levels of varying intensities, within a hierarchy of the organization of attention. By 1953 he was using the concept of "attention cathexis" in a more ambitious manner to provide the foundation for a theory of the formation of psychic structure, particularly that of thought organization (1967, pp. 558ff). This theory was stated more fully in 1959 in preparation for a program of experimental testing which Rapaport did not live to carry out (pp. 778–794); however, this work was continued by some of his collaborators (Schwartz and Schiller, 1970; Schwartz, 1973).

Rapaport's statement of the foregoing hypothesis starts with the assumption that the genetic aspect of cognitive processes is central for psychological development in general. All previous cognitive theories, including his own book, *Emotions and Memory* (Rapaport, 1942), had failed to account for the persistence of structures established by conditioning. Now he felt that the concepts of attention cathexis (Freud, 1900), automatization, and secondary autonomy (Hartmann, 1939) could be used to overcome this problem. Rapaport wrote: ". . . such an attempt is conceived for the purpose of exploring whether or not structures can be expressed in the dimension of cathexes . . . organized under very specific conditions of restriction (binding)" (1967, p. 779). The theory of attention cathexis therefore implies the elimination of the previously assumed dichotomy between perception and cognition; at the same time, it is understood that the deployment of attention cathexis does not necessarily imply the attainment of consciousness. Rapaport listed a formidable array of variables that must be considered in a unified learning theory based on the economic point of view (p. 780). They aim to introduce psychoanalytic economic concepts into experimental psychology through the differentiation of three sets of variables: structure, motivation, and cathexis. These variables might be determinate under varying experimental conditions.[6]

In December 1960, at the threshold of submitting his hypotheses to experimental validation, David Rapaport died. In the next 15 years, his coworkers saw to the publication of his planned experiments. Nonetheless, without his charismatic presence, most of his disciples soon changed the direction of their own psychoanalytic work, and Rapaport's reputation suffered a considerable decline. Rapaport thought that in his time psychoanalysis had reached a proper balance in conceptualizing the roles of unconscious motivation and of man's social niche for the determination of his behavior and adaptation. His immediate successors have clearly disagreed.

Rapaport's career thus coincided with the end of an era in psychoanalysis. Although he was prescient enough to predict that the next phase of analysis would involve the development of a metapsychologically sound theory of self, his own psychoanalytic work, centered on cognitive psychology, could not possibly have led in that direction. The era of ego psychology has been succeeded by a new breakthrough into man's psychological depths—a development I discuss in detail in the chapters to follow. Rapaport's espousal of Erikson's psychosocial theory as an adequate schema of ego development appears today to have been an uncharacteristic historical misjudgment; for the evolution of psychoanalysis, Erikson turned out to be a peripheral figure who did not focus primarily on man's inner life.

But what of David Rapaport himself? What was the significance of his contribution, in view of the fact that psychoanalysis has turned away from the work of Heinz Hartmann? If he is not to be remembered for his specific contributions to ego psychology, does he deserve a permanent place in our history for a more enduring accomplishment? Cognitive psychology has not occupied a place within the core of psychoanalysis. Sigmund Freud's personal creation is a uniquely humanistic discipline in the tradition of introspective poets

---

[6]In spite of his commitment to the theory of psychic energy, in a 1950 review of Norbert Wiener's *Cybernetics*, Rapaport was willing to accept information theory as a superior model for the description of the secondary process (1967, pp. 329–333). He did insist, however on the necessity for energic constructs with regard to the primary process.

like Shakespeare and Cervantes; 400 years ago the tradition of which psychoanalysis forms a part found its first systematizer in Michel de Montaigne (cf., Rieff, 1959; Gedo and Wolf, 1976). The birth of physical science in the 17th century, based on the dualistic epistemology of Descartes, relegated this moral philosophy to the domain of literature. The resulting materialist bias of the culture of science was to be corrected only by Nietzsche and Freud. Psychoanalysis may be said, then, to pursue the way of Montaigne. Rapaport has been its only major figure who stems from a different tradition—that of Kant.

Rapaport described the contrast between these intellectual strains as follows:

> It may seem surprising that Freud was . . . tardy in "bringing the psychological significance of the real outer world into the structure of . . . [his] theory." Therefore, it will be important to remind ourselves of some historical relationships. Philosophical psychology, the ancestor of scientific psychology, was a subsidiary of epistemology. Its major query was: How do we acquire our knowledge of the world of reality? It studied psychic functions mainly in their relation to the acquisition of knowledge of reality. Though there were exceptions to this, the milestones of psychology . . . were written in the service of epistemology. In its beginnings, scientific psychology did not radically change this focus of interest. It was centered in stimulus and reaction, that is, in evaluation by the psychic apparatus of the impingements of external reality, though some studies employing introspection were already concerned with intrapsychic reality.
>
> Freud's point of departure was different: he was concerned with the evaluation by the psychic apparatus of *internal stimuli* (drives, needs) rather than *external stimuli*. . . . Thus it occurred that only after considerable exploration of psychic reality and in the wake of observations concerning maladaptations to external reality did Freud have to face the problem of reality adaptation. . . .
>
> For the theory of thinking, it may be of some advantage to note that his manner of facing the problem . . . . shows some similarity to Leibnitz's formulation of the problem of epistemology. Leibnitz asked: How is it possible that reasoning arrives at conclusions which coincide with the outcome of processes occurring in reality? or in his own words: How can there be a correspondence between *"vérité de fait"* and *"vérité de raison"*? Freud's problem was: How can the apparatus regulated by

the pleasure-principle (drives) be also adapted to reality? [1951, pp. 316–317, n. 6].

Rapaport's publications contain the sophisticated epistemological expertise that is essential for psychoanalysis if we are ever to answer the question posed by Leibnitz. As early as 1947, he tried to demonstrate that although epistemology is in fact a branch of psychology, the empirical, psychologistic, genetic analysis of "knowledge" will never obviate the need for "*aprioristic* philosophical analysis of the conditions of gaining valid knowledge" (1967, p. 291). He thus prepared the way for the successful efforts of his students to demonstrate the epistemological weaknesses of traditional metapsychology.

Rapaport's dissertation was a detailed review of the history of efforts to define conditions for gaining valid knowledge since the resumption, early in the 17th century, of serious philosophizing, which had been dormant since the Hellenistic period. He began his account (1974, p. 7) with Bacon's pioneering attempt to define the obstacles to inductive thinking—the varied psychological factors that predispose everyone to make unwarranted assumptions. Rapaport went on to describe the polarization of epistemology into rationalist and empiricist camps. This intellectual dichotomy came into being under the aegis of Descartes, who split the cognitive realm in two, separating matters amenable to reason (*res cogitans*) from those pertaining to the physical world (*res extensa*) perceived through the senses.

Rapaport (1974, p. 33) thought that this Cartesian solution had once been essential: it had permitted science to study the problems of the physical world by empirical methods. In psychology, this strategy produced a physiological approach that in the 20th century no longer seems adequate for the study of "mind." Consequently, Cartesian dualism has been rejected in our times, and Descartes' contribution to the birth of empiricism tends to be overlooked. Rapaport (p. 35) credits Hobbes with building the empiricist tradition eventually formalized by Locke, who was first to base his hypotheses consistently on empirical data (p. 85). However, a truly psychological perspective was to be achieved only by Hume: "For him, the problem of knowledge was . . . a purely psychological question. He . . . asks *why* we see phenomena the way we actually do" (p. 183).

Of course, the rationalist tradition also had its source in Descartes. As Rapaport wrote:

> The conception of "innate ideas" assumes that we are born with certain ideas, the existence of which explains how it is that we have general concepts even though the sources of our knowledge—sensory impressions—are concrete. This is the diametrical opposite of the "*tabula rasa*" conception, according to which the mind is a *clean slate* at birth and all mental contents are acquired by experience. Descartes . . . assumed that the idea of God, as well as the ideas of all universally valid and necessary truths, are innate, and that sensory impressions do not create concepts but only provide the occasion for concepts to become conscious in us [1951, pp. 176–177, n. 5].

> *A priorism* is a specific form of the conception of innate ideas. Its most systematic presentation is Kant's *The Critique of Pure Reason*. . . . Kant maintained that the validity of a priori synthetic propositions (as for instance Euclid's postulates) cannot derive from experience. To explain the origin of their validity he asserted that the mind synthesizes all experiences in terms of the a priori forms of sensibility, that is, space and time; and in terms of the categories of pure reason, which he classified as categories of quantity, quality, relation, and modification. The validity of synthetic (a priori) propositions derives from the fact that all impingements of the environment are synthesized by the pure mind in terms of these forms and categories, and this synthesis lends them validity [1951, p. 177, n. 6].

Because Kantian transcendentalism successfully bridged the gap between the polarized philosophical traditions of empiricism and rationalism, Rapaport thought that it could perform a similar function within psychology, specifically, that psychoanalysis might best avoid the solipsistic dangers of the idealist-rationalist position by giving proper weight to the problem of cognitive development. The life work of this psychologist of thinking, who had integrated the theory of psychoanalysis, possesses enduring value as an anchor that can keep depth psychology from drifting into the type of id mythology exemplified by Freud's "death instinct" or certain tenets of Melanie Klein (see chapter 6, this volume).

The ubiquitousness of such temptations was keenly perceived by Rapaport:

> Freud's findings, demonstrating that the "psychological" appears as the determining cause of behavior, and even of some

physiological processes, were hailed by many as a new mine of evidence for idealism, vitalism, spiritualism, etc. The *fin de siècle* reaction against "materialism" is the proper background against which [such] views should be appraised [1951, p. 232, n. 104].

Further,

> . . . modern dynamic psychology has implications suggestive of solipsism. . . . The epistemological paradox of dynamic psychology is: how account for an adequate knowledge of reality when consciousness, the medium for gaining knowledge, is determined by intrapsychic laws? This paradox—implicit to the psychoanalytic concept of "reality testing" and amenable to psychological solution—is rarely tackled [1951, p. 519, n. 2].

Psychoanalysts as scientists still have difficulty in taking the last step in reality testing, the consensual validation of their clinical conclusions. This fact demonstrates the relevance of Rapaport's comment:

> Piaget, the philosopher-epistemologist and student of science, was struck by the similarity of the child's conception of physical phenomena to that of pre-Socratic, peripatetic, and Aristotelian physics. . . . Indeed, the struggle of the Milesians, Eleatics, Heraclitus, the Sophists, and Socrates-Plato to distinguish "appearance" and "truth" is in essence similar both to the development of reasoning, of the world picture, of causality, etc., in the child described by Piaget and to the development of "reality testing" described by psychoanalysis. The thought-products of these philosophies are often astoundingly similar to those of our children [1951, p. 155, n. 7–8].

Rapaport serves as a continual antidote to the bent of clinicians to focus on the content of thinking at the expense of observing thought processes, that is, the biological substrate of mental operations. In other words, if Rapaport seems somewhat alien to clinicians, it is because as a Kantian he is less interested in behavior (the outcome of mental processes) than in its mediation (the question of how the mind works). Coming from a master of psychoanalytic theory, his warnings that there are more things in heaven and earth than are dreamed of in our philosophy should yet gain a hearing. This may well prove to be David Rapaport's greatest contribution to psychoanalysis.

6

The Doctrine of Melanie Klein

Vitalism, Innate Ideas, and the Subversion of Reason

THE SCHOOL FOUNDED BY MELANIE KLEIN has proved to be the most
enduring and, at the same time, the most widespread of the dissident
movements within psychoanalysis. Mrs. Klein's earliest publications
appeared shortly after the first World War, while she was moving
from Budapest to Berlin, from analysis with Ferenczi to study and
treatment with Abraham, interrupted by the latter's premature demise. She began her career as an analyst of children, and her future as
a "dissident" may have been foreordained by virtue of the circumstance that her chief competitor for the leadership of this exciting
expansion of psychoanalysis was Freud's daughter Anna. By 1927,
the divergent views of Miss Freud and Mrs. Klein concerning many
aspects of child analysis were publicly debated, and Klein (encouraged by Ernest Jones) transferred her base of operations to London. A
decade later, political events were to bring her rival to the British
capital as well; by that time, however, Klein's influence within English psychoanalysis was ineradicable. She remained active until
1963, when she died at the age of 81; students from many parts of the
world, Latin America in particular, were trained in London in accord
with her ideas and spread her influence far and wide.

Melanie Klein earned her reputation because of two major accomplishments: first, by pioneering in giving due weight to human aggression in neurosogenesis (see 1948, p. 41[1]); second, by besting

---

[1]In this chapter, references to Klein's own works will be listed by date, without

Anna Freud in most respects in the arguments about child analysis. Klein listed the principal points of their disagreements in her Introduction to *The Psychoanalysis of Children:* she insisted on an interpretive technique analogous to that used with adults; she claimed that by using her method, a transference neurosis can be elicited and the negative transference can be subjected to analytic scrutiny (1932, pp. xv–xvi). Klein's analytic technique was based on the assumption that the spontaneous play of children is equivalent to free associations and may be interpreted symbolically (1927a, pp. 145–152; 1927b, p. 175; 1932, p. 7). In other words, she correctly grasped the fact that young children are better able to communicate meaningfully through enactments than by using words (1926, p. 135; 1932, p. 63). With the sure intuition of a gifted therapist, Klein focused her interventions on the affects that cause suffering, that is, anxiety and guilt (1927a, p. 145); she tried to relieve her patients by putting into words their unacceptable fantasies (1932, p. 27). Careful not to claim that she was able to obtain complete cures through these methods (1932, p. 280), Klein asserted that she was successful in mitigating anxiety and guilt by reducing sadism and strengthening the ego (1932, p. 279). Her therapeutic aim was to permit the child's development to resume its course (1926, p. 134).

Despite her difficult and turgid writing style, Klein was clearly masterful in communicating with children, a gift amply demonstrated in her book-length *Narrative of a Child Analysis* (1961). She worked hard to develop a "shared language" (Gedo, 1984a, chapter 8) with her patients (see 1932, p. 32). She was aware that Anna Freud believed that in the process Klein was putting words into the mouths of her child patients (1932, p. 9), and she effectively refuted this objection by pointing out that her interpretations of play were analogous to those of the dreams of adult patients (1926, p. 134). In other words, in practice analysts may often put words into the mouths of their patients, but *in principle* this pitfall is no worse in trying to comprehend the unconscious meanings of childhood play than in attempting to interpret dreams, for children respond to interpretations with further enactments analogous to adult analysands' associations in response to interpretations (see also 1955a, p. 137).

---

repeating her authorship, and by page number in the definitive, four-volume edition of her writings, Klein (1984).

Melanie Klein's views have gained general acceptance, and she is widely credited with establishing child analysis as a viable therapeutic discipline. She was undoubtedly the first to analyze pre-latency children, the youngest, her patient "Rita," at the age of two and three quarters (1932, chapter 1; see also 1927b, p. 169). Klein's initial papers have an evangelical tone about the benefits for children of early analytic intervention. Convinced that favorable emotional development is all but impossible (see 1932, p. 100), she recommended the prophylactic use of child analysis for all three year olds (1923). She also had a tendency to dismiss the premature interruption of many of her analytic efforts as caused by "external reasons" (see 1932, p. 30), rather than mistakes in her own performance. But these signs of excessive enthusiasm did not distinguish Klein from other analysts of her generation; if anything, her ideological position in the 1920s might be called ultraorthodox. After all, she boasted that her work with children, unlike that of Anna Freud or that of their predecessor, Hermione Hug-Hellmuth, amounted to "regular analysis" (1927a, p. 45).

If we are able, nonetheless, to detect the germ of the Kleinian dissidence in Mrs. Klein's early writings, this retrospective ability depends on grasping the significance of her original contributions to developmental psychology. On the basis of her reconstructive efforts (about which I have more to say later), Klein dated the genesis of the Oedipus complex at the beginning of the second year of life and attributed early castration anxiety to the deprivations imposed by the mother (1926, p. 131). She reasoned that such reactions were caused by the guilt produced through the stimulation of the child's aggression. At first, she believed that the crucial frustration setting in motion this entire sequence is caused by weaning, usually late in the first year (1927a, p. 161; 1927b, p. 171). Because the cycle of aggression, guilt, and anxiety tends to be endlessly repeated (1927b, p. 173), Klein attributed the genesis of human character to such early "oedipal" experience (1927b, p. 171). In other words, she gave the Oedipus complex a wholly pregenital anlage; she even postulated superego functioning in infants around the end of their first year of life (1928, pp. 186–187; 1932, p. 7). Because of the intense sadism she attributed to small children, Klein viewed this early superego as necessarily cruel (1928, p. 189); she thought that the introjection of an early, terrifying superego might be the cause of later psychosis (1929, p. 207).

By 1932, Klein appears to have changed her mind about the genesis of infantile aggression; although she still attributed this to "oral frustration," she now asserted that such frustrations lead to oedipal developments by six months of age (p. 132), and she ascribed these inevitable maturational sequences not to actual experience but to the influence of the death instinct (pp. 125–126; see also 1933, pp. 250–251). The fact that Klein invokes the death instinct to account for the inevitability of infantile aggression yet describes the potentiation of this mental activity as entirely reactive to oral frustration appears to be paradoxical. Yet, as we shall see later, the seeming paradox merely reflects Klein's deep pessimism about the human condition—her view of man as victim of fate because his constitutional endowment is poorly adapted to the environment for which he is destined. Implicitly at least, Heinz Hartmann's (1939) monograph on the problem of adaptation, proposing an evolutionary fit between genotype and the expectable challenge of the environment, was a reasoned challenge to Klein's espousal of this arbitrary pessimism.[2] Elsewhere (Gedo, 1984a, chapter 9), I have characterized Klein's position as analogous to that of Pelagius, a heretical churchman committed to the view that man is irredeemably wicked (viz., aggressive). Freud's position, as Hartmann specified it, paralleled that of orthodox believers in avoiding extremes of optimism or pessimism.

Klein believed in the inevitable emergence of a variety of unrealistic primitive fantasies that grossly distort the actualities of the infant's relations with the caretakers (1927a, p. 155; 1932, p. 133; 1940, p. 345), and she thought that these early conflicts could be overcome only with sufficient parental love (1932, p. 148). She called the unavoidable anxieties generated by these primitive conflicts "psychotic" (p. 155), and she insisted that the emergence of such material in treatment betokens not only regression from more mature forms of castration fear but also a fixation on these primitive issues (p. 159). Klein asserted, for example, that, although their neurosis becomes structured in latency, the excessive sadism encountered in obsessional patients is stimulated by crucial events in the anal stage (pp. 160–163). The best statement of her original ideas in *The Psychoanalysis of Children* is Klein's dictum that early anxiety situations are never entirely given up (p. 193).

---

[2]For a masterful evaluation of Hartmann's total contribution to psychoanalysis, consult Schafer (1976, chapter 4).

As the editors of *The Writings of Melanie Klein* have noted (vol. I, p. 432), she began to enunciate her mature theories in 1935. By that time, Klein had acquired a fair amount of clinical experience with adult patients, including several encounters with psychotic analysands (see 1932, pp. 255–260, 264ff.; 1946, p. 17). Her novel ideas were based on clinical findings in the cases with pathology referable to the earliest fixations; in other words, they were built on the assumption that expectable developments in the earliest phases of life can best be illuminated through the study of archaic pathology. As Klein put it, the infant's inner life during the early months is comparable to a psychosis (1935, p. 262; 1946, p. 1). This hypothesis presupposes that the infant has the capacity to fantasy shortly after birth (1936, p. 290)—an assumption contradicted by research on cognitive development (see chapters 10 and 11, this volume). According to Klein, these fantasies revolve around themes of oral aggression and guilt (1937, p. 309). As she was later to state (1957, p. 187), in her view the infant is caught in a vicious circle of greed, envy, and persecutory anxiety, albeit this may be counterbalanced by love and gratitude. In 1946, Klein named the conditions in this initial phase of postnatal life "the paranoid-schizoid position," which she regarded as the point of fixation for the schizophrenias (p. 2; see also 1935, p. 263).

Klein postulated that, around three months, the infant begins to want to preserve "the good object" (1935, p. 264). This need sets in motion a change to the "depressive position," wherein the child, overcome by guilt, wishes to restore the object, damaged in fantasy, to a state of perfection (pp. 270, 286).[3] In Klein's view, the depressive position is central in determining personal destiny. If anxiety about damaging the object is too severe, the child may defensively regress to the paranoid position (1935, p. 274; 1948, p. 37; 1952c, p. 73), a move leading to schizophrenia (1946, p. 15); or there may be resort to manic denial and fantasies of omnipotence (1935, p. 277; 1952c, p. 73). If the balance between hatred and love is more favorable, the infant's later development may avoid such pathological fixations (1935, p. 289). Mourning will inevitably revive the depressive position, includ-

---

[3]Klein refers to such a postulated mental state as "depressive" because of the assumption, generally accepted by psychoanalysts at the time, that depression amounts to self-punitive aggression, initiated by guilt about destructiveness toward another (cf. Freud, 1917a).

ing the propensity to use manic defenses (1940, pp. 344, 349); the success of mourning will depend on mastery of this transitory regressive state (1940, p. 354) by reestablishment of the disrupted inner world (1952a, p. 77). In parallel with her convictions about the etiology of schizophrenia, Klein asserted that manic-depressive psychosis is caused by fixation in the depressive position (1946, p. 3).

In Klein's view, the depressive position is transcended after the infant becomes capable of integrating the representation of mother as a whole object. In her opinion, this development occurs at around six months of age—a timetable of cognitive achievement no longer acceptable today (see chapters 10 and 11, this volume). At any rate, according to Klein, this developmental achievement forms the watershed between psychosis and neurosis (1946, pp. 3, 14). At the same time, the self-representation (in Klein's terminology, the "ego") ceases being an unintegrated assembly of bits (1952c, p. 62). Henceforth, it may lose its coherence through regression (1946, p. 4) or because of defensively motivated splitting (p. 5)[4]—tendencies to be overcome through maternal love (1946, p. 10; 1952c, p. 64). In more abstract terms, Klein believed that the infant's destructiveness is mitigated by instinctual fusion (1952c, p. 66), but she also thought that the child inhibits its aggression because it experiences guilt about it (p. 70). At this point, according to Klein, the child enters the arena of oedipal fantasies wherein the paternal phallus takes the place of the maternal breast (1952c, p. 78).

Although Melanie Klein's timetable of development is markedly faster than that of any other theorist, disagreement about the pace of maturational sequences in early life would not, in itself, constitute a dissidence. In terms of its consequences for clinical work, the specific age of the infant when particular developmental changes typically take place is not a matter of primary importance. Although Klein's formulations about infantile mentation attribute to young children symbolic capacities that do not begin to manifest themselves until the second year of life (see 1952c, p. 83), this objection could be applied equally to Freud's hypotheses about infancy (1895a, pp. 318, 327, 361; 1900, pp. 588, 622)—a matter taken up in greater detail in later chapters about observational research on infancy. Hence Klein's growing

---

[4]As we saw in chapter 3, this concept originated with Ferenczi.

reputation as the originator of a dissident school has additional and weightier determinants.

We may find it easier to approach the heart of this matter by slightly shifting our focus to the field of therapeutics. From that viewpoint, Melanie Klein may be seen as the successor of her first analyst and mentor, Ferenczi, in expanding the range of applicability of the analytic method. She successfully accomplished this task in the realm of child analysis in Ferenczi's lifetime; after his relegation to the limbo of dissidence and subsequent death, she continued the effort to do so in the area of psychotic disturbances. Klein profited from Ferenczi's example: she did not repeat his failure to gain a proper hearing by presenting herself as a technical innovator, although, as I show later, she did significantly modify analytic technique. Instead, she laid ceaseless emphasis on the importance of giving due weight to fixations on the earliest states of mind in the treatment of disturbances more severe than the neuroses. As early as 1926 (p. 136), she noted that in the analysis of children it is easier to uncover oedipal material than it is to reach the pregenital determinants of the pathology. She soon followed this claim with another equally bold, asserting that analytic success depends on overcoming the patient's pregenital fixations (1927a, p. 161) or, as she put it later, dealing with his deepest anxieties (1932, p. 52). Like Ferenczi, she reiterated the overriding importance of allowing negative transferences that echo early infantile frustrations to be reexperienced in the course of psychoanalysis (1952c, pp. 90–91). She ascribed a variety of inhibitions, including intellectual ones, to the stimulation of the child's hatred by early experiences of confusion (1928, p. 188). She presented convincing descriptions of young children suffering from outright paranoia (1931, p. 246; 1932, pp. 44, 57) or from obsessional neurosis before the age of three (1932, p. 3). Although her developmental schema placed these children into a phase she called "oedipal," from the psychosexual vantage point, she explicitly understood that their pathology was pregenital.[5] Klein believed that such obsessionalism serves to bind paranoid anxieties (1935, p. 263). She noted that even children in latency may eventually disclose a paranoia screened by their oedipal material (1932, p. 71). Another way Klein stated this was to claim that

---

[5]In other words, Klein's usage of the term "oedipal" stretched its meaning, far beyond that intended by Freud, to designate the establishment of any kind of object relationship with someone other than the mother.

the infantile neurosis serves to bind psychotic anxieties (1952c, p. 81). Her emphasis on the possibility that a neurotic character structure may overlie a hidden psychosis (1932, p. 103) probably shows that, in the 1930s, Klein was making an effort to integrate the findings of Ferenczi about archaic syndromes with the views accepted by the psychoanalytic mainstream of the day. (For one mention of Ferenczi's influence on Klein, see 1946, p. 5). Be it remembered that in her system, paranoia is a fantasy of relentless persecution by internalized "bad objects," a regression from the depressive position wherein the "good object" is felt to be worthy of preservation (1935, pp. 268, 271).

Melanie Klein's most extensive case report, her *Narrative of a Child Analysis* (1961), presents a sample of her pioneering work, a brief treatment of 93 sessions performed in mid-1941. The patient was a depressed 10-year-old boy, phobic, hypochondriacal, encopretic, pre-occupied with world destruction, and subject to lapses into paranoia. Klein's detailed notes profusely document the emergence of psychotic material, transient delusions, states of manic excitement and incoherence. Klein had no illusions about the fragmentary nature of this heroic effort, constrained from the first by the inevitability of arbitrary termination at the end of the summer. Her purpose in writing such a detailed report was to give an account of her clinical method (more of which later). At the same time, this narrative demonstrates that in her maturity Klein's analytic work paralleled American therapeutic experiments with psychotics by such clinicians as Harry Stack Sullivan and Frieda Fromm-Reichmann. In 1952 (1952a, p. 54), Klein made the explicit claim that her methods permit the analysis of schizophrenic patients—presumably those capable of functioning outside an institution.

Klein always eschewed the temptation to systematize her hypotheses. One disadvantage of her preference for doctrinal flexibility is that many of her ideas were relegated to obscurity: she put them forward almost casually and might never return to them. Many of her flirtations with novel concepts subsequently found support among later analytic authors, often without acknowledgement of her having had the same idea earlier. I was startled to find, for example, that as long ago as 1929 (p. 205) Klein played with a hypothesis I believed to be one of my better contributions to psychoanalysis, that of neurosis as an inability to integrate disparate memory clusters from earliest childhood (Gedo and Goldberg, 1973; Gedo, 1979)! I am certain that I had not read the specific paper in which Klein proposed her notion before I arrived at it "on my own." But I have been familiar with the corpus of her writings for a long time, and the concept of integrating such clusters (what I call "nuclei of the self") is implicit throughout the body of her work. I assume that other contributors who have borrowed from Klein have similarly been lulled into self-deception about their originality.

One of the themes within Klein's oeuvre appropriated by Heinz Kohut is that of the infant's propensity to idealize the caretakers. She first alluded to this finding in *The Psychoanalysis of Children*, pointing out that the initial attitude toward the father is not fear but admiration (1932, p. 137). Klein was aware that in describing the development of object relations, she was focusing on matters beyond the boundaries of the libido theory (1940, p. 348; 1952a, p. 51). As I describe in chapter 7, Kohut did not at first grasp this truth and for a long time tried to fit similar observations into the mold of the vicissitudes of narcissistic libido. At any rate, Klein was the first to focus on the young child's simultaneous tendencies to idealize others and to resort to fantasies of omnipotence (1940, p. 349). It is true that she believed that these developments are brought about by defensive denial of prior fantasies of persecution by "bad" inner objects (1946, pp. 507), but the controversial nature of this developmental proposition does not diminish the importance of her clinical discovery.

Another Kleinian idea now widely credited to self psychology is the occurrence of states of disorganization, subjectively experienced through feelings of "deadness." Klein described the fact that patients with such a vulnerability will experience profound anxiety whenever they are threatened with the possibility of disintegration (1946, p. 21; 1955b, p. 144). She noted correctly that the conscious content of such fears is often of impending death (1948, p. 30; 1952b, p. 57). She viewed the regressive tendency to disintegrate in the context of Freud's hypotheses about life and death instincts: for her, the former *is* the natural propensity for integration, the latter for entropy (1952c, pp. 65–66). She also understood that children whose development reaches the phase at which genital libido predominates are no longer at risk for disintegration of "the self" (1952c, p. 86).

Finally, Kohut's concept of the "selfobject" (which is taken up further in chapters 7 & 8 this volume), as he first enunciated it, also seems to have unacknowledged roots in Melanie Klein's work. As long as Kohut used this term to designate the representation of another person whose independent volition is denied, he was merely giving another name to Klein's concept that through "projective identification" it is possible in fantasy to "take over the object"—in other words, to make it into an extension of oneself (1952c, p. 68).

I have singled out for mention those of Klein's neglected ideas later taken up by analysts eager to extend the scope of psychoanalysis as a method of treatment. Yet it has been possible to espouse a great number of Kleinian contributions without being labeled a dissident, as the example of an influential author like Otto Kernberg demonstrates. Melanie Klein chose the path of dissidence not so much through her own contributions as through her adamant refusal to accept those of the ego psychologists (see chapter 5, this volume), notably Anna Freud. She was untroubled by accusations of having remained an "id psychologist" (see 1932, p. 27). As late as 1961 (p. 27), Klein dismissed the alleged desirability of giving priority to the analysis of defensive operations, although she included the defenses among the phenomena she brought to the attention of analysands (p. 365).

It is difficult to avoid the conclusion that Klein was unimpressed with the utility of ego psychology because this orientation was ill suited to her therapeutic style. From the beginning of her psychoanalytic career, she found that her interpretations were easily accepted (1926, p. 135). There is no doubt that one reason for this unusual success was Klein's unhesitating certainty about her views (see Brome, 1983, p. 155). This attitude is illustrated by her assertion that if a child is afraid of falling into a hole, this symptom is "obviously" an indication of birth anxiety (Klein, 1923, p. 82). Almost twenty years later, in her wartime treatment of the psychotic boy she described in her *Narrative,* (1961) Klein responded to the patient's failure to accept interpretations in the fifth session with a barrage of arguments in which she arbitrarily asserted that all the patient's subsequent associations confirmed her prior statements. When, in the next session, the boy reported that he had been afraid to return, Klein interpreted this reaction as an indication that he wanted to have intercourse with her (pp. 35–36). Under the circumstances, most analysts would have considered the possibility that the child might simply have been frightened by her insistence on interpretations that made no sense to him. Some weeks after this incident, when the patient expressed doubt that Klein knew everything about him and made *only* valid interpretations, she understood these statements as signs of his paranoid mistrust (pp. 111–112). Perhaps the child's pathetic fantasy, in his last analytic session, that Klein was broadcasting to the world, "I shall give the right kind of peace to everybody," (p. 462) was not simply an expression of his need to idealize her but also a valid perception of her self-concept.

Klein did not overlook the tendency of analysands to disavow the significance of the material she brought to their attention (1926, p. 137). In the analysis of children, she found that they resisted acknowledging the relevance of their play activities to important issues in their daily life. Klein simply overrode such resistance by her authority (1932, p. 11). She explicitly conceived the analyst's task to be to confront the analysand with the content of the Unconscious (1955a, p. 129). In her view, confidently articulating id interpretations in the face of resistance diminishes the patient's anxiety and opens the door to the Unconscious (1932, pp. 22–24). She was satisfied that her interpretations were valid if she observed clinical improvement; she overlooked the therapeutic effect of forming a bond with a healer experienced as omniscient (1932, p. 29). I am not implying that Klein was less likely than any other analyst to make valid interpretations, only that she was ready to interpret on the basis of evidence that would fail to satisfy others. Moreover, Klein did not lose her self-confidence even in the absence of adaptive improvements: she blithely assumed that her interpretations would do their beneficial "work" in any case (see 1961, p. 70).

In light of these gnostic attitudes about perceiving her patients' inner life, it is something of a surprise to discover that Melanie Klein's conception of the effect of treatment was seemingly unrelated to the acquisition of insight. Late in her career, she wrote, ". . . during an analysis repeated experiences of the effectiveness and truth of the interpretations given leads to the analyst—and retrospectively the primal object—being built up as good figures" (1957, p. 233). Because of Klein's commitment to the view that only exceptional nurture will save babies from psychosis, that statement can mean only that the aim of treatment is to correct the unfortunate sequelae of having introjected an insufficiency of good objects in infancy. Thus, Kleinian analysis is designed to be a "replacement therapy." If this is one's therapeutic aim, the value of an interpretation does not depend *primarily* on its validity but rather on its effectiveness in mitigating the patient's suffering. Obviously, the therapist's interventions cannot be effective unless the patient accepts their "truth," but validity may have less to do with acceptance than may factors such as the therapist's charisma and the comfort or reassurance provided. Indeed, Klein repeatedly stressed the effectiveness of her interventions in mitigating the anxieties of her patients, that is, her success in soothing their distress. It is notable in this connection that nowhere in her *Narrative of a Child Analysis* (1961) does Klein concern herself with issues of analytic process or the unfolding of the transference. She concerns herself exclusively with current dynamics: reconstructions are never attempted, presumably because the principal issues dealt with in Klein's system are present in unchanged form from the cradle to the grave. The whole effort concentrates on relieving distress in the here and now.

The Kleinian theory of cure is logically related to her conception of early psychological development. It will be recalled that in Klein's mature theory, the expectable vicissitudes of early infancy lead to psychosis unless they are overcome by happy experiences provided by the caretakers (1935, p. 287). In her view, these favorable developments take place through the establishment of good inner objects (1940, p. 347). Elsewhere, she wrote about this process as the introjection of the good breast (1936, p. 291; 1957, p. 178). She believed that this was a prerequisite for the predominance of integrating forces within the personality—in her terminology, for the prevalence of the life instinct over the death instinct (1948, p. 32). In turn, the introjection of the good object enhances the infant's capacity to love (1952c, p. 67); it forms the core of the ego (1957, p. 180).[6]

To grasp Klein's rationale for her espousal of corrective experience as the vehicle of psychoanalytic cure we must therefore investigate how she arrived at her convictions about infantile mental life. In her writings, she consistently reported that she learned these truths through clinical experience with patients suffering from what I prefer to call archaic fixations, especially from work with young children whose material she believed to be particularly illuminating about conditions in early life. We must exercise great caution with regard to these claims because of Klein's general overconfidence about the validity of her interpretations. By 1928, without ever having published supporting evidence, she claimed that she could describe the fantasies of a one-year-old child, before the child acquired any capacity for speech (1928, p. 187). We may gain an impression of Klein's read-

---

[6]Note the echoes of Ferenczi's conception of the absence of good care underlying the pathological development of "the wise baby" (chapter 3, this volume).

iness to leap to conclusions from her assumption that the analytic material she obtained in treating children was a direct reflection of mental life during their first year (see 1932, chapter 1; 1957, p. 204; 1961, pp. 155, 335, 338).

In fact, Klein never indicated *how* she had reached her hypotheses about development. She probably thought theories are adequately validated if they prove to be useful in the therapeutic arena. As we shall see later, in the chapters devoted to developmental studies, this assumption has not proven to be valid. None of the numerous clinical vignettes she published casts doubt on what one may infer from reading her *Narrative of a Child Analysis* (1961). Klein made no effort to develop inductive propositions on the basis of her clinical observations. On the contrary, she classified all the phenomena she encountered in working with the patient according to a detailed set of predetermined categories. In her single-minded concentration on these putative human universals, Klein seems deliberately to disregard the significance of individual differences.

Late in her career, Klein stated that her theoretical position is *based on* the concepts of Freud and Abraham concerning oral libido and fantasies of cannibalism (1952c, p. 76). This statement correctly identifies the source of Klein's ideas in metapsychological abstractions and shows her conceptualizations to have been entirely deductive. If this process resulted in a system of Kleinian propositions unacceptable to most of Freud's followers, this surprising outcome is probably due to the fact that Klein failed to grasp some of Freud's intended meanings. When she uses Freud's construct language, his terms tend to take on new (generally simplified) connotations. For instance, she often concretized the idea of a death instinct; she believed Freud had "discovered" (rather than conceptualized) it (1957, p. 177). She asserted that the infant experiences the force of this instinct as an interal persecution (1946, pp. 4–5); consequently, the instinct is said to produce fears of annihilation (1952c, p. 61). She also concretized and anthropomorphized the psychic agencies of Freud's tripartite model of the mind: she wrote about them as if they were living participants in the activities of the individual (1929, p. 200). Her conception of the superego was, in addition, idiosyncratic: she understood any introjection of parental attitudes or commands as superego formation (1926, p. 133; 1932, pp. 156ff.). It was for this reason that she asserted that such a structure is established in the first year of life (1928, p.

188). In his correspondence with Jones, Freud explicitly repudiated
this distortion of his views (see Brome, 1983, p. 155).

To put the foregoing summary of Klein's intellectual course another way, the Kleinian dissidence seems to have been the inadver-
tent result of her consistent adherence to an idiosyncratic metapsychology that she looked upon as biological truth (see Gedo, 1984a,
chapter 9). To clarify the nature of Klein's metapsychology, we need
to strip it of its veneer of Freudian terms, lest we fail to grasp *her*
intended meanings. Throughout her writings, Klein emphasized the
primacy of constitutional factors in psychic development (1928, p.
191), paying particular attention to the "strength" of various instincts, for example, "oral sadism" (1932, pp. 49, 124; 1952c, p. 62;
1957, p. 176). She postulated the universal occurrence of "phylogenetic" fantasies (1932, pp. 131, 137) starting at birth, involving
envy or greed. Yet she conceded that, initially, thinking does not
make use of words (1946, p. 8).[7] She conceived of fantasy as "the
mental corollary of an instinct" (1952b, p. 58); at the same time, she
looked upon fantasy content as if it were always a valid representation of mental structures or processes (1946, pp. 8, 22–24; 1952b, p.
58; 1959, p. 250; see also 1961, p. 85)—the ultimate reality of mind.
For instance, Klein believed that in case of object loss, the grief of
mourning betokens that unconsciously the inner good object is also
lost (1940, p. 353), destroyed by the mourner's aggression.

As a corollary of the foregoing view of mental disposition as fantasy, the genesis of all pathology must, in the Kleinian system, consist of a fantasy that persists (see 1961, p. 87). The individual's destiny
is determined primarily by the constitutional balance between his life
and death instincts (1952a, p. 54; 1958, p. 236), although the influence
of nurture is also given some weight (1952c, p. 67; 1952d, p. 96). This
influence is acknowledged in the dictum that object relations are initiated at birth (1946, p. 2; 1952a, p. 51; 1952b, p. 57). Klein also postulated that the instinctual constitution determines the degree of ego
strength or weakness (1957, p. 229). In Klein's system, the ego is
assumed to be operative at birth (1952b, p. 57; 1952c, p. 62), having at
its disposal the mechanisms of projection, introjection, and splitting

---

[7]Nonetheless, she attributed to the infant the capacity to make sophisticated
judgments, such as seeing excrements as "bad" or understanding that devouring the
breast would reduce it to fragments.

(1946, pp. 2, 8; 1952c, p. 71). The ego can develop through introjective processes that provide it with good inner objects (1952c, p. 67), but it may be weakened through projective identification (1946, p. 8) because this process leads to confusing the self and the object (1957, p. 192). Through its defensive mechanisms, the ego must deflect the death instinct outward (1957, p. 191) lest persecutory anxiety lead to excessive splitting (1946, pp. 2, 24).

This metapsychological system tightly links mental contents to the instincts on an a priori basis: for Klein, fantasy is the mental corollary of instinct. In its arbitrariness, this hypothesis constitutes a biological myth, a doctrine attributing vital forces to fictive entities.[8] On the purely psychological level, it deals exclusively with a limited set of stereotyped, constitutionally predetermined fantasies or innate ideas. These involve three variables: inside/outside, satisfaction/frustration, and love/hate. The same dichotomies might also be called self/object, good/bad, and repair/destroy. This system is simple enough to have universal relevance for humans, once they develop ability for symbolic thought. Mrs. Klein was convinced that, armed with this biopsychological conception of the core of our humanity, she could discern the basic significance of all symbolic communications. Her opponents saw this claim as a pathetic error or, alternatively, as the triumph of banality. However that may be, Klein's therapeutic prescription, the provision of repair/love so that the self/inside shall be filled with satisfaction/goodness (1945, pp. 408–410), is a logical corollary of her metapsychology.

It is very difficult to judge how literally we should take Melanie Klein's theory of psychoanalytic technique: her actual procedures may well have been more complex than her descriptions lead one to believe. She provided us with her *Narrative of a Child Analysis* (1961) as a repository of evidence in this regard, but the fragmentary treatment reported in that book may not do full justice to Klein's clinical skills. In the management of this barely compensated psychosis, she did stake everything on promoting the internalization of a "good object"

---

[8]Recent criticisms of Freud's metapsychology, particularly of his postulate of psychic energy (see Gill and Holzman, 1976), regard his conceptualization as equally vulnerable to this criticism, now that Freud's assumptions have been left behind by neurobiology (Gedo, 1984a, chapter 10). As Swanson (1977) has shown, however, Freud's hypotheses were scientifically respectable when he devised them. If we take the "principle of constancy" (Freud, 1892) as the keystone of his metapsychological edifice, we may conclude that subsequent research has proved this theory to be *incorrect*. In contrast, Klein's hypotheses have remained *untestable*.

by offering herself in that guise (pp. 427, 457). Consequently, she made almost no effort to correlate the transactions between herself and her patient to the actualities of the latter's life situation.

She focused instead on the content of his bizarre fantasies, occasionally attributing to him ideas he was far from articulating—ostensibly because she was convinced of their universality. Before long, the child seemed to accept Klein as a kindred spirit, a visionary at ease with his inner landscape populated by monsters, and her calmness when confronted with experiences he found terrifying did exert a soothing effect on him. I remain skeptical about the validity of many interpretations Klein offered in this sample of her work, but on a level I consider more basic and essential—creating a "holding environment" wherein further therapeutic efforts become feasible—I consider Klein's work to have been most impressive (see Gedo, 1984a, chapter 3). In the last week of treatment, the patient had a dream (Klein, 1961, p. 449) in which the bus he had to take to reach Klein did not have its conductress. Her interpretation was beyond dispute: the imminent loss of the analysis was about to leave the boy without guidance.

To be sure, psychoanalysis as a method of treatment requires more than the establishment of a stable working relationship or, to paraphrase Klein's patient, the provision of the right kind of peace for the analysand. Even if the analyst's benign attitudes were securely transmitted to the patient, as Klein postulated they would be (a highly dubious proposition, judging by the clinical experience of most therapists!), the resulting identification could not *eliminate* the structured mental dispositions that constitute psychopathology. Whatever the benefits of treatment conducted in accord with Klein's principles might be, her system is radically different from that of psychoanalysts, whose therapeutic goals involve the alteration of mental structure.[9] Incidentally, it is curious that despite Klein's candor about her philosophy of treatment, Kleinians are seldom dismissed as mere "psychotherapists." It would seem that adherence to analytic ar-

---

[9]As I discuss at some length in the chapters devoted to the work of Heinz Kohut, one requirement of psychoanalytic work (in contrast to other forms of therapy) is refusal to exploit as a vehicle of cure positive transference, especially the ubiquitous tendency of patients to idealize the analyst. Klein's insistence on detecting hostility behind the analysand's idealizations fails to address the issue of the transference of infantile experiences of a positive nature. Nor did she ever discuss the cardinal issue of the conditions required for permanent structuralization of favorable adaptive changes: how is the internalization of the good object preserved after analytic termination?

rangements with regard to schedules and physical setup, the basic rule of free association, and the therapist's verbal responses as an "interpreter" suffice to qualify Kleinians as fellow analysts (see Gedo, 1984a, chapter 10).

For better or for worse, therefore, psychoanalysis includes a school of thought with radically different presuppositions about human nature from those of the Freudian majority. Klein's concretization of a "life instinct" in continuous conflict with a "death instinct" that threatens to flood the organism with self-destructive impulses (1958, pp. 236–239) amounts to the invention of biological forces that explain survival. In other words, it is a doctrine of vitalism. This point of view has been losing respectability within biological science for well over a century; it was anathema to Sigmund Freud, the disciple of Brücke and Helmholtz.[10]

Moreover, Melanie Klein's commitment to the notion of phylogenetically determined innate ideas in the form of a variety of primal fantasies carries the Kantian reliance on *a priori* categories in thinking to extremism. It is one thing to assume that it is part of being human to conceptualize sequences in terms of the abstraction we call time; it is quite another matter to expect that everyone will divide the day into 24 equal units. In other words, Klein's resort to a rationalist epistemology is more apparent that real; in actuality, she simply refused to submit matters that require it to undergo empirical investigation. By overextending the domain of pure reason in this way, Klein managed altogether to subvert reason.

---

[10]Paul Stepansky (personal communication) has pointed out that early in the 20th century, there was a recrudescence of vitalistic thinking in some quarters: Alfred Adler was one representative of this trend. According to Stepansky, Adler transposed the "life instinct" to the social arena via his notion of *Gemeinschaftgefühl*—community feeling. Adler construed pathology as maladaptation proceeding from inadequate potentiation of this one great vital principle. Stepansky rightly calls Freud's opposition of Eros and Thanatos, in his late work, a reversion to vitalistic theorizing. I would add that this may account for the fact that this aspect of Freud's work has failed to gain acceptance among psychoanalysts, except for Melanie Klein!

7

A Hero of Our Time

The Dissidence of Heinz Kohut

WITHOUT A DOUBT, HEINZ KOHUT's "Self Psychology" is the most powerful dissident movement on the contemporary psychoanalytic scene. Kohut himself was clearly distressed about this institutional development; in his concluding remarks (1978a, pp. 931–38) for a two-volume collection of his papers, for example, he asserted that his work was, in fact, the latest evolutionary phase of the psychoanalytic mainstream. Even later (1980c, p. 547) he expressed concern about the divisive potentials of his followers' overenthusiasm, cliquishness, and arrogance. Over and over again, he affirmed the continuity between his work and the tradition within psychoanalysis exemplified by Anna Freud and Heinz Hartmann (see 1978a, p. 934)—a claim convincingly substantiated by his sole account of his early clinical work, that of the first analysis of "Mr. Z." (1979, pp. 3–9), a treatment performed in a rigidly conservative manner.

In 1973, on the occasion of Kohut's 60th birthday, the Chicago psychoanalytic community entrusted me with the task of paying him public homage for his scientific contributions (see Gedo, 1975a). At the time, far from being regarded as a dissident, Kohut was rightly seen as a scion of the psychoanalytic establishment. I believe I was giving voice to a widely held consensus when I summarized his role in psychoanalytic history as that of an extender of "the boundaries of the field we are able to survey under the aegis of the basic rule of free association" (p. 319). I added that the resulting insights "invalidated little of significance in our previous clinical theories," although they called into question the universality of some psychoanalytic propositions. I noted that consequently Kohut's work did transcend "the paradigm of psychoanalysis as we have known it," a fact most of his readers until then had overlooked as a result of the unyielding conservatism of Kohut's conceptual armamentarium (p. 317). To be precise, he had tried to reduce complex and novel clinical observations to a narrow modification of metapsychology: he postulated independent lines of development for narcissism and object love, described some putative waystations in the maturation of narcissism, and hypothesized that archaic narcissism may be transformed into certain valued assets of the personality.[1]

In my judgment, the clinical data that Kohut condensed into these theoretical proposals did indeed constitute a scientific discovery of major significance (Gedo, 1975a, p. 318). This discovery was tantamount to Kohut's observation that when the analyst refrained from nonanalytic efforts to educate patients morally and from unwarranted relegation of material referable to archaic developmental phases to the category of defenses against oedipal conflicts, individuals with personality disorders previously impervious to analytic treatment proved to be analyzable by means of the standard analytic method. He reported (1968, 1971) that, in properly conducted analyses, patients with "narcissistic" personality disorders develop stable, transference-like conditions in which an intense relationship to the analyst revives the archaic experience of regarding the caretaker as part of the child's own volitional system. As I understood him, Kohut claimed that "interpretation of the disturbances of these archaic bonds to the analyst permits genetic insights and gradual mastery of fixations at immature levels of object relations" (Gedo, 1975a, p. 318).

Kohut was by no means alone among the analysts of his generation in exploring previously unplumbed layers of the human depths. Let me document this assertion by quoting from my 1972 review of Phyllis Greenacre's *Emotional Growth* (1971):

The common thread uniting [the] varied strands of Greenacre's research is the finding that traditional psychoanalytic theory could not account for her observations . . . all of which seemed to be decisively influenced by the course of infantile develop-

---

[1]These echoes of ideas Lou Salomé communicated to Freud were probably the result of independently arrived at conclusions, although one cannot rule out the possibility that Kohut may have had access to the Freud-Salomé Letters before their publication in German in 1966, and he certainly must have read her *Journal* (Leavy, 1964).

ment prior to the evolution of the Oedipus complex, the decisive experience in neurosogenesis. Greenacre's careful and detailed descriptions of the relevant clinical data thus prepared the way for [a] major reformulation of the clinical theory of psycho-analysis. . . . Greenacre distinguished the castration anxieties of neurotic personalities [from] fears about dissolution of the integrity of the self [that] characterize perverts. She also noted the greater degree of aggression and narcissism in perversions. She understood perverted sexuality as a symptom of the need to guard against [subjective] fragmentation by affirming phallic integrity. She attempted important differentiations between the frantic, defensive use of the oedipal situation by children who have been traumatized in earlier developmental phases and the true 'infantile neurosis' of the child who is developing satisfactorily. . . . In 1967, Greenacre placed these syndromes into the framework of disorders of narcissism, and [later] she repeated that the key to understanding early emotional growth lies in this aspect of analytic theory [Gedo, 1972b, pp. 828–29].

I do not wish to overstate the consensus in the early 1970s between Kohut and other pioneering contributors, such as Greenacre; I quote my contemporaneous assessment of her work only to demonstrate that efforts to explore the role of preoedipal issues in pathogenesis certainly did not condemn anyone to assume the burdens of psychoanalytic dissidence. By 1973, it was becoming clear that Kohut's challenge transcended his extension of the boundaries of the psychoanalytic universe—as I then stated, that "the significance of [his] achievement [was] not dependent on its specific details" (Gedo, 1975a, p. 314). It is true that by that time Kohut had gradually shifted his emphasis: he was already defining the crux of the clinical problem in "narcissistic disorders" in terms of the "insecure achievement of self-cohesion, subject to temporary fragmentation under the impact of certain specific types of frustration" (p. 318).

Perhaps the earliest rendering of Kohut's concepts as an "Emerging Psychology of the Self" is to be found in the monograph I coauthored with Arnold Goldberg in 1973, *Models of the Mind.* In that work, we assumed that novel theories were needed to illuminate hitherto neglected modes of psychic functioning—the archaic modes poorly explained through the constructs of the ego psychology then prevalent in America (see pp. 53–55). For those who could not accommodate their clinical findings within the tripartite model of the mind, Kohut's attempt to correlate narcissistic issues and the formation and vicissitudes of a structured "self" promised a new resolution of a theoretical impasse in psychoanalysis.[2]

The years between his Brill Lecture to the New York Psychoanalytic Society (Kohut, 1972) and the publication of *The Restoration of the Self* (1977) marked Kohut's transition from the avant-garde of the psychoanalytic mainstream to a position of dissidence.[3] These were difficult years for Kohut, marked by the onset of the chronic illness that was to end his life within a decade and by gradual loss of the support of many colleagues who had initially greeted his innovative proposals with enthusiasm. His essay of 1976 on Freud's self-analysis already contains a thinly veiled counterattack against those who would enshrine Freud's theories in order to satisfy their envy and diminish their humiliation vis-à-vis contemporary rivals who make significant contributions necessitating theoretical revision (1976, pp. 801–04; see also 1973a, pp. 667–68). In a letter of August 1977, Kohut attributed his adherence through 1972 to the classical libido theory solely to the necessity to present his findings in a language known to his American colleagues (1978c, pp. 927–28). I think we may legitimately infer that his increasing tendency in later years to revise accepted theories was propelled by the realization that clothing his convictions in the traditional garb of Freud's construct language would not earn him the support of psychoanalytic conservatives.

As late as 1976, Kohut could still resort to explanations in terms of energic cathexes, specifically vicissitudes of narcissistic libido (1976, pp. 800–01); he understood the need of creative persons for fantasied merger with a powerful alter ego on the basis of the depletion of the self because of the investment of narcissistic energy in the created product (pp. 816–18). Yet, as early as January 1973, he claimed that he used the terminology of the libido theory *allusively*, to refer to "an introspected and/or empathically grasped reality" (1978c, p. 870); by June 1975, he was asserting that Freud's psychobiological concepts are mere metaphors that refer to psychological relationships (p. 904). Both *The Restoration of the Self* (1977) and the 1978 Casebook edited by

---

[2]Kohut himself first wrote of a "psychology of the self" in May 1974 in a public letter to one of his followers (see 1978b, p. 752n).

[3]As one of Kohut's former students and a sometime collaborator with whom he shared his unpublished ideas, I was among the first to detect this change. It was I who challenged him about the adequacy of the analytic work with the patient called "Mr. M." (Goldberg, 1978, chapter 3), and it was in response to my intervention that Kohut wrote his defense of that work—the initial chapter of his 1977 book.

Goldberg "with the collaboration of Heinz Kohut," contain several statements about the flow of narcissistic libido.[4] Only the publications that follow the transitional period, culminating in the posthumous *How Does Analysis Cure?* (1984), are entirely free of such anachronistic uses of libido theory.

To recapitulate, Kohut's abandonment of Freud's metapsychology paralleled the fate of that theoretical framework in the psychoanalytic community at large. Far from rendering him a radical dissident, the cautious evolution of his views ranks Kohut as *retardataire* in comparison to contemporary theoreticians such as Schafer (1976), George Klein (1976), Rubinstein (1965, 1967, 1974, 1976a), Rosenblatt and Thickstun (1977), or Kohut's own follower, M. F. Basch (1975a, 1975b, 1976a, 1976b, 1976c, 1977). For an explanation of the divisive impact of Kohut's contributions, we must therefore look elsewhere. The earliest clues are perhaps to be found in some of Kohut's less familiar works, rather than in major statements of his ideas, such as *The Analysis of the Self* (1971).

Around 1970, Kohut began to emphasize certain conclusions drawn from his new clinical theories, conclusions he believed to have general applicability in the broadest human sense. He asserted (1973b) that the theory of narcissism would unlock the mysteries of group psychological phenomena, such as the mass appeal of messianic leaders (p. 532). A few years later, he predicted that the primacy of "truth values" in psychoanalytic contexts would give ground to empathy (1973a, pp. 668, 676–78). He called empathy an "essential psychic nutriment" (p. 707) that counteracts despair and a sense of existential meaninglessness (p. 713)—a considerable shift in his position about this aspect of the analyst's therapeutic armamentarium, one to which I return in chapter 8. Kohut's implicit claims for the primacy of his contributions to psychoanalysis soon became manifest in his further writings about clinical matters. In April 1975, Kohut defined the normal atmosphere one should provide for patients in the psychoanalytic situation as one of empathic acceptance (1978c, p. 899). In his 1977 book, he stated that the transferences encountered in analysis amount to a "reactivated attempt to build a cohesive self *by means of the empathic response of the self-object*" (p. 262, italics added. Kohut's reasons for calling the analyst a "self-object" are discussed later in this chapter). In an address he was working on at the time he

---

[4]See Kohut, 1977, pp. 23, 97; Goldberg, 1978, pp. 8, 123, 152, 440.

died, Kohut repeated the assertion that empathy has therapeutic value in its own right (1982, p. 397; see also 1983, p. 398). In his posthumous book, he specified his view that the decisive curative step in
psychoanalysis takes place through the establishment of a "new
channel of empathy," that of the dyad being "in tune" on a mature
level (1984, p. 66).

Kohut's claims for the effectiveness of "empathic science" (1973c,
p. 700) as a tool in both the therapeutic arena and in the broadest
social contexts probably caused the earliest ripples of disquiet about
his work in psychoanalytic circles. Eventually, Kohut became aware
that his views might be understood as a recommendation to provide
healing by means of a "corrective emotional experience," perhaps
even through the personal magic of the charismatic therapist, and he
was at pains to disclaim such inferences. Kohut stressed that he
regarded empathy solely as a mode of observation—cognition at-
tuned to perceive complex psychological configurations (1971, p.
300). He called upon analysts to overcome their magical wishes to
effect cures through loving understanding (p. 307). He reiterated that
the beneficial effects of empathy are nonspecific and stated, moreover, that empathy cannot be used to formulate interpretations, for it
is merely a method of data collection (1980c, p. 485).

In later attempts to clarify his position on this crucial matter, Kohut
(1982) stated that the analyst's actions should be informed by empathy, but that the needs of the analysand cannot be met through proper attitudes as such, that only effective interventions can do the job
(1982, p. 397). In his last reference to this issue (1984), he acknowledged that empathy has always been a ubiquitous feature of psychoanalysis; hence it is used no differently by "self psychologists" than
by anyone else (pp. 173, 176). However, Kohut also stated that the
empathic bond in analysis can be maintained only through the ongoing performance of "selfobject functions" by the analyst (pp. 184–
85).[5] Goldberg (1978), in his Introduction to *The Psychology of the Self*,
had already made the same point: he defined empathy as "the proper
feeling for and fitting together of the patient's needs and the analyst's
response" (p. 8).

---

[5]Kohut introduced some confusion in making this statement, for it implies that
the analyst must meet the patient's demands within the archaic transference. Yet he
goes on to say that it is sufficient to explain these childhood needs to the patient (1984),
as if a psychoanalytic interpretation were in itself a "selfobject function." The concept
of "selfobject" is discussed later.

THE DISSIDENCE OF HEINZ KOHUT

I trust I have succeeded in showing that Kohut's attitude about the role of empathy in psychoanalysis was inconsistent. When challenged on narrowly clinical grounds, he responded with orthodox pronouncements on the subject. When he was spontaneously describing his preferred technique of analysis, however, his recommendations for an empathic ambiance belied his disclaimers that empathy is merely a method of cognition (e.g., 1978c,; see also Wolf, 1976). And in his sermonizing calls for empathic scholarship (e.g., Kohut, 1973c, pp. 721–22)—or, for that matter, in his emphasis on the need to respond to archaic transferences with empathic *acceptance* (1978c, p. 899), he seemed to imply that the empathy of a psychoanalyst must directly lead to certain *activities* on behalf of others. These implicit but disavowed recommendations for unspecified, noninterpretive interventions on the part of the analyst constitute a radical departure from traditional psychoanalytic technique.

If Kohut was interested in preventing his own slide into dissidence, as I believe he was, the most serious tactical mistake he made was to maintain that there was no need to integrate his clinical findings about archaic transferences with those of Freud about the "transference neuroses" (1977, p. 206). It will be recalled that Kohut originally subsumed his work within the rubric of "The Psychoanalytic Treatment of Narcissistic Personality Disorders" (1968), implying that he was highlighting the special problems encountered in dealing with a hitherto neglected nosological entity. I covered the history of the progressive evolution of this idea in chapter 1; here, I shall only repeat that as he became accustomed to paying close attention to the wishes of patients to receive affirmation and to idealize the analyst, Kohut gradually came to realize that these "narcissistic" issues emerged much more frequently than he initially had believed. Because their presence within the transference was not tightly correlated with primary disturbances of self-cohesion, the nosological schema Kohut presented in chapter 1 of *The Analysis of the Self* was in need of modification.

It will be recalled that in 1971 Kohut defined narcissistic personality disorders as conditions wherein representations of the self and its archaic objects are either insufficiently cathected with narcissistic libido or remain split off from the mature aspects of the personality (1971, p. 19). It was in a lecture delivered in Berlin in October 1970 that he first called these conditions those of a "disordered self" (1978d, p. 554). The rationale for this shift has never been explained, for there is nothing in Kohut's 1971 book to justify its title, *The Analysis of the Self:* descriptions of the vicissitudes of narcissistic libido do not require a conception of "self" as a psychoanalytic construct.

Well into the mid-1970s, Kohut continued to use the term as Hartmann (1956) had defined it, that is, to mean one's own person. In the Preface to the 1971 book, Kohut gave credit to his friend Charles Kligerman for suggesting its title. I do not know if he was aware at the time of the radical implications of characterizing his work in this manner. I do know that I was among those who strongly urged him in 1970 to adopt that title, for I was confident that the logic of his evolving theorizing would impel Kohut in the radical direction his work ultimately did take.

At any rate, Kohut (1972) soon began implicitly to acknowledge that self disorders cannot be detected merely from the presence of one of the narcissistic transferences, for both the classical neuroses and disorders of the self may initially present themselves in the guise of phenomenology characteristic of the other cluster (p. 626). Yet, by the mid-1970s, Kohut was asserting that narcissistic disturbances are the characteristic pathology of our time (p. 680)—a shift from the neuroses of Freud's era, that Kohut attributed to faulty child-rearing practices (p. 713). Kohut must have reached this conclusion because he had found narcissistic transferences in more and more patients.

At about this time, the concept of "Tragic Man" made its appearance in Kohut's discourse (1978b, p. 754) to characterize individuals whose main problems lie in the existential realm, beyond the pleasure principle. Kohut differentiated these people from those with intrapsychic conflicts concerning sexuality and aggression, to whom he assigned the appellation of "Guilty Man." Early in 1975, he was still acknowledging that certain patients in analysis oscillate between these clusters of difficulty (1978c, pp. 897–98), but by the time he published *The Restoration of the Self,* he took the position that such "mixed cases" were scarce (1977, p. 225). In other words, Kohut was less and less inclined to *give weight* to the oedipal material he encountered in Tragic Men as he gained confidence in the power and relevance of his own contribution to clinical psychoanalysis.

In his posthumous book, Kohut (1984, p. 167) reiterated that the Oedipus complex is practically ubiquitous. We must therefore conclude that in minimizing the proportion of Guilty Men encountered in analytic practice, he was simply discounting the *centrality* of oedipal conflicts in Tragic Man. Indeed, from 1977, Kohut became increasingly explicit in claiming that the resolution of the Oedipus complex in analysis is contingent on our degree of success in penetrating to the deeper anxieties, those about self-cohesion, that undergird the oedipal problem (see 1984, p. 22).[6]

At the same time, the change in terminology from disorders of narcissism to the problems of Tragic Man was a necessary concomitant of Kohut's gradual abandonment of Freud's metapsychology. After all, narcissism as a concept is part and parcel of the libido theory. Yet, in the way he effected this terminological rectification, Kohut introduced a measure of inconsistency into his theoretical system, for he failed to modify the etiological propositions he had earlier used to account for the differences between oedipal and narcissistic pathologies.

It will be recalled that Kohut postulated separate lines of development for narcissism and object love. On this basis, he was led to the conclusion that each strand of the libido could be involved in distinct and characteristic pathological vicissitudes (1971, pp. 19–20). The distinction between Guilty Man and Tragic Man superficially echoes that between pathological developments of object libidinal and narcissistic cathexes, but is, in fact, a proposition of an entirely different kind. In order to reach the relatively well-differentiated conditions characteristic of Guilty Man, a cohesive self must already have been formed—only under those fortunate circumstances can Tragic Man's more ominous fate be averted (1977, p. 227). The object-libidinal difficulties of Guilty Man supervene only after healthy narcissistic development has taken place. This is in contrast to the schema of 1971, where the separate strands of narcissistic and object-libidinal development were symmetrical in their ability to account for equally primary types of pathology.

In his clearest statement on this subject (1977, pp. 132–33), Kohut all but acknowledged that the dichotomy of Guilty Man versus Tragic Man is *not* a nosological distinction at all but the alternative application of competing psychoanalytic hypotheses to the same phenomena. Hence, it comes as no surprise that Kohut ultimately con-

---

[6]Kohut (1984, p. 5) nonetheless continued to maintain that oedipal neuroses in pure culture are still to be found—although he acknowledged that he had not analyzed such a case for many years. Basch (personal communication) is making identical statements to this very day, buttressing his view with a case he is supervising. Notwithstanding this exception, the likelihood is that it is the self-psychologically naive supervisee who evokes only oedipal material.

cluded that oedipal problems are caused by self-pathology (1984, pp. 10–11). Thus, he finally resolved the seeming discrepancy between his clinical theory and that of Freud by asserting that Freud's was inapplicable to most people and was in error in the small proportion of cases for which it does have relevance. With this claim, Kohut consciously embraced dissidence and, from beyond the grave, invited his followers to organize a secession.

One might say that the seeds of secession were already planted by the time Kohut conceived the idea that the self-representation is normally formed in early childhood, if not earlier, through processes that parallel the repair of a "fragmented or enfeebled self" in analytic treatment. He first spoke in that vein in the Berlin lecture I have already cited (see 1978d, p. 557), where he announced that the secure establishment of the "self" depends on parental performance in the realms of "mirroring" (i.e., affirming the child's worth) and idealization. Note that for some time past 1970, Kohut continued to use the term self to refer only to mental *contents*. At the 1969 Rome Congress, for instance, he disputed Douglas Levin's (1970) attempt to define self as a structure (see Kohut, 1970, pp. 579, 582–85), despite his own claim that a "nuclear self" debilitated by narcissistic traumata constitutes the nodal pathogenic condition in the disturbances on which his work was focused (see also Kohut, 1971, p. xv).[7] In his 1977 book, Kohut acknowledged that his usage of the term "self" in the narrow sense of mental contents up to that time had been out of keeping with the clinical phenomena he was trying to illuminate (p. 207n.).

It was the broader (I would say structural) definition of this crucial term Kohut espoused in 1977 that alerted most readers to the fact that "self psychology" constitutes a radical challenge to both Freudian and Kleinian traditions within psychoanalysis. Henceforth Kohut threw caution to the winds as far as the expectable reactions of analytic conservatives were concerned. He wrote more and more candidly about his hope that his conceptual system would replace all previous psychoanalytic schools (1980c, pp. 507–515). At the same time, he and his followers began to argue the merits of their selfpsychology as if it were the only alternative to psychoanalysis as Freud had left it at his death. It seems that in Kohut's mind there was

---

[7]Like Levin, I tried to push Kohut in the direction of a structural definition of "self." Kohut's first public response to my position was a discussion in May 1972 at the Chicago Psychoanalytic Society, when he reiterated his adherence to a definition in terms of mental contents (see 1978e, pp. 659–60).

no doubt that only Freud's work and his own merited serious consideration by psychoanalysts (1980c, p. 515; see 1984, p. 41).

Yet in *The Restoration of the Self* (1977), Kohut's discussion of self-as-
structure remained quite sketchy at best. He was particularly vague
about the formation of such a structure in earliest childhood, simply
asserting that a "nuclear self" comes into being through internalizations (p. 177). He described the functioning of the self by means of a
metaphor many readers have found puzzling: he compared it with an
"energic tension arc" that runs from a "pole" consisting of ambitions
to another consisting of idealized goals by way of the specific skills at
the person's command (pp. 178, 243). This poetic image was repeated
in a collaborative paper Kohut published about a year later (Kohut
and Wolf, 1978). At that time, Kohut added that the status of the self
may be assessed in terms of criteria of coherence, vitality, and harmony. These qualities could refer only to the "program of action" or
subjective experience of goals that Kohut defined as the nuclear self.
At other times, however, he wrote about "the self" in a manner that
reified and anthropomorphized the concept, as in his statement that
intense experiences such as love or physical exertion "strengthen the
self" (1984, p. 53). One also gains the impression that Kohut tended
to concretize structural concepts from his metaphoric explanation of
the formation of the self in terms of protein synthesis within the
organism from the metabolized components of ingested foreign pro-
teins (p. 160).

We may summarize by stating that as soon as Kohut decided to
propose an all-inclusive psychoanalytic schema intended to supersede those of his predecessors, he was faced with the task of replacing Freud's drive theory of motivation with a new alternative. Although he consistently posed his arguments on this score in terms of
the putative disadvantages of Freud's metapsychology (see 1984, p.
41), I shall attempt to demonstrate that his actual proposals would
constitute total abandonment of Freud's motivational psychology
even if metapsychological considerations were left out of account
altogether. Kohut argued (1977, pp. 94, 118, 123) that both sexual and
aggressive behaviors in early childhood are manifestations of some
breakdown of the adaptational family matrix—he saw the Oedipus
complex as a pathological variant rather than the developmental
norm (1977, p. 246; 1982, pp. 401–404). In his view, the basic units of
motivation are the ambitions and idealized goals of the "nuclear self"
(1977, p. 245), although he acknowledged that the former crystallize

sometime between the second and fourth year of life and the latter form even later, between the fourth and the sixth year (p. 79).

In other words, Kohut failed to account for the emergence of these structured motives in the young child. In *The Restoration of the Self* (1977), he still noted this gap in his theory: he ended the book with the admission that he had nowhere defined the term "self" (p. 311), and he also implied that the question of how the self is formed was left unanswered (p. 245). In the last five years of his life, Kohut did struggle to solve these conceptual problems. He committed himself to the view that, for better and for worse, the self is formed through early childhood experiences, the crux of which is the caretakers' providing confirmation of the infant's sense of his own perfection and that of his parents (Kohut and Wolf, 1978, p. 414; Kohut, 1984, p. 70).[8]

Because Kohut asserted that all his concepts were derived from the data he had collected in the clinical situation (1980c, p. 501), one must conclude that his developmental hypotheses are extrapolated from propositions about the manner in which his therapeutic work effected "the restoration of the self." Of course, it would not be reasonable to accept at face value Kohut's description of his methodology as entirely inductive, for he continued to explain all structure formation as a process he called "transmuting internalization" (1977, pp. xiii, 32, 173; 1984, p. 172). For Kohut, this term meant learning by identification with the activities of the caretaker. He was convinced that this process is set in motion when the child's needs are met with "optimal frustration" (1977, pp. 87–88n.; 1984, p. 70).[9] Obviously, these propositions are a priori assumptions rather than inferences necessitated by the data of observation. I am not implying that there is anything wrong with using such assumptions in constructing scientific theories; my point is merely that Kohut did not seem to be aware that at the core of his theory he continued to rely on *indispensable* concepts borrowed from the traditional metapsychology he thought he was rejecting root and branch.

---

[8]It follows that Kohut attributed all deficiences in self-formation to parental failures in the optimal provision of such experiences (1977, p. 87; 1980c, p. 524; 1984, p. 53; Kohut and Wolf, 1978, p. 414). This viewpoint comes close to Melanie Klein's innate pessimism about the adaptive capacities of human infants.

[9]Basch (in press) has shown that the hypothesis that learning is facilitated by frustration, even if that is deemed optimal, is untenable. See also Lichtenberg (1983) and chapter 11 of this volume.

It should be recalled that the concept of transmuting internalization preceded the work on narcissism in Kohut's oeuvre. It found its
first definitive expression in the sole metatheoretical essay Kohut ever
attempted, his collaborative paper with Philip Seitz (1963). In that
effort to amend Freud's last model of the mind by taking into account
the possibilities of conflict-free functioning, the authors postulated a
broad psychic sector wherein drive energies were curbed not by
means of defensive countercathexes but through "progressive neutralization" (p. 368). When Kohut later announced his new theory of
narcissism, he put it entirely in terms of the various transformations
narcissistic libido may undergo in the course of development (1966a,
p. 430). He also affirmed the view that new structure is laid down
through introjection brought about by nontraumatic frustrations (p.
431)—an assertion that could refer only to the neutralization of narcissistic libido through these "optimal frustrations." In the 1968 paper
on narcissistic disturbances, Kohut added that such pathology is
caused by narcissistic traumata (1968, p. 478; see also 1971, pp. 8–11)
and that its cure depends on the transformation of the energy of
hitherto unneutralized narcissistic libido (1968, p. 498) into "a particle
of inner psychological structure" (1971, p. 66). It is evident that the
term "transmuting internalization" (p. 50) is simply a condensation
of these sequential concepts into one elegant phrase.[10]

In consequence of the fact that Kohut never ceased to assert that
the formation of the self in early childhood (Kohut & Wolf, 1978, p.
416) as well as its functional rehabilitation in the course of analysis
(Kohut, 1984, p. 172) takes place as a result of the transmuting internalization promoted by optimal frustration, one is led to conclude
that in its essence his theory still depends on the concepts of psychic
energy and its neutralization. In contrast to Kohut's avowed "abandonment" of traditional metapsychology and related claim that his

---

[10]In *The Analysis of the Self,* Kohut still referred to archaic grandiosity as the
"instinctual fuel" of man's ambitions (1971, p. 27) and to "idealizing libido" as the fuel
of his creativity (p. 40). This usage demonstrates that by "transmuting internalization"
he continued to mean the partial neutralization of archaic energies. Apparently he also
believed that structuralization promoted further taming of the drives, for he also spoke
of structure as the "neutralizing fabric of the psyche" (1971, pp. 42, 298). As Friedman
(1982) has noted, Roy Schafer (1968) formerly exposed the centrality of "internalization" as a concept bridging the world of mental mechanism and that of human meanings, but soon repudiated this view. In his more recent work, Schafer (1976, pp. 155ff,)
dismisses the notion of "taking inside" as the concretization of a fantasy; he explicitly
criticized Kohut (p. 156, n.) for failure to address this theoretic deficiency.

prior use of its terminology was to be taken only metaphorically (1980c, p. 488; 1984, p. 114), we are led to an entirely different probability—namely, that he failed to provide any theoretical explanation of these central issues for his psychological system and covered over this lack with meaningless jargon.

On the basis of Kohut's published work, it is not possible to decide which of these judgments better fits the facts—Kohut most likely wavered between these incompatible alternatives. Even when he was explicit about using metaphorical language, his choice most often fell on images having to do with the concept of energy. Recall that he described the bipolar self in terms of a "tension arc" (1977, p. 179). Even in his posthumous book, he used an energy metaphor to characterize the outcome of an intrapsychic conflict (p. 10). On the other hand, on occasion he would write about an "energic continuum" (p. 43) in a manner that asks to be taken literally. The puzzlement many readers felt about his late work thus seems to reflect Kohut's failure to clarify his conceptualizations.

In private discussions prior to 1974, Kohut sometimes shared with me his concern that he would gain many followers simply by virtue of personal charisma: he was keenly aware that many readers became enthusiastic about his work without having grasped its meaning (see Gedo, 1975a, p. 320). In a letter of December 1973, he expressed anxiety about his work's being spoiled by the "unwelcome influence of some self-appointed disciples" (Kohut, 1978c, p. 884). His sensitivity to such matters is reflected in his penetrating discussion of both charismatic and messianic personalities (1976, pp. 823–32). He used Winston Churchill to exemplify the charismatic leader, but I am certain that this portrait was at the same time an attempt at self-description.[11] It is therefore quite striking that, by and large, neither his supporters nor his intellectual opponents have given detailed attention to the specifics of his writings so that the merits of particular ideas might be assessed.

If one does examine Kohut's writings with an eye to specifics, a linked pair of hitherto overlooked problems emerges for consideration. I have already mentioned his substitution of metaphors for actual concepts during the last phase of his career—a cavalier procedure

---

[11]The skeptical reader is reminded that Kohut wrote this essay at my request, that it was first published in a book I conceived and coedited (Gedo and Pollock, 1976), and that I had many opportunities to discuss it with Kohut before it appeared in its printed version.

through which he made it impossible to assess properly the nature of his hypotheses. Earlier, Kohut's use of theory showed occasional lapses of the opposite kind: he had a tendency to reify concepts to an unacceptable degree. Thus his conception of "libido" often turned that abstraction into the equivalent of somatic processes; for instance, he believed that shame is a direct result of the "damming up" of unneutralized "exhibitionistic libido" and that hypochondriasis or self-consciousness are also caused by such obstacles to the "discharge" of narcissism (1971, p. 144; see also 1966b, p. 439). *Per contra*, he postulated that taming archaic narcissism leads to its "transformation" into creativity, wisdom, humor, and empathy (1971, p. 299). He once attempted to explain pruritus as libidinal regression that leads to hyperchathexis of the body surface (1978f, p. 260), and he gave essentially the same explanation for the pallor and/or blushing that accompany the reaction of shame (1972, p. 655).[12]

I suspect that the cloudiness of Kohut's late metaphors was an attempt to escape this propensity to collapse abstractions into "thingness." When the demands of theorizing finally pushed him into consistent reliance on the concept of "self," he once again lapsed into unacceptable concreteness, as in his repeated references to disintegration of self-cohesion as "fragmentation," or his comments about the self having more or less "strength" (e.g., 1984, p. 52). He listed qualities of the self as introspectively accessible subjective experiences, and he fluctuated arbitrarily between these incompatible frames of reference (p. 65). Perhaps, when all is said and done, Kohut ultimately failed to address himself to the task of systematizing his innumerable uncoordinated propositions because he correctly judged himself no longer to be qualified for an assignment that demands exacting attention to details.

In his ultimate psychoanalytic position paper, Kohut (1983, p. 391) acknowledged that in most of his theoretical writings he had illegitimately (but knowingly!) discussed intrapsychic processes as if they were experiences taking place in a social context. He claimed the right to do so in the interest of effective communication, and he did

---

[12]Kohut (1978b, pp. 746–47) corrected the most serious error he committed because of his difficulty in focusing his thinking at a purely abstract level—his unwarranted claim that the stage of autoerotism involves the cathexis of discrete parts of the body with narcissistic libido (1968, p. 478; 1971, pp. 29, 119, 251). He had clearly leaped to this inference from the reports of traumatized patients who experienced themselves as if they were smashed into fragments.

not bother to examine the effect of this self-indulgence on his theorizing. But this careless habit not only vitiated Kohut's ability to adhere to his own definition of the self as a *program* of action (rather than an actor on the stage of actuality), it created even graver difficulties in arriving at a consistent usage for Kohut's most original concept, the "selfobject." This term was originally defined (1971, p. xiv) as an intrapsychic representation of another that is experienced as part of the self-representation. In terms of the metapsychology Kohut was then using, this meant that such an object is cathected with narcissistic libido; in fact, Kohut stated that such archaic cathexes become neutralized by virtue of their "passage" through the idealized selfobject (p. 43). In the paper of 1972 on narcissistic rage that supplemented *The Analysis of the Self* (1971), Kohut asserted that self-cohesion is the consequence of vicissitudes of the "self-selfobject unit" (p. 624); I believe it is impossible to discern whether this statement refers to intrapsychic processes or to events involving the infant and its caretakers.[13] However, when Kohut writes (as he did in a letter of September 1972) that structuralization can take place only through the loss of the prestructural selfobject (1978c, p. 869), there is no doubt that he is referring to circumstances in the external world, for the memories that constitute a psychic representation are ineradicable.

In *The Restoration of the Self* (1977), Kohut began to call the repetition of archaic object relationships in the psychoanalytic setting "self-object transferences" (p. xiii) and to denote the tasks of providing affirmation of the analysand's worth and making possible the idealization of others selfobject functions (p. 33). Clearly, these statements must also refer to the caretakers' actual behaviors. Thereafter Kohut invariably referred to both parents and therapists simply as selfobjects (pp. 85, 100), and one could never again know whether he concerned himself with the inner world at all, and if he did, in which contexts. From the perspective of the child or the analysand, these transactions are selfobject needs (p. 172). Such needs are normally said to persist throughout life (1980a, p. 453). In other words, for Kohut, man forever "lives in a matrix of selfobjects" (p. 473).

Once he began to assert that the need for selfobjects is both normal and permanent, Kohut no longer emphasized that such objects are *by*

---

[13]In either case, this proposition places Kohut's theoretical system into the class of object relations theories; to differentiate it from other members of the class, it might be well to call it a theory of selfobject relations!

definition experienced as part of one's own person: he now classified the need for affirmation itself as a need for a selfobject (1980a, p. 495).[14] Thus Kohut's definition of selfobject now changed to that of an entity supporting the cohesion, strength, and harmony of the self (1984, p. 52).

In summary, in his last works Heinz Kohut put forward a totally novel conception of Human Nature, a view almost diametrically opposed to Freud's conception of the human being as a creature in uneasy equipoise among the demands of conscience, appetite, and social reality. For Kohut, the search for perfection—either through idealizing the Other or by means of the fulfillment of personal ambitions—is the dominant issue for human psychic life. In this schema, psychopathology results from an unwholesome family matrix (Kohut and Wolf, 1978, p. 416): the caretakers fail to affirm the child's worth and/or traumatically disillusion him about their own.[15] By abandoning Freud's insistence on the equal importance of nature and nurture on the development of personality, Kohut carried his Self Psychology into the camp of those psychological systems based solely on the remediable effects of environment (see Gedo, 1984, chapter 10). I discuss the implications of this emergence of utopian optimism in Kohut's late writings in the chapter to follow.

---

[14]As a logical corollary of this shift of emphasis from an intrapsychic frame of reference to one focused on social interactions, Kohut now began to underplay his previous hypothesis that oedipal neuroses are libidinal problems superimposed on a well-structured "self." He proposed instead that these *problems* of the oedipal phase of development are brought about by unempathic responses on the part of "the selfobjects" to the child's age appropriate expansiveness (1977, p. 247; see also 1983, p. 389; 1984, pp. 6, 24, 68). For Kohut, oedipal pathology is based on depression and narcissistic rage in reaction to interpersonal events; a normal oedipal experience, by contrast, involves the family's joyful participation in the child's growth (1977, p. 233; 1982, p. 404; 1984, pp. 14, 188). Although Kohut does acknowledge that in pathological instances the child's fantasy life becomes filled with reality distortions about the family matrix (1984, p. 25), he consistently overlooks the likelihood that such pathogenic distortions may come about no matter how the oedipal parents behave in the present— by virtue of earlier structuralization, for example.

[15]In *How Does Analysis Cure?* (1984) Kohut introduced a minor refinement into his system: because his definition of "the self" now included a set of personal skills, he defined the need for a "silent double" (or alter ego) as a third "selfobject function" (p. 197). The "twinship" transference was thus removed from the list of "mirror" transferences and given separate status (p. 193). Through this casual change in his clinical theory, Kohut implicitly acknowledged that his developmental schemata did not correspond to the actualities found in the consulting room, but he did not make a full retraction on this score. He did admit, however, that even his latest classification of transferences must be regarded as tentative (p. 203).

8

Barred from the Promised Land

Heinz Kohut in the Wilderness

HEINZ KOHUT'S UNSUCCESSFUL STRUGGLE to maintain the position of Self Psychology within the organizational and conceptual framework of psychoanalysis probably constitutes the most telling example of the decisive significance of the theoretician's commitment to a priori philosophical positions upon the formation of his psychological hypotheses. As I reviewed in the preceding chapter, Kohut's psychoanalytic position began as an extension of Hartmann's metapsychology. In the effort to focus these theoretical tools on clinical problems referable to the legacy of early childhood developmental vicissitudes, Kohut became increasingly impressed with the frequent occurrence of archaic transference constellations wherein the analyst is experienced as an animate tool in the service of buttressing the analysand's tenuous self-esteem and/or sense of self (1971, p. xiv; 1984, p. 6; Kohut and Wolf, 1978, p. 413). Convinced that he had achieved a breakthrough in expanding the power of psychoanalysis empathically to grasp the nature of archaic experiences (1984, p. 84), Kohut gradually shifted the focus of clinical theory away from the vicissitudes of the drives to the consequences of transactions between the child and the caretakers—or, as he put it, "the self" and "the selfobject."

This new theory was enunciated in *The Restoration of the Self* (1977) as a complement to Freud's classical theory of the transference neuroses (pp. xvii–xviii). A year later, in a collaborative paper, Kohut

outlined "the disorders of the self and their treatment" (Kohut and
Wolf, 1978, p. 413). By March 1978, he was committed to the view
that the etiology of these disorders is to be found in the failures of
what he called the selfobject (1978c, p. 929). In other words, Kohut
had decisively abandoned the Freudian position that psychopathology is determined by complementary influences from both nature
and nurture (see 1972, p. 649). By 1980 (1980c, p. 486; see also 1984, p.
216), his psychoanalytic program consisted of the study of self-selfobject relations exclusively, and he challenged his readers to try out his
proposals as a unitary system preferable to traditional psychoanalysis
(1980c, p. 515). In his self-assessment, Kohut was admirably clear
about the fact that his basic difference with Freud was philosophical:
he rejected the primacy of the values emphasized by psychoanalysis,
knowledge and *independence* (1982, p. 400).

In other contexts, Kohut articulated his disagreement with the psychoanalytic commitment to the quest for knowledge by challenging
Freud's concept that psychological cures are brought about by the
mastery that insight makes possible (1984, p. 56). Another way he
stated the same point was to claim that neither reason nor expanded
cognition leads to cure (1984, p. 108)—that therapeutic change comes
about only as a result of "optimal frustration" (p. 101).[1] For Kohut,
interpretation became epiphenomenal within the analytic process
(see 1984, p. 153). Whatever its content, he believed that the provision of information in lieu of gratification is frustrating enough to
produce those internalizations whereby functions previously performed by the selfobject-analyst become available to the analysand
(1984, pp. 160, 172). I have already noted (chapter 7, n 10) that the
concept of internalization is no longer acceptable to many theoreticians who have repudiated traditional metapsychology. Even if these
objections are set aside, Kohut's use of this concept to subvert the
traditional theory of cure is astonishing. How radical a departure
from psychoanalytic thinking this point of view represents may be
gauged from the fact that in *The Analysis of the Self* (1971, p. 291) Kohut
still asserted that the therapeutic aim of psychoanalysis was mastery
by means of insight.

The beginnings of this reversal of outlook about the role of knowledge in the regulation of behavior are discernible in Kohut's writings

---

[1]As a corollary of this view, Kohut believed that self-analytic efforts after the
termination of analytic treatment do not betoken a good result. On the contrary, he felt
that such efforts at self-inquiry prove that the analysis was incomplete (1984, p. 154).

of the mid-1970s. At that time, he made several efforts to characterize psychoanalysis as the "empathic science" (1973c, p. 721). In that context, he attacked the "tool and method pride" concerning intellectual mastery of the conventional scientist (1973a, p. 677; 1973c, p. 691). However, it was in his discussion of the analysis of "Mr. M." in *The Restoration of the Self* (1977, p. 31) that Kohut first asserted that cure in psychoanalysis is never achieved through insight, that it always is the result of internalization. It should be noted that Kohut put forward this revolutionary claim in the service of defending his decision, in the supervision of the analysis of Mr. M., not to pursue the investigation of the analysand's psychological depths, wherever that inquiry might lead. He tried to justify his policy on the ground that the analysand's fear that he might disintegrate if transference developments should replicate the circumstances of his earliest childhood were well founded (1977, p. 19). In other words, Kohut apparently realized that he did not believe in the efficacy of valid interpretation when he was challenged about the conduct of the case of Mr. M., one of those included in *The Psychology of the Self* (Goldberg, 1978, chapter 3).[2]

In his posthumous book, Kohut claimed (1984, p. 4) that his 1977 defense of the conduct of this analysis had been widely misunderstood. He now *denied* that his decision was based on shying away from a putative "basic defect" of Mr. M.'s personality; he asserted that the decisive issue was restoration of the patient's adaptive capacities. In making this claim, however, Kohut demonstrated, from yet another vantage point, how his theory of therapy and conception of cure departed from the fundamental program of psychoanalysis—the fullest possible exploration of the inner life. For Kohut, the "restoration" of "adaptive capacities" was often a therapeutic expedient (viz, a "compensatory" outcome) premised on his belief that certain patients' "basic defects" ought not to be explored and altered to the

---

[2]It will be recalled that I intended to participate in the preparation of such a casebook and decided to leave the project because of Kohut's reaction when I criticized the conduct of the analysis of Mr. M. In a private discussion at the time (June 1974), Kohut was still unaware of his attitude about interpretation: he then explained his rationale for allowing the analysis to be discontinued on the ground that he feared that the student-analyst (a woman) would not be able to cope with the patient's sadism. Be it noted that the case report opens with an account of the patient's conflict about articulating the sadistic fantasies stimulated in him when he perceived the Jewishness, as well as a minor physical defect of the analyst's—a percept he associated with his mother's illness during his childhood (Goldberg, 1978, pp. 128–29).

extent made possible by the psychoanalytic method. Consider his notion of the aim of treatment as facilitating the completion of the individual's "nuclear program," that is, the pursuit of his ambitions and ideals (1984, p. 154).

I can think of no better way to articulate the point that patients may achieve great progress in pursing their ambitions and holding to their ideals without having obtained a satisfactory analytic result than to quote from my original commentary on the case of Mr. M. (unpublished memo of March 1974.) I questioned the appropriateness of the decision to terminate this analysis in the following terms:

> [Mr. M.'s] concern about becoming addicted to analysis raises the possibility that the rapid and therapeutically gratifying termination is an enactment of the need to be a "good" patient and avoids working through that aspect of the negative transference expressed in his sadistic fantasies. In relation to the analyst, these were echoed in [a recent] dream of a Jewish Ball; [the analyst's Jewishness] had stimulated his sadism in the initial interview. I would feel more secure [about an analytic outcome] if there were some sign that [Mr. M.] could accept the analyst's pleasure in her own success.

In other words, I suspected that the patient was able to sustain his ideals only by disavowing his continuing hatred of his analyst-mother.

In addition to his skepticism about the value of interpretations, Kohut also stressed the inability of many patients to *accept* them—their insistence on feeling "understood" instead (1977, p. 88). Kohut was explicit about his position that such a feeling has no correlation with the communication of valid knowledge about the analysand. In order to promote such a feeling in patients, it probably is necessary to follow Kohut's technical advice (1984, p. 174) to focus exclusively on the patient's "psychic reality." In accord with this technique, the analyst must then show his understanding of what the patient feels by describing that inner state (pp. 176–77).

Although in his late work Kohut made the point that therapeutic change does not come about through insight, he did not proscribe the use of interpretations. In fact, on one occasion he stated (1984, p. 192) that explanations about the patient's need for "selfobject functions" are the essential steps in treatment. Several clinical vignettes Kohut provided in this period also show that his actual practice relied largely on interpretive interventions. Most revealing in this respect is his

account of a session with a patient who had engaged in dangerous
driving and provocative behavior toward the police on his way to
Kohut's office (1984, p. 74). Kohut responded by telling this man
affectfully that he was acting idiotically.[3] The nature of this intervention demonstrates that Kohut's technical procedures were probably
much more complex than his reductionist prescriptions would lead
one to believe.

Regrettably, Kohut failed to publish very much in the way of case
reports. Goldberg's 1978 casebook contains clinical work by six of
Kohut's students. Although he supervised most of these analyses, it
is never possible to judge to what degree Kohut concurred with the
analyst's technical decisions. Consequently, one would not be justified in drawing from these accounts any conclusions about his scientific views.[4] The only report about Kohut's own analytic work that
presents a longitudinal narrative is his 1979 paper on "the two analyses of Mr. Z." Kohut obviously presented this material to demonstrate the differing effects of treating the same problem on the basis of
the different clinical theories he espoused before and after his transformation into a self psychologist. From this account, as well as his
later references to the same case (1980a, pp. 449–453; 1984, pp. 88ff.),
we can discern that Kohut certainly continued actively to offer interpretations as well as reconstructions of childhood circumstances. If
Kohut himself was critical of his unwarranted confidence in the validity and relevance of the interpretations he had used in Mr. Z.'s first
analysis (1979, p. 9), his readers are in no position to disagree. However, this inference does not call into question the theory Kohut was
applying with such misguided vigor, as he would have us conclude.
Rather, it throws light on the fact that attitudes of omniscience are out
of place in psychoanalytic work.

Obviously, Kohut was not alone in bringing these authoritarian
attitudes to the analytic task—they are practically ubiquitous in a

---

[3]Not only does this intervention disregard the patient's psychic reality in favor
of highlighting the latter's disregard of realities of great immediate moment, it goes
"beyond interpretation" in the manner I have recommended for some time (see Gedo,
1979; 1981b, chapter 11; 1984a, chapters 8 & 9).

[4]If we were to use *The Psychology of the Self* (Goldberg, 1978) as an integral part of
the corpus of Kohut's writings, what could we make of the fact that the book starts out
by stressing the prominence of oedipal material in narcissistic disturbances (p. 5)? And
what about the convincing interpretation of the Oedipus complex in the case where the
analysis was carried to an unequivocal termination (p. 354)?

profession that draws upon the traditions of clinical medicine. Nor should Kohut be blamed for the fact that his personal style appears to have changed little when he substituted his own clinical theory for Freud's in his interpretive schema: when he offers a reinterpretation of one of Z.'s dreams from the first analysis (1984, p. 86), he does so with just as much unwarranted confidence as he demonstrated during the clinical work with his patient. Although he always paid lip service to the ideal of closely following the patient's associations in order to discover their meaning, Kohut actually proposed a rigid interpretive schema focused on a narrow range of selfobject needs (cf. 1984, p. 68).

I do not mean to imply that in any specific instance the interpretation Kohut proposed was invalid; I do wish to point out that he *never* offers sufficient evidence to allow the reader to form a judgment about its validity. Little wonder that, as Kohut eventually discovered (1979, pp. 14–16), Mr. Z. experienced his analysis as the replication of his childhood with a messianic mother! With other patients, such as "Miss F.," (1968, pp. 503–08), who responded to Kohut by insisting on taking full control of the analysis, he acknowledged that, for "a prolonged period . . . I was inclined to argue with the patient about the correctness of my interpretations and to suspect the presence of stubborn hidden resistances" (p. 504).

In the hands of an analyst handicapped by such an excess of certitude,[5] (or blessed, as Kohut put it about himself, with "the ability to inspire enthusiasm in others" [1978e, p. 661]) interpretation does become a dubious tool, at best. Of necessity, the crux of treatment conducted under such a messianic aura is continuous attention to the subtleties of interaction within the therapeutic dyad (see Gill, 1983). I assume, therefore, that Kohut's personal experience as a clinician led him to a conclusion valid for his own therapeutic efforts but not necessarily for those of others—he repudiated the quest for valid

---

[5]To gain an impression of the pervasiveness of this trait of Kohut's thinking, see his discussion (1977, p. 40) of the termination of the analysis of Mr. M., which consists entirely of explanations deduced from Kohut's theoretical system, or his arbitrary invention of an infantile history for this patient (1977, pp. 24–25) on the same basis. Let me quote Kohut's own evaluation of his countertransference problem with Miss F.: "There was a residual insistence, related to deep and old fixation points, on seeing myself in the narcissistic center of the stage. . . . For a long time I insisted, therefore, that the patient's reproaches related to specific transference fantasies" (1971, p. 288).

knowledge as the primary aim of psychoanalysis.[6] This *parti pris* permitted him at the same time to concede graciously that many analysts had obtained excellent therapeutic results before the advent of Self Psychology as a consequence of unintended byproducts of the therapeutic process—that is, despite the application of an invalid interpretive schema (1977, p. 72). Elsewhere (1984, p. 94), Kohut correctly noted that the importance of nonlexical aspects of psychoanalytic interventions has been understated.[7]

To turn from Kohut's rejection of insight to his equally emphatic attack on the value of "independence," this aspect of Self Psychology also represents an abrupt about-face on his part. In his 1968 paper on the treatment of narcissistic disorders, Kohut still defined cure in terms of "ego dominance and ego autonomy" (p. 499). In the 1972 Brill Lecture, he equated it with the maturation of narcissism (p. 652). Even in *The Restoration of the Self* (1977), Kohut noted that individuals threatened with encroachments on the boundaries of their self (as I would put it, on the autonomy of their volitional system) will necessarily respond with negativism (p. 149). The first mention of Kohut's reversal of position occurred in a letter to a follower (1980a, p. 455); there, Kohut dissociated himself from the views of Margaret Mahler because of her commitment to the value of independence. He ended this communication by asserting that an individual's independence is a measure of that person's pathology (p. 456).

------

[6]Kohut deserves credit for grasping the fact that the analyst's personal contribution to the process whereby analytic data are collected has been greatly underestimated (see Gardner, 1983). He first made the point (1977, pp. 264–65) in a discussion of one of the cases in Goldberg's (1978) collection (chapter 4). In that instance, the analyst was unable to deal with an intense need to idealize her. As a result, for better and for worse, the treatment settled into the mold of a mirror transference. In his posthumous book, Kohut broadened the issue, showing that analysis evokes only specific possibilities from each patient, apart from the analyst's *limitations*. He noted (1984, p. 9) that the inner chaos he thought to be characteristic of borderline states is not a function of the patient's condition but of the observer's perceptual capacity (see also p. 37). Kohut correctly noted that so-called borderline cases become analyzable when an analyst succeeds in organizing their bewildering phenomenology in terms of his available cognitive schemata (p. 183).

[7]Nor was this conclusion simply an argument in the political wars to promote Self Psychology. Kohut espoused this point of view as early as 1957, at the height of his reputation as a psychoanalytic conservative. During a discussion of the psychology of music, he took up the issue of archaic mentation and stated that for the pathological sequelae of early phases of organization, forms of therapy designed to deal with aspects of the "structuralized personality" will provide only indirect help, insofar as they prove to be soothing, for example (1957, p. 245).

In his summarizing "Reflections" for the Chicago "Conference on the Psychology of the Self" (1980c), Kohut explicitly stated that he was opposed to Freud's "maturation morality", (p. 486); for him, normal development does not lead from "merger" to "autonomy." Elsewhere (1984, p. 7), he declared that both Freudian and Kleinian criteria of health are erroneous; he also expressed the belief (p. 63) that psychoanalysts who fail to accept Self Psychology do so because they cannot tolerate Kohut's idea that autonomy is, in fact, impossible to achieve.[8] In line with his a priori assumption about independence, Kohut now declared (1984, p. 154) that the aim of psychoanalytic treatment is to assist patients to make better use of selfobjects.

In Kohut's mind, "independence" was apparently illegitimately equated with an anxious inability to rely on human assistance—a homologue of the situation wherein a traumatized analysand "turns back from his reliance on empathy" (1984, p. 66). By construing this matter in this way, as an issue in the interpersonal realm, Kohut distorted the views of his opponents; for the concept of autonomy as used by Hartmann, Rapaport, and other ego psychologists was to be understood within an intrapsychic context (see chapter 5, this volume)—it does not refer to the specifics of an object relationship but to the degree of personal initiative without undue influence either from the side of biological constraints or from those stemming in social reality. This concept is no different from Kohut's statement (p. 72) that every person must have "an independent self." I believe that Kohut also misstated his own position about these matters in the heat of this argument—he was no more opposed to the value of autonomy than is any other psychoanalyst.

My conclusion finds support in Kohut's account of the second analysis of Mr. Z. (1979, see esp. p. 13). It will be recalled that this patient had long been afflicted with masochistic masturbatory fantasies wherein he was enslaved by women. As I have already mentioned, this issue was enacted in the first analysis through the patient's submission to Kohut's insistence on the validity of dubious interpretations alleging that the masochism served to expiate guilt about sexual aggression (pp. 5–6). In the interval between the two

---

[8]Although relatively few among those who rejected Kohut's system were aware at the time they made this decision that Kohut would ultimately repudiate the value of independence, I suspect that Kohut was correct in his belief that this aspect of his theories would be unacceptable to both Freudians and Kleinians.

analyses, the masochistic enactment shifted into the arena of Mr. Z.'s vocational activities. In the second analysis, the transference soon emerged in the form of fantasies of merger with the analyst, but a merger from which Mr. Z. struggled to disentangle himself (p. 13)! It is in this context, replicating the patient's childhood enslavement by his mother, that anxiety about the possibility of disintegration was reexperienced. Kohut ultimately understood (p. 15) that Mr. Z. feared that his efforts to achieve independence would evoke disruptive responses from the analyst, as they had from his bizarre mother in childhood. Whether Kohut's hypothesis about Mr. Z. was valid or not, his view about this transaction actually shows that his analytic effort in helping Mr. Z. to master anxiety about disintegration when left to his own devices was intended to enable the patient to function autonomously. The genuine therapeutic progress Kohut reports was betokened not by a change to more mature uses of the selfobject analyst but through mastery of fears about the consequences of relinquishing the analytic relationship in favor of independence. I think these considerations demonstrate that Kohut's claims equating independence with pathology constitute mere rhetorical overkill.[9]

At the same time, beyond this confusing set of misstatements on Kohut's part, I suspect that he was correct that his conception of expectable adult functioning is radically different from that of most psychoanalysts. At the core of this difference is not Kohut's failure to appreciate that every person must remain master of his own volition, the issue that forms the kernel of individual independence. It is, instead, in the realm of normative standards: according to Kohut, the human norm throughout the life cycle is the requirement for selfobjects—that is, for more or less continuous opportunities to idealize others, to experience them as alter egos, and to receive from them affirmation of one's worth (1977, pp. 187–88n.). Kohut maintained this controversial position despite his realization that many people are capable of performing for themselves the functions he attributed to a selfobject. He acknowledged (1984, p. 76) that some individuals

---

[9]The point could also be made by citing Kohut's excellent explanation for the genesis of agoraphobia (1984, pp. 28–32) as the failure to develop self-soothing abilities, as a result of being raised by a caretaker who, because of her own pathological needs, tries to tie the child to herself by discouraging the acquisition of essential psychological skills. In essence, his hypothesis that defenses are necessitated by the requirement to safeguard "the nuclear self" (p. 115) also speaks for my conclusion: Kohut even saw resistances in analytic treatment as healthy adaptive measures to protect the self (p. 148).

hallucinate selfobjects, while others use their culture to provide them with selfobject functions (1984, p. 220).

One cannot escape the conclusion that in this, as in many other matters, Kohut fell into conceptual incoherence by engaging in ad hoc argumentation. As a result, many readers (and certainly all who study only portions of Kohut's *oeuvre*) will form idiosyncratic impressions of Kohut's intended meanings, projecting their own prejudices about Self Psychology into this sprawling and ambiguous corpus of writings. I believe this circumstance accounts for the fact that Kohut's followers often defend him by asserting that critics have misunderstood his work. In my judgment, every conceivable reading of Kohut involves a reduction of this internally inconsistent system of ad hoc propositions into spurious coherence. If the majority of psychoanalysts have rejected Self Psychology, despite the acknowledged value of many of Kohut's clinical findings (see Gedo, 1975a), this collective decision must be the result of a conviction that, in the final analysis, it is the more radical version of Self Psychology that most accurately reflects Kohut's point of view.[10]

In these radical versions, Self Psychology cannot be regarded as a dissident school within psychoanalysis, comparable to those of Ferenczi or Melanie Klein; rather, it has become an independent therapeutic movement, comparable to those of Adler (see Stepansky, 1983) or C. G. Jung (Homans, 1982). The principal characteristics of this nonanalytic version of Self Psychology might be listed as follows:

1. Its field of observation is defined by empathy (Kohut, 1977, p. 306). Since Kohut defined empathy as vicarious introspection (1973c, pp. 700–05; 1977, p. 89; and esp., 1980a, pp. 459–60), this therapeutic method relies exclusively on the integrative efforts of the therapist (see 1984, p. 84).

2. Its subject matter is the study of self-selfobject relations (1980c, p. 479) or of the "selfobject transference" (1984, p. 216). In other words, interpretations in such therapies focus on issues of idealization and wishes for affirmation or for a silent double.

---

[10]Moderates within Self Psychology will doubtless feel that such radical variants caricature *their* views. However, Kohut has made it emotionally difficult for critics to give him the benefit of the doubt, for his own restatements of the positions of intellectual opponents (see 1984, pp. 116–21, 148) did not make the best case possible for other viewpoints.

3. Its method for changing mental functioning is the promotion of "structuralization" (1984, p. 27), a process brought about by means of "optimal frustration" (p. 71). However, according to Kohut, the extent of structuralization treatment can achieve in adults is limited (p. 77).

4. Its minimally acceptable therapeutic aim is fulfilled through partial internalizations (1984, p. 160) that make at least two of the three selfobject functions previously provided by the therapist accessible to the patient as "compensatory structures" (p. 205). In other words, Kohut is satisfied with improved adaptation as a therapeutic outcome, however that goal has been achieved (1977, p. 134), despite his own clinical report (p. 58) that such results can be impermanent.

5. Its theory of pathogenesis focuses on the putative failures of the selfobjects in childhood—a formula Kohut applied even to unfavorable resolution of oedipal experience (1984, p. 68; Kohut & Wolf, 1978, p. 416; 1980c, p. 524; see also Goldberg, 1978, p. 17). Kohut's exclusive focus on the individual's "nuclear" program of action (1984, p. 400) conceives of human life in terms that exclude biological considerations. Although this viewpoint does not demand that the caretakers perform with perfection (1984, p. 15), it does expect exactly the right degree of imperfection, even with the most difficult of children (1977, p. 29; 1984, p. 33).

6. Its view of expectable functioning in adult life accepts man's inevitable dependence on selfobjects, albeit in Kohut's view (1984, p. 52) normality implies evolution in the nature of the selfobject from a state of merger with "the self" to more mature forms (p. 71). A logical corollary of this concept is the preference for terminating treatment whenever the use of selfobjects improves adaptation, without necessarily exploring the legacy of vicissitudes in the earliest phases of development (1977, p. 219; 1984, pp. 7, 44).

7. Because "optimal frustration" can occur only within an empathic milieu (Kohut & Wolf, 1978, p. 416), this kind of treatment must be conducted in an ambience of active empathic responsiveness (1977, p. 251). This requirement may lead the therapist to accede to unusual demands by the patient (as Kohut [1984, p. 83] described briefly in a case vignette), to refrain from interpreting if such activity is "traumatic" (p. 177), and to accept transference-reproaches as if they were realistically justified (p. 182). Gauging the need to depart from analytic technical strategies in these ways is necessarily left to the therapist's judgment; in Kohut's system, however, the bias is

clearly in favor of departures from a technique that may increase the patient's level of frustration.

Although Kohut's work may be used by many followers in accord with the nonanalytic schema I have just outlined or with one very much like it, I believe that much of Self Psychology can just as easily be characterized in a manner that keeps it safely within the boundaries of psychoanalysis (e.g., Basch, in press). Had Kohut merely devised a system of therapy based on assumptions entirely different from those of psychoanalysis, Self Psychology would not continue to command the attention it receives from the analytic community. It must never be forgotten that Kohut earned a respected place among recent contributors to the field before the formation of the Self Psychology movement, and that he never repudiated most of the empirical and some of the conceptual work that gained him that reputation. Whatever the limitations of his views during the last decade of his life may have been, Kohut cannot be deprived of credit for a body of important contributions to psychoanalysis.

Among these lasting accomplishments, I would rank highest Kohut's challenge to psychoanalysts not to seek alibis—above all, never to blame patients!—when analytic efforts fail as a consequence of the contemporary limitations of knowledge (see 1977, p. 282). He presented brief but suggestive clinical examples (such as "Mr. W." in 1977, pp. 152–70) concerning individuals whose problems in living seemed to represent sequelae of vicissitudes within the earliest phases of development; the resulting pathology could not properly be placed in the category of neurotic disturbances. At least two of the analyses summarized in Goldberg's (1978) casebook, *The Psychology of the Self*, dealt with problems of tension regulation as the central issue of the psychopathology (chapters 2 and 7), one of these (pp. 381–429) to the virtual exclusion of other matters, with strikingly beneficial results. As Homer Curtis recently stated (personal communication, November 1984), it is Kohut's emphasis on these sequelae of defective structure formation in early childhood (e.g., 1971, pp. 46–47; 1972; 1977, pp. 23, 89) that psychoanalysis needs to accommodate within its clinical theory.[11]

---

[11]This does not mean, however, that Kohut was justified in assuming, as he did on many occasions (as in the case of Mr. W. in *The Restoration of the Self* [1977]) that the defect in tension regulation constitutes direct evidence that selfobject needs had been frustrated.

In the theoretical realm, Kohut rightly espoused the need for new concepts to integrate such novel observations about archaic transferences; as he put it (1980c, p. 546), the traditional theories of ego psychology, which lack the concept of a nuclear program of personal aims, do not illuminate the dilemmas of "Tragic Man." He pointed to such issues as low anxiety tolerance (1984, p. 27) or imperative needs for appetite satisfaction (p. 215), for external stimulation (pp. 170–71) or for muted responses from the environment (1977, p. 257) as illustrations of important matters previously neglected in psychoanalytic discourse.

Kohut was by no means alone, of course, in proposing that some construct that encompasses in a holistic manner the individual's structured potentials for action is the key to this conceptual dilemma—as I mentioned in the previous chapter, in *Models of the Mind* (Gedo and Goldberg, 1973) my coauthor and I made such a suggestion several years before Kohut accepted the necessity of theoretical revision dictated by his clinical findings. Kohut deserves credit, however, for reporting in his publications from 1966 to 1972 systematic analytic observations about primitive mental states persuasively enough to initiate the search for new clinical hypotheses. It should also be recalled that most theoretical revisionists, such as George Klein (1976) and Roy Schafer (1976), have been motivated by epistemological objections to Freud's metapsychology; the purely *clinical* grounds Goldberg and I adduced for abandoning exclusive reliance on traditional models originated with Heinz Kohut.

Kohut deserves all the more credit for his clinical discoveries because they had their origin not in the consulting room but, as he proudly avowed on many occasions, in his own introspective efforts. In the psychoanalytic climate of the 1980s, it may be difficult to recall the atmosphere of the era of analytic optimism and smugness of the years following World War II. At that time, most analysts assumed that, on the whole, we had plumbed the depths of human mental life; Kohut's (1959) insistence that psychoanalytic psychology must focus on data obtained through the introspective–empathic method was at first widely regarded as dissident in itself! On this score, the climate of opinion has gradually shifted in Kohut's favor, and it is only his excessive emphasis on the primacy of empathy (perhaps even at the expense of the analysand's own introspective efforts?) that seems to break with the present-day consensus.

At the same time, Kohut's methodological position seemed gradually to shift. In 1959, he asserted only that data from observational settings that do not use the method of free association cannot be directly integrated with psychoanalytic evidence. (The cogency of this argument is once more demonstrated in the chapters of this book devoted to current problems in validating psychoanalytic propositions on the basis of the data of infant observation.) In his late work, however, Kohut also seems to have claimed that the only valid evidence collected within the psychoanalytic setting is whatever the analyst perceives through empathy (1980a, pp. 459–560). This viewpoint is unduly restrictive. In addition to this hermeneutic dimension, the analytic situation also provides opportunities to make inferences about mental *functions*, in the manner of a natural scientist, and it requires the analyst to assist the analysand's self-inquiry in the stance of an interested, sympathetic companion listener (Gedo, 1984b; Lichtenberg, 1984).

Despite the one-sidedness of his ultimate viewpoint about the observational method of psychoanalysis, Kohut's clinical contributions have had some influence on resolving older ideological splits within the field. Most important in this regard has been the fact that Kohut's work has actually provided a bridge between American psychoanalysis and the school of Melanie Klein, a conclusion confirmed by the commitment of many former American Kleinians to Self Psychology. Kohut himself credited Melanie Klein with greater empathy for archaic mentation than the Freudian tradition possessed (1984, p. 98; see also 1966b, pp. 415–22, where Kohut took some Argentine Kleinians to task for their *excessive* emphasis on the most archaic sectors of the personality.) Kohut's explanation of primitive anxieties as fears of disintegration (1977, p. 104; 1978d, p. 560; 1984, p. 16) and of infantile aggression as narcissistic rage in reaction to threats to the child's vital interests (1972, p. 641; 1977, pp. 115–21) provided reasoned alternatives for such problematic Kleinian concepts as the "paranoid position," without compromising the significance of archaic experiences. He confirmed the importance of certain Kleinian findings, for example, the frequent occurrence of countertransference problems based on fears of enmeshment in a fantasy of psychic merger (1971, pp. 280–82), without concurring in their universality. On the other side, Kohut explicitly disputed the Kleinian notion that children's aggression is a drive in need of discharge (1977, p. 124); he correctly noted that analytic interpretations based on this hypothesis cause damage by unfairly blaming the patient (pp. 125, 260).

In the realm of analytic technique, Kohut's unique emphasis on empathy as a *sine qua non* for therapeutic success had a salutary effect in counteracting the threatened routinization of treatment. He rightly stressed that an empathic ambience creates a powerful bond in the therapeutic dyad (1973c, p. 705). However, the most important outcome of Kohut's work with regard to technique is the conclusion forcefully stated by Schwaber (1981, 1983) that the empathic analyst must always try to understand the analysand's experience from the subjective vantage point of the patient. Elsewhere (Gedo, 1984b), I have outlined some objections to exclusive therapeutic reliance on organizing data within this frame of reference; here, it is appropriate to affirm that such reliance is nonetheless preferable to the distortion of analytic technique that always seems to gain the support of all too many practitioners—namely "interpretation" from an omniscient and pseudoobjective vantage point.

Finally, we should take note of the value of Kohut's developmental propositions. As Robert Emde has noted (personal communication, December 1984), whatever flaws these propositions may possess with regard to details, Kohut's insistence (e.g., 1983, p. 389) that infancy must be viewed in terms of vicissitudes within a self-selfobject unit provides the most useful observational perspective for illuminating the phenomenology of the preverbal stages of development, although this viewpoint is not sufficient for the study of later stages. As Lichtenberg (1983) has also pointed out, because of Kohut's consistent reliance on an interactional framework of this kind, there is relatively little discrepancy between his developmental hypotheses and the findings of researchers who make direct observations of infants in their family matrix (see chapters 10 and 11, this volume).

My review of the entire corpus of Kohut's writings has led me to conclude that every one of these important contributions was, at least implicitly, already part of his analytic armamentarium prior to 1970, when he was writing *The Analysis of the Self*.[12] On the other side of the

---

[12]At the level of the clinical management of archaic transferences, Kohut's teaching was based on these propositions as early as 1962 or 1963. I had occasion to present the analysis of such a patient in a termination seminar at the Chicago Institute at that time; Kohut's illuminating response to precisely those aspects of the case that my supervisor had insisted on trying to sweep under the rug confirmed me in my chronic dissatisfaction with existing clinical theories. Conversely, I am sure that my presenta-

coin, the nonanalytic aspects of Self Psychology did not surface until about 1974, when Kohut was already suffering from his lingering terminal illness and felt under great pressure to complete his life's work as quickly as possible. The change in the nature of his commitments from being an innovative psychoanalyst to his emergence as a Self Psychologist may be looked on from one viewpoint as the personal tragedy of a vulnerable pioneer; from the vantage point of his sectarian followers, the same alteration doubtless seems like the apotheosis of a modern hero.

---

tion led Kohut to single me out among analysts of my generation as a most likely recruit to the cause of theoretical revision.

INTERMEZZO

9

The Lessons of History and the Challenge of Scientific Method

My survey of three waves of dissent within psychoanalysis, each chronologically separated from the next by the passage of a full generation, usually followed by ecumenical efforts grounded in epistemology, suggests the conclusion that the intellectual history of the discipline is destined to be marred by factionalism based on the personal subjectivity of charismatic leaders. In his lifetime, Sigmund Freud was the unquestioned fountainhead who defined the nature of the discipline he created, although he was challenged by would-be rivals with their own share of charisma, Alfred Adler and Carl Jung.

In retrospect one can only applaud the good judgment of Lou Salomé as the epistemological referee of the Adler and Jung secessions: without overlooking the unsolved theoretical problems of Freud's system, she refused to throw out the baby with the bathwater and dismissed the schools founded by these former adherents of psychoanalysis for disavowing the significance of its clinical discoveries. As I noted in chapter 4, Salomé's confidence in the empirical validity of the discipline was based in large measure on her recognition that Ferenczi's clinical observations would ultimately supplement those of Freud and would correct what she looked on as an unfortunate a priori bias of psychoanalytic theory, its assumption that all behavior must be a result of intrapsychic conflict, that everything archaic must be altered or warded off in adult life.

To state these objections within the context of Freud's method of investigation, centered on personal introspection (see Gedo, 1968), prior to 1920 psychoanalysis concerned itself almost exclusively with mental contents, fantasies recoverable by means of self-inquiry. Freud attempted to explain the occurrence of these thoughts with a speculative metapsychological theory derived from the natural science prevalent at the turn of the century (see Sulloway, 1979). The therapeutic technique used before the theoretical reformulations Freud proposed in the 1920s (esp. in Freud, 1923a, 1926) forcefully confronted the analysand with deductive interpretations about the unconscious meanings of behavior in the manner I have illustrated through the work of Melanie Klein (chapter 6, this volume). These interpretations were logically derived from a model of the mind— now usually designated the "topographic model"—applicable only to a narrow segment of the behavior observed in the psychoanalytic setting (Gedo and Goldberg, 1973). However, this model is almost entirely adequate to deal with observations made through introspection, and Freud did propose a supplementary model, the "reflex arc," to take care of the exceptions.

Every wave of dissidence within psychoanalysis has come about because the actualities of clinical observations, which brought to light ever more archaic material as a result of improvements in analytic technique, rendered obsolete the accepted theoretical schemata of the day. In these circumstances, various contributors advanced compelling hypotheses, which, in their turn, proved to encompass too narrow a segment of the observational field—a repetition of the *pars pro toto* fallacy that undermined the edifice of Freud's original theory. Moreover, the opportunity to conceptualize the data collected in previously unexplored areas inevitably induced each innovator to stamp his or her proposals with subjectivity and foreordained their rejection by colleagues who could not share these idiosyncratic assumptions.

This sequence of typical events has been demonstrated with clarity with regard to a dissident I failed to include in my survey, the Viennese analyst Wilhelm Reich. W. Grossman (1976) has carefully shown that Reich "claimed to be the heir to and savior of the fundamental discoveries of Freud's early years."[1] He rejected the theoretical revo-

---

[1]This claim was echoed in more recent years by Jacques Lacan, who also presented his idiosyncratic version of "psychoanalysis" as a return to the essence of the *real* Freud, that is, Freud, the id psychologist.

lution Freud instituted in the 1920s, finding there "only a betrayal of the true concrete biological base of the libido theory" (p. 381). In other words, Reich, in a counterrevolutionary mode, labeled the elderly Freud a dissident from his own origins. Grossman also notes (p. 380) that Reich's assumption of the functional identity of psyche and soma is not *philosophically* untenable—it is merely "totally at variance with conventional scientific wisdom" (p. 384). Because of this heterodoxy, the majority of psychoanalysts have regarded Reich as a crank—or worse!—and dismiss his therapeutic methods as charlatanry.

If Wilhelm Reich can be seen as the messianic leader of an attempted right-wing coup within psychoanalysis around 1930, Ferenczi might be regarded as the ineffectual though widely admired chieftain of a disorganized left-wing opposition during the same period. In chapter 3, I showed that Ferenczi's "deviation" derived from his discovery of the syndrome he named "the wise baby"—a self-description resulting from introspection set in motion by the transference relationship with Freud. Ferenczi conceptualized this pathology not in terms of libidinal vicissitudes but as a distortion of ego development because of early traumata. In other words, he fully accepted the new model of the mind Freud introduced in 1923—after all, much of the evidence that compelled Freud to revise his previous model was collected by Ferenczi (among others) in his work on the war neuroses, general paresis, and various "narcissistic neuroses" deemed unanalyzable by the techniques based on the topographic theory.

Yet, as I suggested in chapter 3, the archaic syndromes studied by Ferenczi are scarcely encompassed by Freud's structural theory of 1923 (see Gedo and Goldberg, 1973). When he attempted to analyze such patients, Ferenczi was compelled to resort to technical modifications that far transcended the analysis of defenses demanded by Freud's introduction of ego psychology. But Ferenczi was far from *rejecting* these new Freudian insights, as Reich did at the time; as early as 1924, he singled out the problem of overcoming resistances, the defensive activities of the ego, as the key to reliving the infantile neurosis within the transference. He was emphatic that this can be accomplished only by analyzing the *function* of resistance, instead of attacking it.

Some of the noninterpretive measures Ferenczi tried out on patients with predominantly pregenital pathology were aimed at increasing tolerance of tension. Half a century after these technical experiments, in my joint work with Goldberg, I tried to find a coherent theoretical rationale for such measures of "pacification" (Gedo and Goldberg, 1973, chapter 4). I mention this sequel to my review of Ferenczi's work in the mid-1960s only to underscore that his technical "deviation" was truly an effort to find solutions for unsolved problems in psychoanalysis that ego psychology did not succeed in ameliorating. Nor should we assume that in scientific controversies the majority is more likely to be right than in political ones; that Ferenczi's contribution was largely unappreciated by his contemporaries does not diminish its value. As Lou Salomé correctly noted, it was an effective counterweight for Freud's exclusive emphasis on the neurosogenic conflicts of the oedipal period.

Ferenczi's "deviation" did not develop into an organized dissident movement, despite the continuing loyalty of some followers, particularly those trained in Budapest, such as his literary executor, Michael Bálint. The first organized dissidence within psychoanalysis was led by Melanie Klein—from a historical vantage point probably the most important of Ferenczi's students. As reported in chapter 6, she succeeded in the assignment he gave her, to extend psychoanalytic treatment into the early childhood era. By doing so, Klein decisively demonstrated that pathogenesis cannot be attributed exclusively to the oedipal period, as Freud had claimed. She thus found convincing support for Ferenczi's reconstructive conclusions, based on work with narcissistic syndromes.

Melanie Klein was not a systematic thinker, nor did she seem to be interested in metapsychology. Through 1932, when she published her best received contribution, *The Psycho-Analysis of Children*, both her technical prescriptions and her use of theory adhered closely to the Freudian tradition—as she understood or misunderstood it. We do not know what emboldened Mrs. Klein to become the charismatic leader of a dissident school between 1932 and 1935, but it is by no means far fetched to assume that the unreasoning rejection of Ferenczi's late work by the leadership of psychoanalysis and his tragic death—events that unfolded during that interval—may have played a role in her transformation. She certainly did pick up the banner of the fallen leader to guide those who would persist in heroic efforts to offer psychoanalytic assistance to the sickest of patients.

As the dissidence of Ferenczi is illuminated through a comparison with the contemporaneous schism provoked by Reich, so that of Melanie Klein may be clarified by invoking another secession, that of Karen Horney, which took place at approximately the same time. For this comparison, I rely once again on the thoughtful work of Grossman (1984), who concluded that behind its manifest controversies about clinical matters, the Freud-Horney schism was determined by the latent force of Horney's need to look for explanatory models that invoke primarily sociocultural factors. I would add that her use of such models allies Horney with Alfred Adler. In contrast, Melanie Klein devised an explanatory system that echoes the *Weltanschauung* of C. G. Jung—a doctrine of vitalism and innate ideas (like Jung's "archetypes") presented in a pseudobiological guise.

The Kleinian dissidence that has lasted for half a century despite the threadbareness of its conceptualizations cannot have depended for its longevity on Mrs. Klein's charisma alone. In my judgment, it was assisted by the ossification of the Freudian "mainstream" in reaction to the death of Freud and under the understandably conservative guardianship of his daughter. It is true that Heinz Hartmann (1939) led American psychoanalysis out of the theoretical impasse of too literal adherence to the structural theory of 1923 by making allowance for the great sphere of conflict-free functioning—a conceptual refinement still under the rubric of ego psychology. This modification of Freud's last paradigm blunts the force of Lou Salomé's objection to the reductionism of Freudian theory. But Hartmann's important contributions (1964; see also Hartmann, Kris and Loewenstein, 1964) were in the systematization and clarification of metapsychology. On the clinical level, the majority of Freudians were content to accentuate the cardinal importance of the intrapsychic conflicts discovered before 1920 and neglected the issues Ferenczi began to address. Even in regard to classical subject matter, Klein stole some of the thunder by showing that the traditional view had not given due weight to issues of primitive aggression.

The second epistemological referee whose work I review in this volume is David Rapaport. Having systematized psychoanalytic theory (1959), he concluded that even Hartmann's important addenda had failed to broaden it sufficiently to deal with the phenomena Freud had classified under the rubric of narcissism—hence the contemporary proliferation of clinical propositions centered on (internalized) object relations, theories incapable of correlation with previous conceptualizations in psychoanalysis. Rapaport accurately predicted that advances in theory would take the direction indicated by Hartmann's specification of an "adaptive viewpoint" within metapsychology, that is, theories focused on the self-organization (formerly adumbrated under rubric of a "synthetic function"). He insisted that an adequate map of personality organization would have to include archaic functional modes integrated hierarchically with more mature ones, characterized by ego mastery, a prescription I was to follow in developing the hierarchical model (Gedo and Goldberg, 1973). Finally, Rapaport's emphasis on cognitive development as a subject for empirical study was explicitly aimed at arbitrary developmental propositions, such as those of Melanie Klein. In other words, his sophisticated theoretical critique judged all existing psychoanalytic theories to be both incomplete and inconsistent, and some to be untenable too. For good measure, he demanded that in the future we develop hypotheses capable of empirical validation.

It was at this juncture that Heinz Kohut threw his hat into the ring of theoretical discourse in psychoanalysis. As a result of the successful analysis of resistances made possible by ego psychology, he made the important clinical discovery that certain archaic transference constellations referable to phases of development preceding the Oedipus complex are focused on issues of self-esteem and self-cohesion. He then became convinced that under these conditions in particular (and in psychoanalytic work in general) the crux of therapeutic success is the empathic performance of the analyst. In parallel with this shift, Kohut began to see man's existential problems, the tragic difficulties of pursuing his ideals and ambitions, as more central than are conflicts about sexuality and aggression. In other words, he relegated all previous psychoanalytic findings to a position of secondary importance, elevating his own novel observations to primary significance.[2]

This reformulation of clinical theory amounted to an effort to turn about the fate of all previous dissidents: the concerns of Ferenczi and Lou Salomé about the relative neglect of narcissistic issues in psychoanalytic discourse, the emphasis of Melanie Klein on putative transactions in the preverbal era, even the emphasis placed on interpersonal relations by Harry Stack Sullivan and his successors (see Imber, 1984), are retrospectively justified by Kohut's relegation of the empirical discoveries that constitute the core of traditional psychoanalysis to the status of epiphenomena. But Kohut also attempted to supersede

---

[2]In making this choice, Kohut repudiated his previous endorsement of the hierarchical model (Gedo & Goldberg, 1973) as the first psychoanalytic schema to avoid reductionism. My own condemnation of Self Psychology as a reductionistic system inevitably followed.

every dissident school surviving from the past by proposing the search for perfection as the primary motivating force of human nature.

At the same time, Kohut proposed a new value system for psychoanalysis, replacing Freud's parallel quests for knowledge and personal autonomy with a commitment to provide people with optimally empathic selfobject relations (see chapter 8, this volume). A corollary of this proposition is the conception of cure by means of the analyst's promoting internalizations—note the reemergence of Melanie Klein's "good-breast-as-inner-object"!—through active management of the patient's levels of frustration. Predictably, those who accept this prescription will leave organized psychoanalysis and form a schismatic therapeutic movement.

I have summarized the argument of the preceding section of this volume in a manner similar to that of Lou Salomé and David Rapaport as intellectual historians and philosophers of science. I cannot claim to match their degree of objectivity; I was an active participant in the intellectual free-for-all within psychoanalysis for many years, whereas they evaluated contemporaneous controversies as witnesses from the sidelines. Nor have I felt free to survey the gamut of dissident schools, for I am not sufficiently familiar with the intellectual matrix from which French or even British variants of psychoanalysis arose to assess those as I have their Central European and American counterparts. I do not believe that the work of Jacques Lacan can truly make sense to anyone schooled in the two traditions I represent, for example. I am convinced, however, that we may draw reliable conclusions about the intractable differences of opinion among psychoanalysts on the basis of the three major dissidents whose work I have studied in detail.

In the Introductory chapter, I alluded to the fact that around 1920 Freud defined a psychoanalyst as a clinician who accepts the significance of transference and resistance phenomena. In accord with that criterion, Ferenczi, Klein, and Kohut, in contrast to Adler or Jung (see Freud, 1914b), remained psychoanalysts despite their dissident views. Each of the waves of dissidence led by these prestigious analysts reflected the accumulated dissatisfaction of a generation of their colleagues with contemporary psychoanalysis, both as therapy and as a science of mind. The unavoidable imperfection of any scientific enterprise should culminate in such periodic crises within our discipline as long as it retains its vitality. The organizational disruptions caused by these differences of scientific opinion demonstrate our collective inability to make rational choices among competing psychoanalytic hypotheses.

However loudly epistemologists (e.g., Grünbaum, 1984) or methodologists (e.g., Silverman and Silverman, 1984) have protested against the status quo, almost the only efforts at validation to take place within psychoanalysis are the individual activities of clinicians who apply specific theories—more or less faithfully—in the therapeutic arena. As I have discussed in detail elsewhere (Gedo, 1984a, pp. 188–190), theories may capture the allegiance of practitioners on a number of different grounds; unfortunately, however, these may well disregard both validity and pragmatic utility. It is quite likely, as a matter of fact, that analysts will subscribe to that specific school of thought which most closely reflects their individual hierarchy of values. As Kohut well knew, Self Psychology is unlikely to appeal to those of us committed to the primacy of truth.

In addition to these nonrational considerations, our preferences among the alternative clinical hypotheses available must be based on their congruence with the developmental schemata we accept. In the past, every major psychoanalytic theorist enunciated his or her own hypotheses about psychological development. These propositions were, it is to be hoped, correlated with the theorist's clinical experience but, particularly with regard to the earliest stages of life (those preceding the consensual use of speech), they generally did not derive from psychoanalytic evidence. Occasionally, the hypotheses were no more than arbitrary inventions, for example, Melanie Klein's adultopmorphic conception of the infant as a being handicapped by psychotic ideation. More often, developmental hypotheses were borrowed from cognate disciplines; Rapaport's use of Piaget's conclusions about cognitive development is an example.

Only recently has psychological development in the early years of life received serious attention from empirical investigators. The evolving consensus of their conclusions is ultimately bound to tip the scales in favor of the psychoanalytic theories congruent with their findings. These exciting research efforts are conducted, for the most part, outside the psychoanalytic orbit. As a result, they often focus on questions not directly related to psychoanalytic concerns. On the other hand, observational studies conducted by psychoanalysts tend to take for granted some of the assumptions built into existing psychoanalytic theories. All in all, the evolution of developmental psychology as a basic science that will inform psychoanalysis about the biological parameters constraining its own hypotheses is still in its own infancy. As it reaches maturity, we may expect its scientific input to resolve various controversies in our field that were previously decided by popular vote.

In the chapters to follow, I consider the current status of the interface between psychoanalysis and the direct observation of the behavior of young children, as well as some of the methodological problems inherent in correlating these cognate disciplines. These difficulties have by no means been overcome; the verdict of infant research on many psychoanalytic controversies is not yet final. Nor will committed sectarians necessarily heed the voice of reason at first hearing. Witness the recent reaction of a Kleinian spokeswoman (O'Shaughnessy, 1984) to reports calling into question Klein's assumptions about infantile mentation—she confidently predicts that evidence supporting the Kleinian position will be found. It is to be expected that the implication of extraanalytic observations about infancy for questions of psychoanalytic technique may encounter even greater resistance, for many analysts seem to have invested their clinical procedures with the aura of a sacred ritual, as the intensely negative reaction to Ferenczi's technical experimentation already demonstrated.

One of the most important lessons learned from observations of infants in interaction with their caretakers is the astonishing complexity of the nonsymbolic channels of communication through which these relations are mediated. These findings are of the utmost importance for our understanding of psychoanalytic technique, especially to arrive at operational definitions of the processes that constitute empathy. These observations should also restrain the current tendency to follow some of our French colleagues into a conception of psychoanalytic work modeled on decoding the latent meanings of a literary text. I shall therefore devote the last chapter of my methodological section to a critique of this fallacious idea.

METHODOLOGICAL SECTION

10

Caveat Lector

Psychoanalytic Theory and the Direct Observation of Behavior

RESPECTED THEORETICIANS OF SUCH VARIED persuasions as Charles Brenner and Heinz Kohut have expressed marked skepticism about the value of attempts to use data from the direct observation of young children in reformulating psychoanalytic theories. Another school of thought, that of Ernst Kris, Anna Freud, René Spitz, and Margaret Mahler, to name only the pioneers of this movement, is committed to longitudinal observational studies, more or less in the tradition of experiments of nature, in the service of supplementing reconstructive data from the psychoanalysis of children and adults. Whatever the methodological difficulties of translating the behaviors of entirely or largely nonverbal youngsters into the constructs of a psychology of man's inner life, the actualities of adaptation during the earliest phases of development are decisive in permitting a choice among alternative hypotheses about the regulation of infantile behavior.

Most research efforts provide equivocal testimony about this methodological controversy. At the very least, they do bring into the public domain a wealth of well-documented phenomenology; this accomplishment alone is enough to justify observational research into the earliest years of life. The formidable problem of translating the manifest behaviors of children, especially in the preverbal era, into a psychology of motivations has, however, thrown doubt on most attempts to use extra-analytic data to buttress and/or to amend aspects of psychoanalytic theory. The most recent book-length report of research performed to test some psychoanalytic propositions about development, Henri Parens' *The Development of Aggression in Early Child-hood* (1979), is a prototype of the difficulties of such an enterprise.

Parens (1979) is one of the most distinguished of a group of psy-choanalytic investigators who have carried on the tradition of Mar-garet Mahler, observing the behavior of young children over the course of several years in the more or less naturalistic setting of a nursery school. The observations were begun early in infancy, when the mothers started to bring their babies to the school regularly. The investigators had excellent opportunities to gather reliable informa-tion about the overt behaviors of the children; as might be predicted, however, even at this level, the most unequivocal findings reported by Parens pertain to the era after the acquisition of language. For instance, he found gender differences in the modes of "aggressive discharge" in the latter half of the third year of life (pp. 326–329). As Parens has rightly noted (p. 323), the same defensive operations that becloud our perception about this era of childhood in the clinical setting already stand in the way of any direct interpretation of the meanings of the specific actions of toddlers at the age of 24 months, if not earlier.

Nonetheless, about children who can already communicate through speech, Parens made observations that carry conviction–but they do so precisely because they happen to be congruent with our clinical experience! When we deal with issues about which we lack clinical consensus, observational data will fail to resolve our disagree-ments, for those of us whose opinions are not reinforced by the seeming implications of the data will simply call their relevance into question. Witness, for instance, the general failure of the analytic community to heed the findings of Thérèse Décarie (1973) that chal-lenged the connection between "stranger anxiety" around the age of 9 months and presumed attachment to the person of the mother. Established theories die hard.

Let me give a concrete illustration of the operation of these factors in the work of Parens. In his population of subjects, he found that castration fantasies emerged at 27 to 30 months, not at 18 to 24 months as reported by other investigators. I feel that the findings of Parens must be valid, because they tally with my reconstructive con-clusions from clinical practice with a wide spectrum of adults; conse-quently, I prefer to believe that the reports contradicted by Parens may have studied less representative populations than he. The issue of biased sampling in longitudinal studies that require the coopera-tion of volunteer subjects over the span of many years has never been adequately addressed. Neither Parens, Mahler, Pine, and Bergman (1975), nor any of the other investigators who recruited families to participate in time consuming efforts of this variety looked into the complex question of what motivates people to make sacrifices of this kind for the sake of scientific research. In my view, we are unlikely to gain this kind of cooperation from families unless they hope to get professional assistance of some type from the joint effort. If my prejudice is valid, this circumstance raises serious doubts about the generalizability of findings about the families concerned.[1]

To return to the issue of studying the earliest phases of development: With children who are still incapable of using words to communicate about their inner world, the observer's inferences about motivations rest on particularly insecure foundations. No better illustration of this point could be offered than Parens' description (pp. 242–245) of a 19-month-old whose mother had just given birth to a sibling. In this context, the toddler, who was at the threshold of acquiring speech, developed a symptom—bedtime fear. The research team decided on the unusual step of interfering with the natural unfolding of events by making a therapeutic intervention. (So much for naturalistic observations in laboratories run by psychoanalysts!) In the child's presence, the mother was told that her daughter was afraid of being abandoned because of her anger about the advent of the baby.

Clearly, this interpretation was not based on the child's communications but on the investigators' clinical convictions, themselves heavily influenced by a commitment to the Mahlerian schema of emotional development. Because this intervention was followed by symptom relief, Parens assumes that the child understood the interpretation and was reassured by it. In my view, such an assumption is unwarranted; if the intervention was instrumental in removing the symptom (a matter most difficult to determine even in principle and never studied in this specific case), the result was much more likely to have followed from the effects of the explanation on the mother's subsequent response to the child than from any direct verbal comprehension of such a sophisticated message by a preverbal toddler. Further observation revealed that only at the age of 26 months was this particular child able to express her jealousy by means of words.

---

[1]Shortly after publication of her research, I queried Margaret Mahler (at a meeting of Group V of the Center for Advanced Psychoanalytic Study at Princeton) about her views concerning this methodological problem. Mahler simply denied that the reasons for agreeing to cooperate with her research were worthy of further inquiry.

Despite his best efforts to exercise caution, to qualify inferences about motivation made on the basis of overt behaviors, the investigator of early childhood is generally forced to commit himself about highly controversial issues far removed from his observational data. In the work reported by Parens, the ultimate goal of the research was to draw metapsychological inferences on the basis of the spectrum of behaviors rated as aggressive by the investigators. Of course, such ratings are unavoidably arbitrary, for they depend entirely on "vicarious introspection," (Heinz Kohut's designation for empathy [1980a, pp. 459–460])—in fact, Parens nowhere explicitly defines aggression.

To illustrate how investigators may set up categories of doubtful relevance, let me note that Parens even chose to classify the chewing movements of toothless infants as instances of "nonaffective destructiveness," attributing intentionality to subcortically regulated activities and thereby confounding the goals of behavior with its consequences. Ultimately, then, Parens' decisions about what constitutes aggression are *deduced* from an existing model of mental functioning: he uses the a priori assumption that all behaviors are necessarily fueled by the instinctual drives. Thus the four categories of aggression he differentiates permit the inclusion of active, goal-directed behavior of any kind. For better and for worse, the conceptual work of this project took the traditional metapsychology of psychoanalysis for granted.

Because these metapsychological assumptions form the conceptual premises underlying the categories into which all the observations have been fitted, the data collected in the course of this research could in no way lead to any meaningful theoretical revision—the research design required that each piece of behavior be assigned to one of the subdivisions provided by psychoanalytic drive theory. It is true that a number of alternative schemata of the drives have been proposed within psychoanalysis over the years, but these are perfectly adequate to accommodate all the observations reported by Parens. In the psychoanalytic conceptual realm, most research using methods of direct observation of behavior has been guilty of circularity of this kind. (After expanding on this essential aspect of methodology, I shall mention a representative study performed by psychoanalysts that avoided this pitfall.)

Let me underscore this point with a concrete example—how Parens discusses one class of observations about the early months of infancy, a class that seems unequivocally reliable, the occurrence of the affective storms he calls "rage reactions." Parens (p. 20) asserts, that these phenomena cannot be explained without postulating some mechanism that mobilizes destructiveness. This claim is simply inaccurate; affects have been explained on other grounds, even in the psychoanalytic literature. For instance: "[That] there are basic affective expressions common to human infants and adults, as well as other mammals, that are stereotyped, universal, and involuntary, suggests that affect, so-called, is in fact an onto- and phylogenetically early form of communication" (Basch, 1976a, pp. 775–776. More recent statements on this issue from other psychoanalysts are taken up in the next chapter).

It is not to the point to decide here which set of hypotheses about any of these issues is the most tenable; I merely wish to highlight that to argue, as many psychoanalytic investigators (including Parens) have done, that only the explanations psychoanalysis has taken for granted are *thinkable* is to prejudge the issues through the avoidance of or a failure to discover serious alternatives. If the conceptual possibilities were truly limited to the various versions of psychoanalytic metapsychology, we would have no need for empirical data, either from observational research or from the clinical situation, in order to choose among them. Our preference would then have to be based on considerations of internal consistency and that economy in the elaboration of concepts usually called "Occam's razor." Elsewere (Gedo, 1979, pp. 247–249), I have tried to show that by these criteria Freud's proposals of 1920, enunciated in *Beyond the Pleasure Principle*, remain unsurpassed.

To put the matter differently, if one is committed to a set of theoretical assumptions, the potential use of observational data is restricted to an exercise comparable to trying on a number of ready-made suits for optimal fit. It should cause no surprise that the theoretical schemata of Freud or Hartmann fit the observations of Parens reasonably well—although Parens has chosen to tinker with the cuffs and the sleeves, in my judgment more often to the detriment of conceptual order than to its improvement! But I do not wish to enter into the minutiae of these metapsychological questions, for it is the utter disregard Parens shows for alternatives to drive theory that requires comment here.

I must confess that I was initially stunned into disbelief when I perused the list of References in *The Development of Aggression in Early*

Childhood (1979, pp. 373–384). That a book aspiring to draw meta-psychological conclusions could ignore every publication dealing with the theoretical ferment of recent years within psychoanalysis fills me with despair about the possibility of reasoned scientific discourse in our field. I should think that a contemporary reconsideration of the theory of aggression would have to take into account Kohut's clinical challenge (see chapters 7 and 8, this volume) as well as such major theoretical contributions as the monographs of George Klein (1976), Roy Schafer (1976), Gill and Holzman (1976), or Rosenblatt and Thickstun (1977), and the series of papers on this topic by Benjamin Rubinstein (1965, 1967, 1974, 1976a, 1976b), Robert Holt (1965, 1967a, 1967b, 1976), or Michael Basch (1975a, 1975b, 1976a, 1976b, 1976c, 1977).

Rosenblatt and Thickstun (1977), for example, regard behavior as organized into goal-directed units activated by perceptual information about those goals—a hypothesis centrally relevant for the organization of data such as those reported by Parens. A scholar of his stature cannot be unaware of these powerful alternatives proposed to replace the traditional metapsychology of psychoanalysis. He must also know that the objections to the epistemological status of that metapsychology have never been adequately answered. To ignore these issues in 1979 required an act of faith worthy of an Aquinas—it is not psychoanalytic dissidents alone who place ideological passion above reason!

If a priori theoretical assumptions can predetermine the conceptual yield of studies based on the direct observation of behavior, turning their data into illustrations of the investigator's hypotheses, are we justified in dismissing such flawed empirical efforts altogether? Insofar as the primary data are reported in terms of nontechnical descriptions of actual events, we are not justified. Unfortunately, psychoanalytic researchers are often insufficiently cautious about this requirement in reporting observations—many of their accounts are impregnated to an extraordinary extent with theoretical presuppositions. Let me illustrate, once more, by citing some particulars from the work of Parens.

In line with his metapsychological commitments, Parens (1979, p. 146) explicitly assumes that he can directly categorize behaviors observed in the laboratory setting into those fueled by neutralized aggression and those driven by unneutralized aggression. This method leads to entries of the following kind: ". . . because libidinizing the motor apparatus carries with it the expenditure of aggressive energy,

[Mary at age 1-0-13] can tolerate reaching targets slowly without frustrating aggressive impulses" (p. 195). Parens means that a child who has just learned to walk practices this new skill without apparent displeasure about her inefficiency when rated by adult standards. As this example shows, it is usually advisable to translate such statements by investigators, wherever possible, into nontechnical language to free them of built–in theoretical assumptions. If this proves to be feasible, fresh conclusions may be reached from the observations reported.

To continue with the same illustrative example, my reading of the evidence presented by Parens leads to a definition of "aggression" much narrower than the one proposed by the author. Specifically, I do not think it is warranted to include the primary affect of rage among the phenomena classified as aggressive. As Tomkins (1980) has proposed, rage and other basic affects are satisfactorily accounted for by certain characteristic quantitative changes in levels of neural firing. Parens consistently commits the error of imputing subjective motives to an organism whose behavior is not yet cortically regulated. (Alternative explanations are discussed in the next chapter.) When, for example, Parens rates certain motor activities in infancy, such as chewing motions, as "nonaffective destruction," he commits an error in empathy, judging the behavior of a child in the sensorimotor phase of cognitive development by the standards of adulthood. The same kind of misjudgment occurs when Parens, in his ratings of infantile behavior, confounds mere *purposefulness* with a sophisticated motivation, such as his category of "nondestructive aggression."

I could summarize my sense of the phenomena for which a psychoanalytic theory of aggression must account by calling them, in Parens' terms "unpleasure related" and "pleasure related destructiveness." In saying this, of course, I am merely echoing Freud's point of view. But the fact that Parens and I cannot easily agree about the phenomema that appropriately should be included in a study of "aggression" should alert us to the probability that our conceptualizations in this area could lead to the creation of fictive entities. Parens comes all too close to writing about aggression as if it were an autogenous poison perfusing the organism, a poison from which the body must gradually be detoxified— or about the "ego" as a liverish organ designed to accomplish that task. As a version of psychoanalytic drive theory, this is a bit more concrete than most, a contemporary variation on the Renaissance notion of Humours.

Lest I be misunderstood, let me hasten to add that in my own theoretical work I have not called into question the utility of the concept of "drive" [Freud's *Trieb*] in psychoanalytic discourse. In proposing that we abandon the traditional metapsychological framework, however, I have argued that we must fit the drives into our schema of the organization of behavior at the *biological* level (see Basch, in Panel, 1984, p. 582). The observations Parens has collected certainly include instances of unpleasure-related destructiveness occurring before the regulation of behavior can meaningfully be characterized as "psychological" in the sense of employing symbolic thought.

When 13-month-old toddlers strike out at their mothers upon being prevented from moving out of a given play area, for example, it seems likely that this aggressive behavior represents a preprogrammed action pattern automatically activated at subcortical levels. Of course, there are occasional instances of infants being *trained* to respond in certain ways, with response patterns (e.g., defecating when placed on a potty chair) that resemble the cortically mediated behaviors of older children or even of adults. Such learned behaviors are not to be confused, however, with actions based on levels of cognition unavailable in the sensorimotor phase. At any rate, my conception of "drive" is that an automatic, preprogrammed action pattern is brought into operation—admittedly, a definition so different from traditional psychoanalytic usage, that of an inner force seeking discharge, that to propose it risks creating terminological confusion.

It happens that the observational research of Parens yielded evidence of the most compelling sort about the transition from the sensorimotor mode of organization to that of behavior mediated by the cerebral cortex. He reports that at the age of 20 months a child who had for some time been quite angry about having to accommodate to a new sibling suddenly reorganized the "discharge of her aggression." Until that time, this had taken the form of indiscriminately throwing things, crying, or twisting away from the mother's efforts to calm her. Now, with seemingly pleasurable affect, she created a game of throwing a doll off the sofa on which her mother customarily sat during the sessions in the laboratory. Parens interprets this enactment as evidence of "ridding herself of and separating aggressively from the object" (p. 228). Perhaps so—but the main significance of this observation is that it unequivocally shows the operation of symbolic thinking.

I assume that the doll stood for the baby and the child was playing mother; from her behavior we may infer that the child wished her mother to get rid of the baby. Lichtenberg (1982, p. 228) highlights another symbolic meaning one might ascribe to the child's behavior: he proposes that the doll stood for the child herself and that the enactment of picking up the doll after each act of rejecting it was intended to reassure her about her mother's receptivity in the face of the child's anger. Most probably both symbolic interpretations are valid; this level of complexity in thought is a universe different from the automaticity of "drive discharge."

I know, of course, that my definition of what constitutes a "psychological" level of functioning is as narrow as it is possible to make it; in fact, there has to be a transitional period between the "biological" and "psychological" modes of organization I have tried to differentiate so sharply for heuristic purposes here. In my previous work (Gedo and Goldberg, 1973; Gedo, 1979, 1981b, 1984a), I attempted to sidestep these terminological limitations by giving these phases of development numerical designations: Phase I for the biological, Phase II for the transitional, and Phase III for the unequivocally psychological level of organization. I dare say that such a schema is unobjectionable to most, but we have no consensus whatever about the actual age levels represented by these phases.

In my opinion, most psychoanalytic authors, including Parens, consistently overestimate maturational progress in these matters by a wide margin—perhaps not quite as wildly as Kleinian authors, who postulate capacities for fantasy at birth (see chapter 6, this volume), but with unusual abandon nonetheless. I have already alluded to Parens' attributing *motives* to infants under 16 weeks of age; he also assumes that children have *wishes* in the latter half of the first year of life, that infantile affects are *emotions* (i.e., that they are subjectively felt), and that infants are capable of hallucinatory and delusional mentation. Parens (p. 191) even asserts that a 13-month-old child deduced that its mother was going to have a baby! I do not want to commit myself here about a timetable for the acquisition of these various capacities; I merely wish to say that it is not legitimate to address oneself with unwarranted confidence to controversial matters about which reasoned conclusions are difficult to reach. Some of the specific issues that remain controversial are taken up once more in the chapter to follow.

I have described my manifold differences with traditional psychoanalytic views concerning the organization of behavior in the first 18
months of life in order to illustrate the difficulty of making use of
extra-analytic data for theory construction in psychoanalysis. It is
regrettable that one must take such a negative view of the observational work of so many psychoanalyst-researchers, despite essential
sympathy with their aims and methods. As the remainder of this
chapter should demonstrate, the possibility of making use of observational data in our conceptual work cannot be ruled out; I trust that
projects in the tradition of Spitz, Mahler, or Parens will ultimately
produce a great deal we can all endorse with enthusiasm. Clearly,
one prerequisite for such consensus is scrupulous attention to the
sharp differentiation between observational findings and the conclusions the theorist wishes to base upon them.

Even *The Development of Aggression in Early Childhood* contains many
convincing observations of major importance, by no means involved
with issues of aggression exclusively. To begin with, an example
pertaining to Parens' chosen topic: I believe his data demonstrate that
hatred and destructiveness in young children are invariably the result
of excessive frustration. In most instances, this means a relative
failure of the caretakers to provide the child with a manageable environment. This does not mean, of course, that the parents are necessarily responsible for the original noxae, only that the effects of the
latter can be mitigated only through appropriate parental activities.
(As I discussed in chapter 7 and 8, I believe these to be much more
varied than are the "selfobject functions" highlighted by Kohut.)

It is particularly significant that Parens found that traumatized
infants may show a decisive turn to obstinacy and sadism *before* the
onset of the phase of development characterized by "anality." His
data imply that we need to rethink the role in character formation of
struggles around habit training in the second year of life—and, for
that matter, of anal pleasures per se in stimulating these archaic wars.
Not that it is difficult to find reconstructive data from within the
psychoanalytic setting that raise the same questions about traditional
developmental theories, but single case reports are invariably dismissed as potential evidence because of questions about their reliabil-
ity. And skepticism is entirely appropriate on that score—hence the
need for observational research to validate our hypotheses. I present
an illustrative example from clinical practice bearing on these issues
in the next chapter. Nonetheless, the example confirms the findings

of Parens (p. 107) that infantile rage *never* arises spontaneously; it is always a response to specific circumstances, either in the external environment or in the physiological sphere.

Another important observation reported by Parens, but one more distant from the central concerns of his book, is that infants develop the ability to respond appropriately to affectovocal cues from the mother before the age of ten months (p. 179). This incidental finding is a crucial dividend from this research project, because it has profound implications for the art of interpretation, especially whenever the analyst is faced with states of regression into archaic transferences. As I have elsewhere described at some length (Gedo, 1981b, chapter 11; 1984a, chapter 9), it is often necessary to pay close attention to the paraverbal aspects of our communications if we expect our message to be understood. Nowhere is it more valid that *c'est le ton qui fait la musique.*

Further, Parens (p. 184) briefly reports that some toddlers in the first half of the second year of life seem to regard their mothers as responsible for whatever pain they experience. From the adult observer's viewpoint, Parens legitimately sees such an attitude as the attribution of omnipotence to the parent. If this conclusion proves valid, the observation would constitute the earliest evidence uncovered thus far about those attitudes we call "idealization" when they emerge in the analytic transference (see Gedo, 1975b). I predict that this observation *will* be validated, for it is congruent with my clinical experience. Contrary to Kohut's original developmental schema (1971, p. 97), I have found that such primitive idealizations are the very earliest transferences to be encountered in analysis—they invariably antedate attitudes of subject-centered grandiosity. When archaic idealization is accompanied by regression to a mode of behavior characterized by nonverbal enactments, our patients' transferences most closely resemble the behavior of the normal toddlers Parens is describing.

Such a correlation demonstrates the methodological solution we must follow if we wish to make use of the results of our reconstructive work in the psychoanalytic situation for theory construction. But it shows, in addition, that the investigator is more likely to record observations uncontaminated by theoretical presuppositions in those areas of controversy about which he has not committed himself to any one of the competing alternatives. Put differently, scientific research is most likely to yield valid results if it is designed to test more than one hypothesis: it is feasible to refute propositions one by one, but evidence that supports one's favored viewpoint is all too easy to find and is therefore never conclusive.

To illustrate from the perspective of the theoretical problems with which I have been struggling, certain alternatives are refuted by the observations Parens reports about children who have already acquired the ability to communicate through words. The timing of certain occurrences Parens has highlighted confirms my doubts about traditional hypotheses. First, Parens (p. 260) inferred the presence of the defensive operation of *projection* at the age of 20 months—the earliest unequivocally defensive behavior he noted. Parens couples this conclusion with the claim that he detected the operation of reaction formation and splitting at the same time. I cannot accept either of these conclusions, for they depend on dubious arguments that fail to consider more likely alternatives. It is more reasonable to view the tenderness toddlers display as identification with their caretakers than as reaction formations against hostility, for example. At any rate, projection is available to the child before the capacity for repression becomes manifest. A second finding Parens communicates (p. 264) I consider to be even more significant: he notes the acquisition of some superego functions *before* the onset of the oedipal conflict.

At its peril, psychoanalysis disregards such challenges to its accepted assumptions. Yet psychoanalysts have found it extraordinarily difficult to approach the phenomena observable in early childhood without the constraining developmental propositions of their discipline to guide them. Consequently, the most fruitful observations have been made by researchers active in other scientific arenas. In the next chapter, I consider some of the steps through which that new body of work is entering psychoanalytic discourse. Before going on to that task, however, I must redeem my pledge to cite at least one project of infant observation performed by a psychoanalyst in a methodologically sound manner.

Among the available alternatives, the project closest in method to Parens' is one employing long-term studies of children either perceptually impaired from birth or environmentally deprived in other ways. Originally conceived collaboratively by Fraiberg and Freedman (1964), this research culminated in a series of independent publications by each participant. To mention only Freedman's contributions (1979, 1981, 1982, 1984; Freedman and Brown, 1968), he has confirmed that in congenitally blind infants the incidence of autism is extremely high, whereas in the congenitally deaf it is no different than in the general population. Neglected and feral children without perceptual handicaps fall between the general population and the blind infants in the incidence of autism.

Freedman (1984, p. 23) explains the differential effects of blindness and deafness on the grounds of the sequence of myelinization in the relevant portions of the neural system—the visual pathways mature earlier than the auditory ones and are most important in establishing communicative channels between infant and mother. The investigators were able to devise effective interventions to teach mothers of congenitally blind infants to circumvent these limitations and establish adequate communication with their babies, thereby reducing the incidence of autism in this group to its level in the general population.

On the basis of these observations, Freedman concluded that instinctual drives are not the fundamental building blocks of human behavior. On the contrary, their establishment "is the result of a long developmental process that insures that drives will be unique expressions of the psychological history of the individual" (1984, p. 37). In other words, through his research, Freedman has succeeded in testing and, in this instance, decisively refuting certain propositions within the realm of the developmental theories of psychoanalysis. Further work of the same kind is discussed in the following chapter.

11

On the Dawn
of Experience

The Past Recaptured

IN THE HISTORICAL SECTION of this work, I attempted to trace the repeated threat of psychoanalysis' fragmenting into hostile factions heatedly defending ideological *partis pris*. These civil wars have always been byproducts of a limitation of the psychoanalytic method, a constraint that results from the fact that the clinical procedure yields relatively scant evidence about personality development in the preverbal period of life. Consequently, every clinical theory, starting with Freud's initial one in *The Interpretation of Dreams* (1900, pp. 588–622) is perforce based on extra-analytic assumptions about the organization of behavior during infancy. The unreliability of such borrowings has been demonstrated so frequently that influential voices within psychoanalysis (Gill, 1976) have urged that psychoanalysts confine future theoretical enterprises to the systematization of data obtained within the psychoanalytic setting.

By contrast, some authors (see Gedo, 1981c) have expressed skepticism about the possibility of eliminating all a priori assumptions about early development in constructing psychoanalytic theories, no matter how hard one might try to do this. In any case, the psychoanalytic controversies—those pitting Kleinians against Freudians some decades ago or the self psychologists against the ego psychologists more recently—(the array of dissidence I have discussed)—demonstrate that clinical innovators are quick to invent hypotheses about early childhood that are convenient for their purposes. The lack

of valid information about infant behavior has sanctioned the proliferation of arbitrary schemata about early development.

Recent research on infancy therefore promises to impose badly
needed constraints on the collective propensity of psychoanalysts to
engage in free speculation about early mentation. In a comprehensive
study of these investigations, Joseph Lichtenberg (1983) has collected
their results in a wide-ranging and carefully researched monograph.
He has addressed this work to a psychoanalytic readership largely
faithful to the Freudian metapsychology still taught in our training
institutes; his primary focus is on those of the traditional theories that
have either been refuted by or shown to have marginal relevance for
the observational data of an impressive body of infant research. As a
result of Lichtenberg's focus, a casual reader might overlook the fact
that those findings of this corpus of scientific work about which consensus has been reached challenge the adequacy of *every* prominent
psychoanalytic schema about early development, not merely the traditional Freudian one. Not that Lichtenberg has been too easy on
recent proposals proffered as alternatives to those of Freud; he calls a
spade a spade in an even-handed manner, but he deals with Freud's
garden tools at much greater length than he does with those of psychoanalytic dissidents.

In the present context, it is not possible to substantiate my impression that Lichtenberg has surveyed the field of recent infant research
thoroughly enough to have culled from this literature the reliable
evidence it can offer psychoanalysis. (For other assessments of the
adequacy of his survey, see the issue of *Psychoanalytic Inquiry* [1985]
devoted to his book.) If his work suffers from any limitation of perspective, it is his decision to confine his purview to the implications
for psychoanalytic theory of the empirical findings reported about
behavior during the first two years of life. Obviously, these theories
should be assessed from a number of viewpoints at the same time—
as I have tried to demonstrate in the historical chapters of this book.
Because he makes no effort to judge competing theories by such
criteria as epistemological adequacy or internal coherence, Lichtenberg's work cannot constitute a court of last resort about them; it
merely provides one set of minimal guidelines for theory construction, those provided by currently accepted observations of infant behavior. With further research, this consensus may change in various
ways; if and when such increments of knowledge occur, their conse-

quences for the theories of psychoanalysis will once again have to be carefully assayed.[1]

Despite those limitations of his approach, Lichtenberg chose his priorities for understanding behavior regulation in infancy with the most relevant developmental issues in mind: He states that theories of early mentation should emphasize "how each developmental finding fits into a pattern of adaptation . . . . [Hence] the questions to be answered become: How does the particular form of problem solving fit into the infant's interactional matrix? How does the infant move toward disengagement from the interactional matrix? And what relatively independent collateral functioning of child and parents facilitates the development of the toddler's intrapsychic life on a symbolic level?" (1983, pp. 90–91). Lichtenberg notes that such a focus renders irrelevant whether behavior is "drive-inspired or ego-inspired"—not to speak of less fundamental aspects of the structural theory.

The poor fit between the concepts of a psychology of intrapsychic conflicts and the behavioral phenomena of infancy most in need of explication had already been noted by Freud (1895a, pp. 318, 327, 361; 1900, pp. 536–547; see also Gedo and Goldberg, 1973, chapter 4). He therefore proposed a theory of infantile mentation based on the model of the neurological reflex arc. Freud's experience, early in his career, with neuroses of traumatic origin, later confirmed by the work of his students (Abraham et al., 1919; Ferenczi and Hollós, 1922) with war neuroses and similar syndromes, fed his lifelong conviction that at the core of every insoluble intrapsychic conflict there lies an archaic propensity for psychoeconomic imbalance—in Freud's terms, an "actual neurosis."

In the era of ego psychology, Freud's viewpoint about these matters was generally abandoned. Influential voices within psychoanalysis (e.g., Brenner, 1983) continue to insist that its sole subject matter is the mind in conflict. There have always been contrary opinions, to be sure: In *Models of the Mind* (Gedo and Goldberg, 1973), my coauthor and I espoused Freud's viewpoint on the basis of its *clinical* utility in illuminating extreme psychological situations such as nightmares, acute psychotic reactions, and the like (see pp. 49–51.)[2]

---

[1]Lichtenberg has also refrained from correlating his own conclusions with those of theoretical revisionists (e.g., Modell, Loewald, or me), who approach the problems of archaic mentation on the basis of reconstructive data gathered within the psychoanalytic setting.

[2]Freud's metapsychological hypotheses concerning the role of psychic energy in

The conclusion that the constructs of Freud's tripartite model (1923a) are useless in organizing our understanding of infant behavior lends powerful support to my contention that the varied modes of behavior regulation throughout the life cycle call for the use of a variety of conceptual tools. According to Lichtenberg, the model of "intrapsychic regulation of conflict" (i.e., the structural theory) becomes applicable in the latter half of the second year of life at the earliest (1983, p. 35). I do not dispute this statement, but I would add the *caveat* that the initial appearance of these capacities (or of any others, for that matter) should not be confused with the nodal point in development when they assume the role of the predominant or *typical* mode of operation. The ubiquity of transference phenomena referable to the third year of life that reproduce a symbiotic mode of adaptation should remind clinicians that autonomy in self-regulation does not supervene as an expectable feature of children's performance until much later. As a consequence, an array of theories based primarily on the status of relations between self and objects (either on the stage of real life or in the intrapsychic arena) have been proposed to deal with the segment of development transitional between conditions in early infancy and those in the oedipal period (see Gedo and Goldberg, 1973, chapter 5).

Lichtenberg endorses the use of these "interactional" models; in fact, he goes a step further: ". . . it may be that psychoanalysis overstates our separateness, our degree of independence from our animate and inanimate surround . . . we need to retain a view of the interactional context as an explanatory concept with considerable validity throughout the life cycle" (1983, p. 35). On the basis of this conclusion, one can only view the repertory of man's behaviors as a continuously expanding set of potentialities, none of which is ever completely abandoned after its acquisition. In the hierarchical model I developed with Goldberg, these circumstances are depicted along the horizontal axis, which represents the passage of time: the behavioral repertory of previous phases is exactly replicated in each new developmental phase, but each phase is characterized by the addition of still another mode of behavior to the repertory.

---

the earliest functional mode (and throughout development) should be assessed separately from his proposal to differentiate between behavior regulation in the newborn and in later life. In *Models of the Mind* (1973) we chose not to consider the postulate of psychic energy; in my later writings, starting with *Beyond Interpretation* (1979), I have rejected the metapsychology centered on psychic energy.

At any rate, on the basis of the consensus about the findings of infant research, Lichtenberg reached the same conclusions about a valid and relevant theory for archaic behavior regulation that Goldberg and I espoused in the light of therapeutic experience with the psychoanalytic method. As I see it, this consensus places Lichtenberg's work and ours within a new psychoanalytic orientation (not a new dissidence, we hope!), one that rejects the basic theoretical positions promulgated by the ego psychology of Hartmann and his collaborators as well as those of the major "opposition" of the previous generation, the school of Melanie Klein (see chapters 5 and 6, this volume).[3]

Lichtenberg is well aware that through his survey of infant research, he came to abandon the position of what he calls the psychoanalytic "mainstream,"[4] and he has courageously outlined some crucial objections to its theoretical propositions. In particular, Lichtenberg points out that the major questions the traditional theory of development attempted to answer about infancy were based on inferences that seem "unwarranted by the information" he culled from the literature on infant research (1983, p. 67). The questions he singles out as ill conceived are, "How do self and object representations become differentiated within the first year; how does the infant move from a narcissistic or autistic stage (without awareness of the object) through symbiosis (with its merger of representations) to separation from the object and individuation of the self; and how does the infant cope with the innate aggression, envy, and cruelty and achieve concern?" (pp. 66–67).

Perhaps the most direct way of stating the flaw in the theoretical positions that led to asking these questions is that Hartmann, Mahler, and Melanie Klein have all set the age at which infants acquire the ability to form mental representations of self and objects much too early: "It is this hypothesis that . . . supports the notion of the need to differentiate fused or merged representations into separate ones. Mahler's postulated developmental stages rest on this assumption. Similarly, the [Kleinian] concept of cruelty depends on a self inflicting pain on another, while envy [another attitude Klein attributed to

---

[3]If theoreticians who concern themselves primarily with metapsychology are to be included in the discussion, those who come closest to the new orientation are Jules Weiss (1985) and M. F. Basch (see References for his relevant publications).
[4]Like the Yellow River, psychoanalysis has the habit of suddenly changing course! Yesterday's mainstream may easily become a backwater by tomorrow . . .

infants] depends on the self coveting another's property or trait" (Lichtenberg, 1983, p. 67). Although Lichtenberg was less explicit in calling Hartmann's developmental propositions untenable, it is clear that he included "ego psychology" among the psychoanalytic schools that make incorrect assumptions about infancy. Contrary to the hypotheses of most psychoanalytic authors, "the infant emerges [from the studies here reviewed] as a sensory perceiving, acting, feeling person *by virtue of preprogrammed and learned perceptual-action-affective response patterns*" (p. 67; italics added).

It should be noted in this connection that the conclusions of other authors, drawn from the very same portrait of the infant presented in the foregoing quotation, are different from Lichtenberg's —and from mine. It is possible to emphasize that aspect of these new findings that presents the baby as very much more competent than psychoanalytic hypotheses have suggested; such a reading of the evidence may lead to a corresponding deemphasis of the difference between behaviors based on response patterns and those guided by consciousness. However, even those who follow this tack, like Hamilton (1982), agree that the evidence invalidates the traditional hypotheses of psychoanalysis; given these new findings, they tend to support one or another form of object-relations approach.

As I have argued in detail elsewhere (Gedo, 1981b, pp. 236, 241–244), object relations theories are not fully adequate to illuminate early behavior regulation because they cannot take into account the manner in which the infant registers "events" in the interpersonal realm, particularly during the sensorimotor phase of development. This argument has been posed in persuasive detail by David Freedman (1984). Hypotheses such as those of the British school of object relations overestimate the capacity of the infant to register the specifics of early transactions; in my judgment, they are therefore lacking in congruence with the results of infant research. This is even more true of the Kleinian hypotheses about early development, attributing the capacity for fully formed "phantasy" to babies shortly after birth (see chapter 6, this volume). As I discussed in chapter 8, Kohut also overestimates the capacity of infants to form mental representations.

Clearly, the results of studies of infant behavior also invalidate Freud's hypotheses about early mentation. As Lichtenberg puts it, "a unitary view accounting for [infantile] behaviors as simply discharge phenomena cannot be supported. In each observable pattern of infant behavior, stimulus *seeking* is so compelling a force that stimulus seeking and discharge must be seen as complementary governors" (1983, p. 27). To be sure, the notion that the newborn has a fully differentiated repertory of instinctual drives has already been repudiated by a number of authors on *clinical* grounds: Loewald (1971, 1978) has proposed, for instance, that the drives are structured by infantile experience. Others (e.g., Basch, 1975b, 1977; Rubinstein, 1976b) have put forward alternative hypotheses, impelled by a combination of epistemological imperatives, clinical convictions, and neurobiological information.[5]

In terms of the alternatives he espoused to replace traditional psychoanalytic hypotheses about behavior regulation in the period preceding the acquisition of symbolic capacities, Lichtenberg's position—I am happy to say!—once again comes closest to my own published views. Lichtenberg labeled the conditions in the newborn that Goldberg and I simply called "phase I" in development "the biological-neurophysiological-behavioral level of organization" (1983, p. 45). This is another way of describing the fact that the infant's organismic responses are dynamically equilibrated with those of its milieu—the state of "mutual regulation" Lichtenberg also called "interactional" (p. 35).

For psychoanalytic psychology as a whole, the most important finding about this mode of organization is that the satisfaction of bodily appetites—hunger, elimination, sensual pleasure, and sleep— does not constitute the sole motivating force of infantile behavior. This is tantamount to saying that human behavior cannot be reduced to the vicissitudes of the drives; other aspects of man's motivations will continually surface in contexts inexplicable in terms of libido, aggression, and narcissism. As I have repeatedly stressed (e.g., Gedo, 1981c, pp. 313–315), we have had to account for these anomalous events as manifestations of a "compulsion to repeat" certain patterns lacking in symbolic representation.

Lichtenberg suggests that memories of basic units of experience will later serve as organizers of psychic life. Tentatively, he posited that these early memories are "coded in action-affect pattern responses," which may be transformed into evocative memories but may also remain without symbolic representation as "perceptual-ac-

---

[5]My own theoretical work of the past decade is indebted to these pioneers in an alternative metapsychology, but my proposals for a new clinical theory come almost entirely from clinical observations.

tion-affect responses" (1983, p. 80). In my opinion, these are the
archaic behavioral patterns that are compulsively and unconsciously
repeated in an active mode later in life; from the psychological perspective of adulthood, of course, such behaviors are endured passively. I have called the overall hierarchy of these unconscious patterns the "self-organization." Although the experiences on which
they are based take place, for the most part, in an interactional context, they do not constitute a record of early object relations, as the
theorists of the British school would have us think. Because these
transactions lead to innumerable primary identifications with the
caretakers, the relevant memories in fact constitute the *basic fabric* of
the self-organization. It is an adultomorphic distortion to misread the
infant's experience in terms of an objective observer's impression of
the mother-child transaction. This is why I have criticized as mislead-
ing and reductionistic the tendency to center psychoanalytic psychology on the concept of object relations (see Gedo, 1981b, Section III).[6]

Although *Psychoanalysis and Infant Research* is devoted primarily to a
critique of untenable psychoanalytic hypotheses and to the articula-
tion of questions cogent for any valid depth psychology about behavior in the first two years of life, Lichtenberg also reveals his own
preferences as a psychoanalytic theorist: as I read him, he belongs to
the tradition of Heinz Lichtenstein and George Klein. I also consider
my own work to form part of this tradition. I would prefer to designate these theories as psychologies centered on the concept of self, in
the sense of self as a hierarchy of memories of primary experiences.
Unfortunately, the dissident school of Heinz Kohut has preempted
the name Self Psychology, although it belongs to a different category
of conceptualization; as I stated in chapter 7, I believe it would best be
described as a psychology of the selfobject.[7]

Despite the kinship of Lichtenberg's viewpoint and my own, there
is an important difference of emphasis between us. Nowhere does
Lichtenberg stress structural considerations, as I do in proposing the

---

[6]Lichtenberg's conclusions about mentation in the earliest phases of life are
congruent with Piaget's schemata about cognitive development. My concept of the
hierarchical organization of the modes of functioning characteristic of successive
phases makes use of the Piagetian hypothesis that earlier capacities are assimilated into
later, more complex ones.

[7]Such an appellation would clarify that Kohut became progressively more and
more committed to the viewpoint of object relations as the crux of motivation but
differed from other theorists of that persuasion in stressing the propensity to treat the
caretakers as an aspect of one's own self.

concept of self-organization (see Gedo, 1984a, chapter 1). Lichtenberg's self psychology is always grounded in phenomenology; he is
concerned exclusively with the subjective "sense of self" (see 1983, p.
39). His is a point of view that first surfaced in psychoanalytic discourse in the work of Paul Federn (1952), where this crucial experiential datum was named "ego feeling." In those terms, primary significance is assigned to the notion of personal boundaries and to the
distinction between syntonic and dystonic mental contents.

In contrast, I have stressed the importance of the hierarchy of
action patterns developed in the course of "phase I." Because these
patterned behavioral dispositions are devoid of symbolic representation, they form that aspect of the Freudian system *Ucs.* which does
not involve the operation of repression proper. Consequently, action
patterns that constitute important components of the self-organization may, as a result of disavowal induced by environmental requirements, eventually become subjectively dystonic in terms of the *sense* of
self. Hence I believe that we need to look "beyond subjectivity" if we
wish to develop a useful psychology of the self-organization. I feel
this is the strongest argument against the viewpoint of those who
would confine psychoanalysis to a search for meanings.

Lichtenberg's approach may also be compared to that of Kohut.
Kohut's concept of the "bipolar self" refers to a combination of subjective ambitions and ideals; thus his work on this score may be
construed as parallel to that of Lichtenberg. Lichtenberg also read
Kohut in this way, for he bracketed his own past writings on "the
development of a cohesive sense of self" with those of Kohut (1983,
p. 39). On the other hand, he did note that Kohut had failed to
propose any detailed developmental schema, so that his "core concept of self cohesion lends itself to concretization or murkiness as to
its level of abstraction" (p. 191). I would put this more strongly:
because Kohut never addressed himself to the issue of how ambitions
and/or ideals could be formed in infancy so as to yield a sense of
individuality before the end of the second year of life, his concept of
self necessarily remained both murky and reified.[8]

---

[8]As I reviewed in chapter 7, Kohut explained the analytic repair of a faulty "self"
as the "transmuting internalization" of finite identifications with the analyst. He implied that he conceived of the formation of "the self" in infancy in similar terms. I do
not see how such a developmental schema can be justified in view of the evidence
Lichtenberg presents about the infant's limited capacity to grasp the purport of the
activities of the caretakers. I discuss these issues in greater detail in the next chapter.

Perhaps as a result of their essential agreement about the importance of the analyst's empathy in clinical work (Lichtenberg, 1983, pp. 221–225), as well as their shared opposition to the views of Melaine Klein, Kernberg, and other believers in the role of primary aggression in infancy (p. 86), Lichtenberg's references to Kohut's work are generally positive.[9] Yet, as I have already mentioned, his summary of the results of research on infants invalidates some of the basic, if often unstated, assumptions of Kohut's developmental psychology. In my judgment, the most important of these assumptions is that learning will occur only in the context of an empathic interactional matrix. Lichtenberg reports, on the contrary, that the earliest activities that betoken problem solving by the infant occur in the state known as "quiescent wakefulness"—most important, they take place "when the neonate is not being stimulated by the mother" (pp. 45–46). Basch (in press) has also singled out this facet of Kohut's theory as the gravest weakness of Self Psychology.

Because everything the infant has learned by the age of nine months is mastered without an internal representation of the object (Lichtenberg, 1983, p. 62), it does not make sense to postulate that mental functions are acquired through internalization, purportedly stimulated by manageable ruptures in that state of "merger" Kohut attributes to the infant. In this regard, Lichtenberg cites a convincing experiment involving four-month-old infants who were enabled to switch on some lights by fortuitously performing certain head movements: once successful, the babies actively repeated the experience "with gestures and vocalizations of joy" (p. 90). It appears that wherever autonomous competence is attainable, human beings are well able to make do without their fellows! Robert White's concept of "effectance" (1963) already made allusion to this capacity.

As Lichtenberg put it, "Much . . . learning takes place when the infant is not impinged on, either by need urgency or by the mother's active intrusion" (1983, p. 92). He quoted infant researchers such as Louis Sander (1983) to the effect that the child's experience of initiative "begins in relatively brief spans of time, 'open space,' during which there is no requirement for interactive regulation by the mother . . . . These open spaces for the active exploration of stimuli and

---

[9]The only exception to this statement is Lichtenberg's judicious expression of skepticism about the possibility of analytic patients' internalizing hitherto missing functions as a result of interpretation of the persisting need for external provision of those functions (1983, p. 224).

the exercise of initiative in action expand if the mother is sensitive enough not to intrude or co-opt the developing infant's attention" (p. 118).

This is a far cry from "Kohut's baby," as Marian Tolpin (1980) has described that poor creature, trapped in the tarpit of symbiosis.

Whatever our differences may be—and they are considerable, as I have tried to show—Lichtenberg, Kohut, Basch, Weiss, and I agree that sometime after the middle of the second year of life, a structure most of us call "the cohesive self" or "the self-as-a-whole" takes over the regulation of behavior; henceforward, the toddler has a subjective sense of personhood. In *Models of the Mind*, this nodal point in development was designated as the transition into "phase III." Lichtenberg (1983, p. 117) aptly compared this achievement with the change in a functioning institution when a responsible executive takes command. The toddler's new level of organization has been ingeniously demonstrated in experiments involving exposure to his mirror image: early in the second year, children begin to view their reflection as an object of contemplation, without recognizing its connection to their own person. Toward the end of that year, they betray self-recognition by touching smudges or labels on their own bodies when they see them reflected in the mirror (p. 105).

With respect to the maturation of perceptual and cognitive capacities, this change betokens the acquisition of *imaging*—a process that takes place gradually during the first half of the second year. Lichtenberg (1983, pp. 100–101) pointed out that this capacity is a prerequisite for the ability to recognize another person as an external object. From this vantage point, the traditional view of the nine-month-old's "stranger anxiety" as a sign of feeling endangered by separation from the primary caretaker appears to be untenable. (Décarie [1973] has finally been acknowledged by a psychoanalyst to be right!) Lichtenberg argued that these behaviors appear when they do because infants acquire the affect of *fear* at that time (p.60). Stranger anxiety is therefore the behavioral manifestation of the infant's discomfort about the perceptual mismatch between his store of memories and the novel stimuli that confront him. The Mahlerian schema of development during the first year of life is utterly refuted.

Between the perceptual-affective action patterns that characterize phase I and the mode of behavior regulation ushered in by the achievement of self-cohesion (i.e., phase III), much of the second year of life may be viewed as transitional. Lichtenberg (1983, p. 97) labels this phase (called phase II in *Models of the Mind*) as the *emergence* of a sense of self. With the onset of imaging, the biological-neu-rophysiological mode of phase I is superseded by one Lichtenberg called the "sign-signal mode" (p. 131). He described mode II as a set of "experiential traits of the self-in-action" (p. 114). It is these discrete behavioral traits that Goldberg and I named "nuclei of the self" in *Models of the Mind*. I have also described this mode of behavior regula-tion in terms of the lack of a unified hierarchy of personal goals (Gedo, 1979, chapter 12).

As I read *Psychoanalysis and Infant Research,* Lichtenberg's concep-tion of behavior regulation in phase II is largely congruent with my previous proposals (Gedo, 1979). He described the principal issues of the second year of life as follows:

> "Ambitendency in behavioral action responses is observ-able . . [that] may be the precursor of the conceptual represen-tation of opposing urges and functions. Infants at this point can recognize contrasting possibilities for responses and can antici-pate positive and negative outcomes in familiar situations, but they require sensory perceptual cueing to trigger the responses. However . . . until opposing conceptual representations can be clearly organized, the polarities of the infant's life may lead to turbulence within the infant-caretaker interactional matrix but not to intrapsychic conflict in the infant" [pp. 64–65].

Lichtenberg also noted (1983, p. 78) that affects become integrated into a system of symbolic representation in the second year of life and take over the function of anticipatory cuing previously supplied by the caretakers; this is why he used the term sign-signal mode for the manner of behavior regulation in phase II. Moreover, Lichtenberg's position on the establishment of defensive operations stressed that even the earliest of these mental mechanisms, projection, presup-poses a *conceptual* distinction between self and object (p. 81). We therefore cannot attribute defensive capacities to the infant before he achieves the cognitive advances that enable him to make such a dis-tinction (see also chapter 10, this volume). In *Models of the Mind*, we also chose this developmental nodal point as the time of transition from phase I to phase II. Lichtenberg (1983, p. 125) took the position that the splitting of the self as a defense takes place, in cases of excessive traumatization, only after the formation of the cohesive self.[10]

---

[10]This view is certainly in agreement with mine (see Gedo, 1979, pp. 185–194;

All in all, then, Lichtenberg's conclusions about development in the first two years of life come extremely close to the hypotheses I have endorsed on clinical grounds and in the light of the requirements of conceptual coherence. It is true, of course, that my work has been influenced in important ways by the results of infant research (not through direct study of these, but through the mediation of colleagues such as M. F. Basch), and Lichtenberg's assessment of the studies he has surveyed for his book may well have been tipped toward this consensus by his familiarity with my work. Despite these *caveats*, I believe that our independent efforts lend powerful support to each other. Presumptively, the burden of proof now lies upon those who would disagree. As I stated at the beginning of this chapter, these developmental issues have crucial significance for the clinical theory of psychoanalysis; their implications are decisive even for our theory of technique (see Gedo, 1984a). I once again consider these issues in the chapter to follow.

Gedo & Goldberg, 1973, pp. 89–100). I feel that Lichtenberg (1983, p. 125) fell into conceptual imprecision, however, in accepting the conclusion of Stern (1983) that the cohesive self is not formed by unifying prior subsets of experience. It is self-evident, of course, that the toddler's recognition of his personhood is achieved at a specific moment, but *that* developmental advance does not yet amount to the formation of a self-*organization*. Because Lichtenberg focused mostly on the *sense* of self, he generally overlooked the distinction between self-cognition and the achievement of a consistent hierarchy of personal aims.

12

The Legacy of Infancy and the Technique of Psychoanalysis

IN CHAPTERS 10 AND 11 I attempted to survey the methodological problems of extra-analytic validation studies through which the competing developmental hypotheses within psychoanalysis might be assessed, and I reported on the implications for theories of early development of the current consensus about this evidence concerning infant behavior. Here, I extend my review to consider the implications of infant research for issues of psychoanalytic technique. To begin with, I wish to note that in his account of this field, Joseph Lichtenberg (1983, p. 193) echoes the repeated challenge articulated in my own work (Gedo, 1979, 1981b, 1981c, 1984a) that even with patients selected in accord with stringent criteria of analyzability, only illumination of the analysand's presymbolic experience will lead to therapeutic success. This viewpoint is a departure from the traditional psychoanalytic position, which encourages a focus on the infantile neurosis. That time-honored view was based on the assumption that resolution of the complex structures formed during the oedipal period would simultaneously correct unfavorable sequelae of earlier developmental vicissitudes. Kohut's (1984) posthumous recommendation that in the oedipal transference neuroses the analyst should pay particular attention to the manner in which the parents' failures as "selfobjects" *in* the oedipal phase underlie the actual pathogenesis paradoxically conforms to the traditional viewpoint.

In contrast, Lichtenberg admonishes us to broaden our field of observation within the psychoanalytic situation if we wish to uncover derivatives of the archaic phases of infantile organization in our analysands' behaviors, for these derivatives are necessarily encoded in communications that do not use the consensual meaning of words as their medium. In a chapter of his 1983 book that examines the implications of his survey of infant research for psychoanalytic technique, Lichtenberg offers brief case vignettes that illustrate three subtypes of archaic syndromes wherein crucial issues present themselves during analysis by means of nonverbal communications. Lichtenberg discusses syndromes involving basic regulatory deficits, those characterized by bodily symptoms, and problems related to primary cognitive deficiencies. Although I do not regard those three categories as exhaustive and they are in fact overlapping, Lichtenberg's case examples provide a convenient entry point for further discussion of the entire range of archaic syndromes.

An example of deficient basic self-regulation is the incapacity to meet nutritional needs, albeit in some cases this function may become secondarily impaired as a result of specific intrapsychic conflicts. In Lichtenberg's case vignette, the problem resulted from the patient's lack of awareness of the experiences we call hunger and satiation. In order to regulate food intake in accord with physiological needs, such persons have to learn to encode symbolically the somatic events connected with appetite. It should be noted that these generally sophisticated individuals are usually in command of the shared vocabulary needed to discuss these matters, but the relevant words are isolated from the organismic experiences they designate for other people. As a consequence, those experiences never become part of the patient's *subjective* universe. Hence the deficiency in self-regulation may also be seen as a focal defect in cognition.

In teaching his patient to deal with these crucial matters in symbolic terms for the first time, Lichtenberg engaged in analytic operations that go beyond the interpretation of unconscious meanings. This illuminating example demonstrates convincingly the rationale of my contention that psychoanalytic technique must include measures that transcend the description of intrapsychic conflicts (see esp. Gedo, 1981b, 1984a). In my clinical experience, many disturbances in bowel habits (such as chronic constipation) and sexual functions (e.g., some cases of inability to reach orgasm despite adequate sexual arousal) result from analogous deficits in building associative links between physiological systems and behavior regulation by means of voluntary (conscious or preconscious) control. But note that adequate behavior depends on a variety of psychological skills, beyond those of perception and cognition, for pathology of this kind comes about when primary bodily experiences are not *assimilated* into the individual's set of acknowledged personal aims—an achievement contingent not only on the capacity to form symbolic representations of the relevant experience but also on adequate opportunities to exercise autonomous decision making about the matters in question.

Lichtenberg provides an impressive list of syndromes based on arrests in the development of specific psychological skills, without pretending to have mentioned all possibilities. Instead of trying to extend his catalogue here, it is more useful to discuss the usual consequences of such psychological deficits in the realm of the sense of self and of object relations. Whatever the etiology of the maldevelopment may have been, a child who grows up with a gross deficit in behavior regulation must inevitably rely on external assistance to adapt to the escalating demands of life. Hence afflicted children show a persisting need for symbiosis with a cooperative caretaker. Their inevitable realization of their relative inadequacy often drives such persons into illusions of personal grandiosity as well.

In other words, Lichtenberg has not described a novel category of psychopathology through this case example; instead, he has specified one of the possible pathogenic determinants of the archaic syndromes widely discussed in the last two decades. This material suggests that Kohut's contention (1980c, p. 473) that "selfobject needs" persist throughout the life cycle should be treated with the greatest reserve, for imperative symbiotic needs may well disappear if patients succeed in mastering psychological skills they failed to acquire in childhood. In my clinical experience, analysands who overcome chronic deficiencies of this kind thereby repair their previously low self-esteem, and (contrary to Kohut's insistence about the permanence of selfobject needs in more mature forms) will no longer require confirmation of their worth from external sources.

I believe the connection between deficits in self-regulation and the type of character pathology usually termed "narcissistic" deserves emphasis because in most clinical instances (and this was certainly true of Lichtenberg's case example) the presenting clinical picture highlights those aspects of the personality disorder which revolve around the patient's problems in self-esteem and/or object relations. In other words, the fixation at presymbolic levels of functioning is generally masked through the adaptive use of external assistance— and this is what Kohut has misleadingly called the need for a selfobject. It is only through the shift of this requirement into the analytic transference that it may become possible to identify actual psychological deficits. As Lichtenberg reports (p. 196), such an effort may arouse considerable resistance, presumably because of the humiliation involved in facing these handicaps. At any rate, it seems extremely unlikely that either the symbiotic mode of adaptation or the low self-esteem of such patients can be overcome unless the pathogenic legacies of the presymbolic era are first dealt with. In *Models of the Mind* (Gedo & Goldberg, 1973) the requisite therapeutic activities were named "pacification" because in clinical practice the most frequent deficit in behavior regulation one finds is an inability to reduce states of excessive tension.

In contrast to the position I have advocated for the past dozen years, most authors continue to assume that the regressive manifestations encountered within the psychoanalytic situation echo childhood conditions that can be characterized as a series of waystations in the course of more or less expectable development. Parens (1979), for example, continues to adhere to the developmental schemata proposed by Mahler, Pine, and Bergman (1975). According to Mahler, normal toddlers are in need of libidinal "refueling" during a phase of "rapprochement" late in the second year. In Mahlerian observations of young children, like those of Parens, all signs of dysphoria are therefore interpreted as vicissitudes of the child's relations with the caretakers. Because the latter can relieve the child's distress through direct interventions (usually by offering personal contact), Parens finds confirmation of Mahler's thesis of libidinal refueling. The putative implications for psychoanalytic technique are evident: in the transference, patients allegedly experience separation anxiety because they are reliving a normal phase of "separation-individuation," and this is the issue to be interpreted to them.

Such conceptualizations are radically faulty. That parental intervention will often soothe a distressed child and the availability of the therapist may allay the anxieties of distressed patients does not demonstrate a causal connection between the distress and vicissitudes of object relations: headaches are not caused by lack of aspirin! The

distress of toddlers left to their own devices is most often caused by
the confusion they experience when called upon to meet unfamiliar
contingencies that overtax their cognitive capacities. Whenever this is
the case, a parent may soothe the child by countering the stimulus
overload or providing clarifying information. If the caretakers fail
over time to teach the child to accomplish these adaptively essential
tasks for himself—a failure that may or may not be related to the
narcissistic type of parental pathology Kohut (1977, p. 189) implicates
in the genesis of "narcissistic disturbances"—a syndrome will supervene that will strike the observer as a symbiosis between child and
caretaker. These archaic forms of psychopathology are seldom modi-
fiable unless appropriate psychoanalytic treatment is undertaken.
They can be remedied through analysis, however, provided the missing psychological skills are acquired (Gedo, 1984a, chapter 1)—as
Lichtenberg's first case demonstrates.

Lichtenberg's second case exemplifies the occurrence of a bodily
symptom as a "somatic memory" of preverbal experiences. (It should
be noted, once again, that this phenomemon could be conceptualized
as a vicissitude of cognitive development.) We have been familiar
with phenomena of this general kind since Isakower (1938) described
one fairly common variety. Lichtenberg ascribes the persistence of
such behaviors to the fact that they remain encoded "in the percep-
tual-affective-action mode and did not receive later recoding into
symbolic representation" (p. 201). Although his illustrative example
is both simple and clear, it probably fails to convey the extent and
variety of such archaic manifestations, the range of psychosomatic
phenomena—either within the limits of physiological "normality" or
unequivocally pathological—referable to the earliest modes of behavioral organization. That bodily processes can "join in the conversa-
tion" in the course of analysis was already described by Ferenczi
(1908–1914, chapter 7) more than 70 years ago; moreover Freud
(1914a) understood hypochondriasis as a vicissitude of archaic narcissism, lacking in symbolic significance. Thus, Lichtenberg's contention about the recurrence of somatic memories in the course of analysis has solid precedents in psychoanalytic history.

Concerning these bodily symptoms, it should be noted that recurrence in the analytic setting, however dramatic an event, may constitute a relatively trivial incident in terms of overall adaptation; such
symptoms may play a much more important role in the individual's
life. I can offer an illustration from the analysis of a man whose

personality was organized principally around a set of intrapsychic conflicts related to issues of aggression and guilt. During the oedipal years, a syndrome resembling the case history of Little Hans (Freud, 1909) had impelled his family to consult a child analyst. The analytic intervention, focused on the child's exhibitionism and competitive- ness in the phallic sphere, was seemingly successful, just as Freud's participation in the cure of Master Hans's phobia had been. During the second year of our work, the patient experienced an exacerbation of ectopic dermatitis, a condition that began in infancy as severe eczema. In the present, crises of pruritus and exudation could be correlated with frustrated longing for maternal soothing, especially within the transference. The patient's furious scratching, on the other hand, expressed his rage toward his caretakers, as well as his self- hatred for not being omnipotently self-sufficient. Needless to say, this person did not have organized memories about the discomforts of his skin lesions in infancy, although he had been told that when he was a small child his hands had often been bundled up in mittens to prevent him from scratching himself.

Thus far, my example corresponds precisely to the one provided by Lichtenberg. I present this material, however, to highlight the consequences of these important early experiences for the later orga- nization of this man's personality: every developmental phase in this individual's life was characterized by circumstances, regularly pre- cipitated by himself (unless chance saved him the trouble to arrange them), that duplicated the sensations associated with the cycle of excessive bodily excitement, frustrated longing for soothing, rage, and autoaggressive activity he had passively endured as an infant.

In the oedipal phase, for example, his phallic excitement had led him to harrass his mother through endless questions about the pros- pect of marrying her when he grew up. When she eventually became exasperated, the scene would end with a tantrum on his part. Ver- bally, he denied his mother's assertion that his plan of action was impossible, but the heart of the tantrum transcended the words of defiance—it was the outburst of rage, directed primarily at his own helplessness. I believe these phenomena correspond to that "actual neurotic" core that Freud found to be the invariable basis of the psychoneuroses. In adolescence, the pattern was repeated through a series of romantic attachments reminiscent of the ill-fated lovers of *Wuthering Heights*—this modern-day Heathcliff made his own rejec- tion certain by enacting the role of the maddened swain so convinc- ingly that every potential Cathy was quickly frightened into withdrawal. Fury and despair followed, although he did not perfect a way of mortifying his flesh until he took up smoking a few years later, greatly aggravating his tendency for bronchial asthma.

Whenever this experiential pattern was forestalled within the transference, for example, when the recurrence of the dermatitis was brought under control through appropriate professional care (which the patient sought only with great reluctance), a state of empty bewilderment supervened. The patient felt inert and his world seemed derealized. Although he did not like this feeling state, he also made it clear that it was quite different from his customary sequence of stimulation, longing, mounting frustration, helplessness and rage, self-injury, and guilt.

Late in the analysis, the issue was traversed once more on the ground of the patient's smoking. He decided that his "habit" served to avoid awareness of crucial aspects of his inner life, and he realized that he would have to give it up if he wished to bring these obscure forces under conscious control. When this asthmatic man stopped the repetitive enactment of self-injury through smoke inhalation, he no longer felt guilty about misbehavior. On the contrary, he was overtaken by violent surges of rage set off by the unavoidable deprivations of an analytic relationship that echoed a variety of infantile frustrations. The earliest of these he was dimly able to remember, from the second half of the second year of life, concerned his exciting but ultimately disappointing reunions with his mother when he was taken to visit her during a hospitalization lasting several weeks. Thus, by the age of two the cycle of feeling states had decisively shifted into the arena of interpersonal relationships, but its basic constituents and rhythms always remained unchanged, within the template provided by the reactions to his eczema. (Parenthetically, this example demonstrates once again why object relations theories are insufficient to illuminate such a personality configuration: even the earliest relationship to the mother that gained symbolic representation was decisively skewed away from any "objective" version of the transaction by the infant's somatic state.)

Even the termination of his analysis was characterized by the repetition of the usual cycle of this man's affects, albeit in a muted form that recapitulated the pattern within a brief time span. When the patient decided to discontinue his visits, about six weeks prior to the date of his departure, he experienced a crescendo of pleasure. He was rudely disappointed by my failure to respond in the same way, and my persistent dispassionate curiosity provoked his customary reaction of mounting anger. He then proceeded to attempt to induce an emotional response of some kind—any kind!—from me, in order to overcome his sense of helplessness, only to relax with fresh conviction about the appropriateness of his decision to terminate when he realized that he was enacting a repetition of his lifelong experiential pattern.

Among other important lessons to be learned from clinical experiences of this kind is a conclusion also reached by Parens (1979, pp. 106–115): rage does not require *discharge!* It is most effectively overcome through the elimination of the environmental noxae that provoked it. (In this sense, somatic disorders can be classified with such noxae.) To be sure, in analytic treatment we are not dealing with infants, and the primary goal of our efforts is not to appease our analysands but to clarify their own motives for getting into the specific situations that prove to be noxious. The work of Parens is very germane, nonetheless, to the controversy about the appropriate management of archaic transference rage. It shows that interpretations attributing excessive primary hostility to the patient in infancy, as recommended by Kleinian authors (Segal, 1974; see also chapter 6, this volume), or by Kernberg (1975), are always wide of the mark, as Kohut (1977, p. 124) rightly insisted.

I do not mean that we should naively accept at face value the tendency of many patients to blame their destructiveness on their parents. As I tried to show in chapter 8, carried to its logical extreme, that is the ultimate effect of Kohut's unwarranted emphasis on the perpetual need for selfobjects and the ostensible production of psychopathology by the relative failures of the latter. Both the direct observations of Parens and my own clinical experience suggest that to mitigate transference rage we must instead accurately reconstruct the exact nature of the early experiences being echoed in the analytic situation—experiences that provoked the infant's chronic rage and/or defeated the caretakers' efforts to provide appropriate soothing. Such understanding will eliminate the patient's rage within the transference as well as the projection or introjection of blame onto the innocent, but it is by itself not yet curative: my patient had to learn how to manage his skin lesions from his dermatologist. My reconstructive efforts were a necessary prerequisite for his acceptance of such instruction.

It should be noted that Parens never encountered an instance of the turning of aggression against the child's own self in his study of "normal" toddlers (1979, p. 229). Self-hate is a very unusual, patho-logical attitude indeed, presumably the outcome of exceptional cir-cumstances in early life, such as my patient's intractable eczema.[1]

The clinical illustration I have offered also demonstrates that an individual's failure to encode certain issues in a verbal language may take several forms: my patient produced not only *somatic* memories, he also engaged in a variety of dramatic enactments with latent mean-ings as far removed from their ostensible subject matter as that of dreams is different from manifest content. Such mimetic enactments probably constitute a transitional stage between the perceptual-affec-tive-action mode of infancy and the consensual use of words to con-vey meanings. The language of gestures, including posture, is one component of this transition into symbolic modes of communication.[2] But complex enactments differ from "body language" in the same way as the dramatic theater differs from a ballet without narrative content. In order to decode the latent meaning of their message, it is imperative not to dismiss these communications as mere "acting out." In stating this, I am in fact merely echoing a point made by Melaine Klein (1927a, p. 147), who made possible the psychoanalysis of prelatency children by using their (play) activities within the treat-ment setting in lieu of verbal associations as her source of data about the inner world.

Lichtenberg's (1983) last clinical example deals with a person who suffered from a persistent cognitive deficit not amenable to correction by interpretation of his intrapsychic conflicts. In discussing this case, Lichtenberg explicitly recognizes the inevitability of difficulties in self-esteem and needs for symbiotic assistance in children with severe learning disabilities. He correctly points out that such "disorders in processing symbolic modes of organization" (p. 205) eventuate from

---

[1] I have provided another illustration, wherein the self-hate was primarily a consequence of the mother's refusal to accept the child's accurate view of reality, in chapter 3 of *Psychoanalysis and Its Discontents* (Gedo, 1984a).

[2] I have encountered one clinical contingency wherein gestures became the prin-cipal avenue for expressing meanings during crucial periods of the analysis. The pa-tient had lost hope of understanding others or being correctly understood when com-munication took place through speech because several of her childhood caretakers blatantly misused language to manipulate her. I did not learn how she acquired the ability to read the language of gestures as a substitute, but the patient did become an excellent ballet dancer. Many of her most essential communications were encoded in her posture on the couch, in expressive gestures, especially of her hands, and in her gait when entering or leaving the room.

prior developments during the presymbolic era. My clinical experience confirms Lichtenberg's conclusion that therapeutic success with problems of this kind requires simultaneous attention to both aspects of the pathology. The primary cognitive deficit must be repaired in order to transcend the symbiotic modes of adaptation, but it cannot be dealt with unless we help the patient to overcome his inability, usually narcissistically based, to make use of remedial instruction.

All too often, both sides of the problem stem from vicissitudes during the first 18 months of life, usually (but *not* invariably) involving disturbances in the infant-caretaker dyad. I have provided (Gedo, 1984a, chapter 4) a reasonably detailed clinical example illustrating such problems. However, another brief case vignette may help to put this issue into clearer perspective here. I shall give some details about the analysis of a person with a variety of cognitive deficits—a clinical encounter I have described from a different vantage point on a previous occasion (Gedo, 1984a, chapter 8). Here, I shall confine my account to those aspects of a complex analytic encounter most germane to the issue of the influence of primary cognitive deficits on subsequent personality development.

The patient was a professional person with outstanding quantitative skills. He entered treatment largely because of the discrepancy between his actual work performance and what he (and others) expected of himself on the basis of his school record. Crudely grandiose and boastful attitudes, with a tendency for hypomanic excitement, protected him from any long-term acknowledgment of his limitations or lacunae in his skills or knowledge. These defenses developed quite early in childhood, partly in identification with a vocationally successful father struggling to disavow the devastating difficulties of his wife and children, as well as a mother whose personal grandiosity extended to her children in the form of denial of their limitations.

Many years of analytic effort were required to help this patient to understand that his megalomania, both in the past and in the present, was necessitated by his pervasive sense of humiliation about his inadequacies. I will not go into detail about the communicative and cognitive limitations that interfered with his activities in adult life—some aspects of these were, however, described in my previous account.

As for his childhood, it was an unending succession of organismic problems: alarmingly poor motor development and coordination, delayed speech development, severe gastrointestinal disturbances, and a pervasive confusion lasting well into his fourth year of life. As far as the patient could remember, his mother was nonetheless unfailingly supportive of his self-esteem, and he could always rely on her personal assistance in his enterprises—in Kohut's terms, she excelled in fulfilling the child's needs for a "selfobject." It is true that, as I previously reported (1984a, p. 133–135), transference enactments enabled us to reconstruct a brief period characterized by frustration, disgust, and helplessness on the mother's part and negativism on that of the child—a lapse in the generally supportive matrix provided by this family for their impaired child.

The patient's psychopathology in adult life did not involve any deficit in self-esteem regulation, however, so that this temporary disruption in the symbiotic adaptation that protected this child from the potential consequences of his deficits did not prove to be pathogenic. As an adult, the patient was struggling with the continuing need for symbiotic assistance with the very issues he had never learned to manage on his own during his childhood impairment. His persisting need for a selfobject was continually reinforced by his inability, throughout development, to meet age-appropriate challenges independently. This need for assistance outweighed the streak of negativism also left over from his early experiences.

In these circumstances, the mother's *character*—the factor Kohut (1977, p. 189; 1980c, p. 524; 1983, p. 389) singled out in his theory of pathogenesis—plays, at most, a secondary role in the development of subsequent pathology. In the case I am describing, this involved the child's identification with certain undesirable traits of her personality. Her other children also identified with these qualities of this overbearing woman, mostly without falling ill—they merely became markedly offensive individuals. My patient's difficulties were compounded, of course, by his adherence to these obnoxious standards of behavior, but the basic pathology remained the structural deficit that necessitated this "merger" with the mother. In the transference, he experienced rage whenever he perceived that he and I are not exactly alike; but only the acquisition of autonomous skills, and not the clarification of the archaic wish to merge with me, liberated him to *become* different from me.[3]

---

[3]In clinical practice, it may not be easy to differentiate our efforts to clarify archaic merger wishes secondary to developmental lags from our attempts to overcome the deficits in psychological skills that I consider to be the primary pathology. Nonetheless, unlike Kohut, I do not believe that "optimal frustration" will eventuate in the acquisition of compensatory structure (see chapter 8, this volume). I am quite ready to

The theory of psychoanalytic technique has been most deficient in explaining how to correct disorders of early cognition: these problems have received even less attention than the deficiencies in organismic regulation previously discussed. Because cognitive capacities underlie the establishment of the coherent hierarchy of aims I call the self-organization, I have collected the therapeutic activities designed to correct dificiencies in this area under the rubric of "unification" (Gedo & Goldberg, 1973, pp. 162–168; Gedo, 1979, pp. 18–19). But the foregoing case example of severe confusion suggests that some children are so atypical in their maturation that their handicaps in early life as well as in adulthood cannot usefully be conceptualized in terms of the three broad categories listed by Lichtenberg.

Although infant observations have barely begun to explore the area of developmental patterns markedly different from the norm (but see Sander, 1983), so that there are no nosological criteria for disturbances in organismic functioning in the first years of life, clinical experience in using the psychoanalytic method with the broadest variety of patients (see Gedo, 1984a, chapter 2) suggests that the most severe character disorders in adult life are often based on poorly understood early childhood syndromes similar to the one I summarized in the preceding illustration.

In some instances, lengthy and persistent analytic work has yielded information (often grounded in progressively clearer repetitions within the transference) about clinical disturbances in the second, third, and fourth years of life that are so pervasive in terms of functional impairments that they can only be called infantile psychoses. I believe the case example of severe confusion I have provided here may serve as a prototype for these heterogeneous conditions. As D. W. Winnicott (1964) indicated a generation ago, the prognosis of such early disturbances is often more favorable than we might think— in his words, these lesions may spontaneously heal over. I suspect that such "healing" takes place by way of the establishment of essential symbiotic bonds with a willing caretaker. The persistence of these symbiotic bonds into adult life will, however, cause great adapta-

---

believe that many self psychologists *do* succeed in teaching their analysands the requisite psychological skills (as do analysts of every persuasion), but that they do so by providing a direct example, not by frustrating the patient's archaic wishes or needs. In other words, it is the theories of technique and cure espoused by Self Psychology that oversimplify the problem; in practice, skilled clinicians have always engaged in successful "ego building," as such educational activities were once called.

tional difficulties, and it brings a fair number of people into psycho-analytic treatment (see Gedo, in prep.)

To be effective, the analysis of such individuals must allow the repressed and disavowed psychotic core to emerge in the therapeutic setting. The defects in mentation that constitute the infantile patho-logical state will not disappear, however, as a direct result of the relaxation of the customary defensive operations that have held them at bay in adult life or through dissolution of the symbiotic adaptation that has compensated for them. Kohut (1977, chapter 1; 1984, chapter 1) believes that in cases of this type "cure" has been achieved with the operational repair of compensatory structures (as I discussed in chapter 7, this volume). As he himself admitted, however, (1977, p. 58), the flaw in this recommendation is the possibility that adaptive repair may have been effected through the establishment of a silent symbiotic bond with the analyst. Whenever this is the case, termina-tion of the treatment will once again expose the patient's helplessness when he is left to his own devices. Hence I believe that definitive "cure" presupposes the acquisition of those psychological skills that did not properly develop as a result of the childhood illness and the symbiotic solution for compensation of the pathological mental oper-ations. (see Gedo, in prep.)[4]

In any case, hypotheses about the etiology of primitive syndromes of this kind await validation through careful observational studies of children with grossly atypical development.

---

[4]Evidently, the mastery of hitherto missing skills may also depend on the con-tinued availability of the analyst. It is commonly observed that such abilities are re-gressively lost during the analyst's vacations in the middle phases of the analyses. Although the permanence of adaptive improvements can never be guaranteed, I con-tend that the chances of compensatory structuralization are greatly increased if the analytic focus is on the specifics of the patient's deficits (in perception, cognition, or communication skills, for example) and work is devoted to learning these functions in action. In contrast, Kohut recommends reliance on haphazard identifications with the analyst-as-idealized-mentor.

For detailed case reports about the painstaking repair of multiple deficits in patients' skills in language and cognition, see Gedo (1984a, chapters 4 and 5).

13

Relevance or Reductionism in Interpretation

A Reprise of the Psychoanalysis of Kleist's Puppet Theater

IT IS PROBABLY NO COINCIDENCE that in recent years an influential segment of the psychoanalytic community has begun to regard the discipline as a hermeneutic enterprise exclusively concerned with meanings (e.g., Schafer, 1978) and, at the same time, strong doubts about the relevance of analytic interpretation of literary texts continue to be heard (e.g., Crews, 1975: Heller, 1978). To be sure, skeptical voices have expressed similar reservations about the validity of specific interpretations in the clinical setting as well (Grünbaum, 1984), rightly pointing out that the therapeutic efficacy of interventions must not be confused with their truth value (see also Gedo, 1979, Epilogue). If some clinicians are content with the "narrative truth" of interpretations (Spence, 1984), such a standard is unlikely to satisfy most literary critics, despite the efforts of Norman Holland (1975) to focus on the reader's response to the text as the key to analytic interpretation.

Demands for interpretive relevance are, of course, appropriate whether we strive for the illumination of clinical data or of cultural materials, for the plausibility and coherence of interpretations do not guarantee that they are addressed to the principal issues implicit in any set of materials. Erich Heller (1978) calls into question the very idea of psychoanalytic hermeneutics on the basis of the grotesque results of the frequent miscarriage of psychological interpretation. Heller's point deserves serious attention, for the particular thesis he used to demonstrate the irrelevance of such efforts—Margaret Schaefer's (1975) explication of the essay "On the Puppet Theater" by Heinrich von Kleist—is both internally consistent and congruent with certain clinical theories that have found wide acceptance.

Kleist's mysterious essay, a bare six pages long, takes the form of a first-person narrative about an encounter with a ballet dancer in the year 1801. The narrator inquires about the dancer's interest in the local marionette show and receives a series of puzzling responses about the superiority of the motions of puppets to those of human beings. In the ensuing dialogue, the dancer expresses the hope of perfecting the mechanized dance of puppets. As for human dancers, he regards their performance as irredeemably spoiled by self-con-sciousness—the inevitable consequence of having "eaten of the tree of knowledge." The dancer wishes to transcend the consequences of the Fall, thereby to match the achievements of a god. The narrator's skeptical response is to relate an incident in which an adolescent's excessive self-consciousness is the outcome of a disturbance in his sense of identity, that is, it is a mark of psychopathology. The dancer rebuts this reasoning with an anecdote about a fencing match in which he (a self-conscious human) was defeated by a bear with super-natural powers, and the narrator professes to believe this incredible tale. The debaters then agree that mankind must regain the state of innocence by eating a second time of the tree of knowledge. It would seem that the narrator has been converted to the dancer's irrational viewpoint.

Heller's (1978) jeremiad, protesting the interpretation of this mate-rial in psychological terms, led to the publication of an exchange of letters between him and Heinz Kohut (1978h) in which Kohut made an eloquent plea in behalf of the psychoanalytic study of culture. Kohut correctly pointed out that unsuccessful use of the method does not invalidate it in principle, but he could not resist asserting that the central idea of Schaefer's paper, interpreting the behavior of Kleist's protagonists as manifestations of narcissistic personality disorders, is in fact valid.

There can be no question that Heller's objection in the controversy was well taken. Schaefer (and Kohut) base their reading of Kleist's essay on the assumption that its characters, like those of a psychologi-cal novel, represent real human beings. In the first place, this unwarranted inference disregards that a Platonic dialogue such as "On the Puppet Theater" need not adhere to naturalistic conventions. Indeed, as I have mentioned, Kleist introduced overtly supernatural elements into his essay, such as the invincible bear of the climactic fencing match. Even more to the point, Schaefer's reading overlooks the fact that Kleist's oeuvre as a whole does not deal with man's inner life in the usual sense—it is almost exclusively focused on eschatological concerns.

The resultant misunderstanding illustrates the overriding methodological importance of applying analytic tools to an artist's oeuvre in its totality, instead of singling out individual works for interpretation (see Gedo, 1983, pp. 14–16)—particularly works as baffling as those of Kleist. In the clinical situation, it is equally important to make every interpretation of particulars fit into the overall gestalt of the analysand's mental life as revealed over hundreds of hours of observation. Hence one requirement of effective analytic work is the capacity and willingness to delay interpretive closures until most of the potential alternatives have been ruled out by an accumulation of evidence (see Sadow, 1984). Schaefer's (1975) work showed no awareness of the thematic currents of the Kleistian *opus*, for example, its insistence on the significance of Original Sin. This is most tragically depicted in *The Earthquake in Chile*, a story in which humanity is all but destroyed as a result of the sexual defilement of a sacred enclosure. One wonders whether Kohut would have persisted in his espousal of a literal reading of Kleist's essay if he had realized that this philosophical writer continuously portrayed man's fate as an unbearable dilemma—remaining the puppet of a Divine Will whose purposes are unfathomable or, by revolting against God, lapsing into unacceptable states of imperfection and lack of grace.

To ask this question is to suggest a methodological solution that should circumvent Heller's (1978) objection to psychoanalytic approaches to art. As Meredith Skura (1981) has shown in detail, many texts demand the decoding of their allegorical meanings before the resultant literal rendering can be submitted to psychological scrutiny. This process is analogous to the translation of dream imagery into discursive language in the act of communicating the dream to an audience. We are used to this two-step hermeneutic sequence in our efforts to interpret the visual arts, but we tend to overlook the need to follow the same procedure with literary texts, especially those which screen their allegorical meanings behind a seemingly straightforward surface narrative.

If the *premier danseur* of Kleist's essay is reduced to looking upon marionettes with admiration and envy for the perfection of their movements unconstrained by human self-consciousness, this narrative can best be understood in the context of Kleist's oeuvre as a parable about man's loss of contact with the Divine as a result of the Fall of Adam. I do not mean that such a reading amounts to a psychological interpretation of the text; on the contrary, it is *this* concept that calls for analytic scrutiny. Although Heller was correct in dismissing the Kohutian claim that Kleist's dancer exhibits a form of psychopathology, it would seem that he has failed to acknowledge that depth psychology might illuminate some of the mysteries inherent in Kleist's diagnosis of the human condition. But more of that later.

Here I should like to buttress my case about the metaphorical sense of "On the Puppet Theater" by reminding the reader that in his early play, *The Broken Pitcher*, Kleist depicted Adam's Fall, the defloration of Eve, as if this crucial act of rebellion against the Sacred Order were merely a comic incident in the setting of peasant life. However, there is an undercurrent of awe and terror even in this pastoral comedy, for those characters within the play who have Faith understand the action as the work of the devil. The drama seemingly concludes in a happy vein—the only permanent damage done is the shattering of the household's most precious possession, a jug with a provenance from the supreme ruler of the Holy Roman Empire. Things fall apart; the centre cannot hold; Mere anarchy is loosed upon the world . . .

Margret Schaefer was not unaware of Kleist's philosophical intent, but she disregarded its centrality for explicating his work. According to her (1975, p. 381), the argument of the essay is a defensive effort intended to prove that Kleist's pathological self-experience was actually normal, even expectable. Her brief article baldly asserts that this great writer suffered from hypochondriasis and psychotic delusions. Recent biographers (e.g., Maass, 1983) have been more cautious about Kleist's complex and shifting mental status, but in any case it does not seem likely that an author who characterized some of his own actions as inexplicable without medical expertise (p. 95) would devote his best efforts to denying his illness. There can be no doubt that Kleist was able to portray pathological mental states with the insight of one who had undergone such experiences. Nonetheless, when he describes the onset of autism in an adolescent in his essay, he is also making use of observations gathered in the course of visits to institutions for the mentally ill to study the patients (Luke and Reeves, 1978, p. 35). His lengthy psychological illness at the age of 26 (in 1803–04), when in a crisis of despair he destroyed the manuscript of his most ambitious work, the tragedy *Robert Guiscard*, probably aroused his interest in these phenomena.

In their focus on the psychopathology allegedly portrayed in Kleist's essay, Kohut and Schaefer overlooked the fact that the account of an adolescent's psychological crisis is given by the narrator who, in this Platonic dialogue, represents the faltering voice of 18th century rationalism. In other words, the report about a person becoming psychologically ill (in our terms, withdrawing into autism) is proposed as an argument against the deism of the ballet dancer—an effort to explain the mysteries of the cosmos through scientific hypotheses of the very kind the Kohutians now offer as the nub of Kleist's meaning. The *premier danseur's* crushing reproof, that his antagonist "had not read the third chapter of the Book of Genesis with care" (Miller, 1982, p. 214), would seem to apply with equal force to these latter-day rationalists. Consequently, Heller's sarcasm in subtitling his paper "The Dismantling of a Marionette Theater" by psychoanalysts who would misinterpret literature was all too justified! However illuminating the biographical approach to the meanings of works of art may be, to reduce that significance exclusively to the personal vicissitudes of the author is to misunderstand profoundly the goal of literature, the effort to attain universality.

Although the psychopathology Schaefer attributed to Kleist may have been present, the biographical data of greatest import for the understanding of his life's work do not concern the details of his psychological difficulties as an adult. In my judgment, it is the crisis of his late adolescence that is the psychological key to his oeuvre. Offspring of a prominent Junker family, orphan by the age of 15, the future author continued the military career of his forefathers until the age of 22, when he resigned his commission to study philosophy, mathematics and physics; when he considered marriage about a year later, he toyed with the idea of becoming a professor of Kantian philosophy (Maass, 1983, p. 32). But the skepticism he absorbed from Kant shattered the youthful Kleist's *Weltanschauung:* "We can never be certain that what we call Truth is really Truth, or whether it does not merely appear so to us. If the latter . . . my highest goal has sunk from sight, and I have no other" (Miller, 1982, p. 95). "An unspeakable emptiness filled my innermost being" (p. 97), Kleist wrote his fiancée. And to his sister, Ulrike, he confessed, "The very pillar totters that I have clung to in this whirling tide of life" (p. 93). This crisis occurred in 1801; we may, then, conclude that Kleist dated the dialogue in his Platonic essay to that year to indicate that in this work he was dealing with the intellectual issues that had so dramatically disturbed him at the time. The narrator and the ballet dancer each articulate one of Kleist's incompatible intellectual positions.

We may best grasp the gravity of Kleist's crisis by recalling a letter he wrote two years earlier, at the height of his commitment to the values of the Enlightenment. "Existing without a life-plan, without any firm purpose, constantly wavering between uncertain desires, constantly at variance with my duties, the plaything of chance, a puppet on the strings of fate—such an unworthy situation seems so contemptible to me and would make me so wretched that death would be preferable by far" (Luke and Reeves, 1978, p. 7). It seems, then, that after the crisis of 1801, Kleist's ultimate suicide was merely a matter of time—but this brief excursion into details of his life is pertinent here for reasons even more intimately related to the intellectual content of his pivotal essay. For Kleist's anguished confessions reveal that the role of God's puppet suited him no better than did his imperfect humanity; it is the tension between these irreconcilable attitudes that forms the mainspring of Kleist's literary art.

Tempting as it is to explore the ramifications of a personality organization that depends for its integrity on rigid adherence to an arbitrary intellectual schema—in Kleist's case, the rationalism of the Enlightenment—that line of inquiry does not throw light on his literary work, although it would be most fruitful for a study of his creativity. The psychological questions relevant for illuminating his oeuvre lie elsewhere. They concern such issues as the refusal of Kleist, despite the pessimistic deism he came to accept, to acknowledge the possibility that the universe is governed by a Divinity of Hell (like the god of Shakespeare's Iago): "It cannot be an evil spirit that stands at the world's helm, but merely an uncomprehended one," he wrote a friend in 1806 (Miller, 1982, p. 165). The arbitrary power of this incomprehensible deity tosses his helpless puppets about in the most terrifying of Kleist's stories, *The Earthquake in Chile*, *St. Cecilia or the Power of Music*, *The Duel*, *The Foundling*, and *Michael Kohlhaas*. So unbearable is the atmosphere of helplessness vis-à-vis a malign fate that

Kohlhaas has been adapted as a play from which all the supernatural aspects have been eliminated (Luke and Reeves, 1978, p. 27).[1] It makes for a more rational world, but (like the Kohutian view of "On the Puppet Theater"), it is not the cosmos of Heinrich von Kleist.

My aim here is not to make an exhaustive inventory of the Kleistian themes that call for psychological interpretation, for I will close my consideration of his universe by surveying his summarizing masterpiece, the drama *Prince Friedrich of Homburg*. It does behoove me, however, to give a few more examples of typical psychological issues raised by the work of this philosophical author. I should like first to offer the theme of epistemological confusion—the phenomenon at the heart of Kleist's spiritual crisis in his early 20s. In addition to *The Prince of Homburg*, several stories revolve around this quandary, notably *The Marquise of O—, The Duel*, and *The Betrothal in Santo Domingo*, as well as Kleist's dramatic version of the legend of *Amphytrion*. In each of these, the protagonist is caught in a situation wherein an insoluble conflict arises between his or her deepest convictions about reality and the evidence of the senses. In this series of works, Kleist surveys the gamut of alternative resolutions of the dilemma of being torn in this way.

The second example I have chosen to illustrate the autobiographical aspect of Kleist's literary activity is the disintegration of behavior into subsets of mutually incompatible personal goals, each pursued in turn, without regard for the consequences of that choice for all the other aims espoused at the same time. This catastrophic outcome of the failure of Kleist's "life-plan" is depicted most overtly in his last work, *The Prince of Homburg*, but it is already discernible in his Euripidean tragedy *Penthesilea*, completed about three years earlier. Kleist himself wrote, ". . . my innermost being is in this play . . . all the suffering and at the same time all the radiance of my soul" (Maass, 1983, p. 134).

The play has been widely interpreted as an expression of confusion between love and death, and it is evident that Kleist shows the presence of this confusion in characters who hover at the edge of mad-

---

[1]It is noteworthy that in his 1972 discussion of narcissistic rage, Kohut (1972, pp. 616–617) referred to Kleist's Kohlhaas (in tandem with Melville's Captain Ahab) as a prototypical personality victimized by the malignant aggression released by intolerable threats to its self-esteem or integrity. His discussion of both works completely disavows their supernatural content, precisely in the manner used in the dramatic adaptation in question.

ness. However, the crux of the myth is Penthesilea's inability to remain faithful to the creed of the Amazons and the resultant incoherence of her behavior. If she does not know whether she wants to conquer Achilles or to surrender herself to him and adopt his belief system, her indecision leads not to unresolved internal conflict but to uncoordinated actions in the service of each of her incompatible goals. In this drama, the shattering of Sacred Order is no longer emblematic, as it was in *The Broken Pitcher*, the work that launched Kleist's career as a playwright—here the fading of belief shatters the protagonists themselves.

Let us now proceed to a more detailed reading of Kleist's last creation, *Prince Friedrich of Homburg*. This drama is an archaicizing work, one that attempts through the use of verse to recreate the courtliness of the late Baroque period in which the action purportedly takes place.[2] This formal approach achieves an aura of timelessness and mystery. The drama also takes place in a surreal space in which Brandenburg lies on the banks of the Rhine—an echo of Shakespeare's Seacoast of Bohemia. Hence we cannot take literally either the identity of the historical personages who people the action or the dating of 1675. In this artful play, we are involved in a metaphysical inquiry into the human condition, *sub specie aeternitatis*.

Yet the issues are examined in the context of a concrete and specific set of circumstances. On the surface, these concern the establishment of the Kingdom of Prussia by the campaigns of Friedrich Wilhelm, the Great Elector, and the modern reader will easily accept this rendering as naturalistic. Kleist achieves universality by suggesting close parallels to the political events of his own day; on that level, the drama is an allegorical call to action, imploring the reigning monarch, Friedrich Wilhelm III, to rally to the cause of creating a German nation-state. The confusion of Homburg, the protagonist, is a metaphor for the condition of the commonwealth. Or is the political disarray an allegorical representation of Man's Fate?

The Prince of Homburg reverses the actual situation of Prussia when it was written, at the height of Napoleon's ascendancy over Europe.

---

[2]Both the court scenes and the battle pieces recall the sweet and melancholy atmosphere of the paintings of Watteau, splendidly represented in the Prussian Royal Collections since the reign of Frederick the Great. Kleist was a protegé of Queen Louise of Prussia and frequently visited the Royal Palace at Potsdam, where the pictures abounded.

In the play, Kleist recreates the battle of Fehrbellin, in which the Great Elector, Friedrich Wilhelm, routed the allies of Louis XIV in the course of a French attempt to achieve domination over the Continent. This memory of a Prussian triumph fulfills Kleist's wish to undo the contemporary humiliation of German defeats at Jena and Wagram at the hands of Napoleon. Similarly, defiant rejection of the offer of a foreign marriage for a Prussian princess at the climax of the drama erases the real shame of the Corsican upstart's triumphant espousal of Maria Luisa von Habsburg.

Kleist's invaders are thrown back across the Rhine—doubtless into an imaginary Alsace rather than the Eastern provinces named in the play. And the ethic of the French Revolution, which had devoured its sons, is transcended with exquisite delicacy: the Great Elector shows that he is not a Roman patrician who would sacrifice his children on the altar of the Commonwealth. During his residence in Paris, Kleist had ample opportunity to note that Jacques Louis David had ushered in the events of 1789 with a celebrated tableau glorifying the inhumanity of Brutus, who condemned his sons to death for lack of patriotism. During the Terror, the *sansculottes* repeatedly carried the sacrifice of Isaac to its bloody conclusion. By contrast, Kleist's ideal community relies absolutely on the free gifts of responsible men. The admiration of revolutionary France for the Roman Republic is transcended in Kleist's ideal world by a community modeled on the Republic of Plato, as the Old Testament was once superseded by the New.

The *res publica* of Kleist takes the form of a Divine Kingship. Friedrich Wilhelm governs Brandenburg with inspiring wisdom, modesty, justice, and empathy for the needs of his subjects. But even the God of the New Testament refuses to undo man's imperfections—the Great Elector's adoptive son, the Prince of Homburg, persists in disrupting the public order through impulsive actions in the pursuit of personal glory and success in love. Yet the battle of Fehrbellin is won *because* the Prince has eaten of the fruit of the Tree of Knowledge: Homburg violates the orders of the High Command, because he has greater faith in his own judgment. He is a soldier of genius, enthusiastically followed by the army, a tactician whose decision is endorsed by the most experienced commanders, and Friedrich Wilhelm grants him credit for the victory. But the greatest of human achievements falls short of ideal, Divine schemata; hence the Primal

Crime is punished by banishment from Eden. As a consequence, man is faced with the necessity to accept his mortality; the Great Elector condemns Homburg to death because he was responsible for reducing the order of battle to a secular instrument. Kleist has brought us back to the third chapter of *Genesis* once again.

The heart of the drama is the reaction of the human protagonist to the hopelessness of his existence, Kleist's poetic résumé of the crux of man's psychology. In his initial state of innocence, the Prince disavows the significance of his sentence: he cannot imagine that a person of his status and merits could be treated as an ordinary man. This state of mind was to await detailed discussion until the emergence of Kleist's heir, Franz Kafka, whose philosophical novel, *The Trial*, elaborates on the theme. When he finally grasps that Friedrich Wilhelm will not skew the operation of justice in his favor, the Prince is stunned. There follows a remarkable personality change, a reorganization in terms of continuous awareness of human helplessness. Like naive religious believers, Homburg pleads for mercy through the intercession of maternal figures.[3] In panic and with humility, he expresses attachment to life at the simplest level, and he comes as close to the state of beings without consciousness as a human adult can get. Kleist affirms partial adherence to the Christian view of life through the outcome he assigns to this transaction: Repentance leads to Salvation. Friedrich Wilhelm grants the Prince the privilege of deciding his own fate.

In his response to being saved, the Prince embodies post-Christian man and (one might suspect) reflects most revealingly the personal attitudes of Heinrich von Kleist. As if in identification with the nobility of Friedrich Wilhelm as Vicar of Christ, Homburg rejects Salvation in order to achieve Grace. He affirms his own guilt and concurs in his sentence—in other words, he fully accepts the consequences of

---

[3]I am indebted to Professor Harold Bloom for suggesting (in his discussion of this material at the conference on "Transformations in Psychoanalysis," Valencia, CA, March 1985) that Homburg's reactions must echo those of Kleist himself. In his dealings with the Prussian Government, his overt opposition to their policy of appeasement had produced a severe confrontation despite the intercession of his kinswoman Marie von Kleist, who had the ear of the Queen. Prof. Bloom suggests that the actual sentence of death was pronounced not by Friedrich Wilhelm, but by a more significant father-surrogate, Goethe. Indeed, Goethe all but ruined Kleist's literary career by making a travesty of a staging of *The Broken Pitcher* he had arranged at the Court Theatre at Weimar.

his mortality. In this decisive passage, we are able to read the first intimations of Kleist's private determination to triumph over death by eating of the tree of knowledge a second time. He will achieve his triumph not through Christ, but in his own way, by his imminent ecstatic suicide. In this view, philosophical man cannot rest content with God's bounty: revolting against the status of His puppet, the Prince voluntarily abandons the satisfactions of ordinary existence, even the possession of the most desirable of women. The pursuit of perfection has preempted all other aims: the *premier danseur* is determined to outdo God's marionettes. Homburg has increased his insubordination by displacing it from the battlefield to the existential arena: he will not accept the "human condition," as did Socrates or Michel de Montaigne.

Yet, in *The Prince of Homburg,* Kleist still acknowledges the superiority of Divine Wisdom, its power over human presumption. Friedrich Wilhelm pardons the Prince in spite of himself, because he knows that man is ultimately without freedom of will: even Homburg's existential revolt has been Divinely ordained. Indeed, Kleist has cunningly set the action so as to place responsibility for Homburg's behavior on the shoulders of Friedrich Wilhelm. The opening of the play is *mise en scène* in a garden mirroring Eden. Here, the entire court of Brandenburg tricks the Prince into believing that he has only dreamt certain events he has actually witnessed. In the confusion that follows, Homburg becomes incapable of understanding the instructions of the high command for the battle to come. Poor Adam! He does not as yet know that life is but a dream. Kleist is giving us a reprise of Calderón's *La vida es sueño.* And the ways of the gods are truly inscrutable: in the end, the Prince of Homburg lives out his destiny as commander of the Great Elector's cavalry.

Did the *gods* intend Heinrich von Kleist to kill himself, or by ending his life did he succeed in bursting the bonds of necessity that constrained the protagonist of his last work? Behind the manifest ecstasy of Kleist's suicide, his attainment of the status of a prototypical hero of the Romantic Era, a peer of Byron seeking death at Missolonghi, clinicians will doubtless postulate despair caused by inability to accept the meaningfulness of an ordinary life. But matters of that kind did not find their place on the stage until the era of Beckett and Ionesco. Perhaps, after all, they first had to enter the public domain through the findings of Sigmund Freud.

Does my survey of the literary work of Heinrich von Kleist demonstrate that psychoanalytic hermeneutics yield relevant insights about
cultural materials? Some humanist scholars who have heard earlier
versions of my interpretations were willing to grant them some value
as literary criticism informed by a psychoanalytic sensibility, but
questioned whether my proposals are in fact "psychoanalytic." I
have, of course, sedulously avoided the technical vocabulary of psychoanalysis in making these textual interpretations, as I avoid the use
of jargon in my clinical work. I believe my résumé of *The Prince of
Homburg* qualifies as psychoanalytic interpretation even though it is
focused on matters seldom mentioned in analytic discourse: the catastrophic confusion that follows the collapse of a belief system that
sustains a fragile personality, the despair born of the inability to renounce any of a number of incompatible personal goals, the exalta-
tion of a hypomanic quest for perfection.

Although Kleist confines himself to the description of specific instances in his literary works, I believe his corpus purposefully and
consciously highlights human concerns of this kind. Kleist never
names the eschatological issues exemplified by the actions of his characters, just as I tried to refrain from spelling out the psychoanalytic
constructs on which my reading is based. To put the point differently,
my discussion of *The Prince of Homburg* does not interpret its unconscious meaning for its author—or, obviously, for myself. The issues
Kleist manipulates preconsciously to create his art and that I attempt
to render conscious by transposing into discursive language may be
so fraught with conflict for certain readers that they may be unable to
grasp these particular meanings—this segment of the public will in
some manner reject the author's message.

In parallel with the therapeutic situation, the interpreter of texts is
necessarily blinded to those aspects of the material that impinge on
his own conflicts. I too must be oblivious to certain issues in his
oeuvre that Kleist might have regarded as central. Yet the defenses of
most readers will fail to exclude the full impact of the artist's message;
it is this ability to communicate emotion that we call artistic power. At
the most fundamental level of communication, the work of art is able
to produce affective arousal in its audience. Many readers may miss
the philosophical import of Kleist's work or even deny its significance, as Schaefer and Kohut have done. Few will remain unaffected,
however, by the revelation of bravery and terror in *The Prince of Hom-*

burg, even if they know nothing about its history as prelude to the author's suicide.

My interpretation of the Kleistian corpus was built exclusively on the *reading* of his texts and some of his letters—I have never had the opportunity to see any of his drama on the stage.[4] As consumers of the performing arts well know, the affective response of the audience depends in great measure on planned or even unplanned interpretive variations by the performers. The skillful playwright gives the artists who will stage his work a large degree of latitude to infuse the text with their own emotions. To restate the point from the perspective of the audience, drama makes different demands on the viewer than a literary text makes on the reader; instead of requiring the creation of emotionally charged human transactions in the consumer's imagination, it presents the *mise en scène* of such events, enacted by virtuosi in the communication of affects.

The foregoing distinction deserves emphasis because there is no way to explicate in words the evocation of affects in human transactions—it is an automatic process, part of man's constitutional repertory. In a text intended for reading, the author has to build in purely verbal meanings that produce affective reactions by way of the recipient's *conceptual* capabilities. That is not the way affective communication takes place in living transactions: for the most part, it is accomplished through paraverbal means, such as posture, gesture, facial expression, bodily reactions mediated through the autonomic nervous system, and the music of the speaker's vocalization. On the stage, as in everyday life or in the psychoanalytic situation, a transcription of the communications encoded in words is insufficient for one to grasp the full message.[5] *Per contra*, the author of narrative fiction must in some manner put the ineffable subtleties of human discourse into words. In the story or novel, dialogue is never sufficient to accomplish this end.

---

[4]Paradoxically, a seeming exception to this statement is the dramatization of the novella, *The Marquise of O—*, as a motion picture. Although Eric Rohmer's screen version was unusually faithful to the original, transposition into a medium not intended by the author actually removed the work from Kleist's oeuvre.

[5]The point can also be made by noting that disorder of communication wherein an individual speaks in the mode of the narrator of a work of literature. Such speeches do not qualify as conversations; unless the speaker has the gifts of an epic poet, listening to this type of communication tends to be both boring and outrageous, for the audience is forced into a passive position against its will.

In the psychoanalytic situation, where the observer is simultaneously participant in the dyad, the relative importance of processing the lexical meaning of the verbal interchange is even smaller than it is during a dramatic performance. I would compare it to my experience at the opera: if I am provided with a synopsis of the action, I seldom miss having a precise understanding of the words; when I read the libretto without hearing the music, I find the text to be without interest and fail to respond in any way. I know that my claim about the weighting of verbal material in the clinical encounter goes well beyond prevalent views (for an exception, see Gardner, 1983). I suppose my opinion constitutes the polar opposite of the enormous stress French psychoanalysis has placed upon language as a result of the impact of Jacques Lacan's work.

Paul Ricoeur (1978) has protested against the conception of psychoanalytic experience through the "universe of discourse" of language; he proposed instead that it is the *image* that forms the most appropriate conceptual category in this regard. Obviously, I concede that both words and images are indispensable constituents of the analyst's mental stock-in-trade. But I also believe that the analyst achieves his specialized insights in the clinical setting because he has trained himself to respond to the music of human behavior, beyond language and even beyond imagery. This training is usually accomplished by means of consistent introspective effort, initially in the course of a personal analysis, later through the challenge and consensual validation of performing analyses with the assistance of supervision. When Freud repeatedly stated that analysis must take place through the response of the analyst's "unconscious" to that of the patient, I believe he was alluding to these coenesthetic channels of communication.

Perhaps it is the lack of opportunity to exercise these specific tools of clinical psychoanalysis that leads all too many efforts to apply the analytic method to cultural materials into unproductive channels.

EPILOGUE

14

More on the Essence of Psychoanalysis

Self-Creation and Vocabularies of Moral Deliberation

ABOUT A GENERATION HAS PASSED since Philip Rieff, in two magisterial volumes (1959, 1966), described psychoanalysis as a science of morality and, by virtue of that role of the discipline in Western intellectual life, credited Freud with creating the only feasible model for a post-theist community. Rieff did not believe that as a doctrine offering no salvation and no faith, psychoanalysis would prove to be palatable to a significant number of people—like Plato, he took the sardonic view that the masses need myths and slogans for their edification. That, at least in the short run, his pessimism was justified is affirmed by the scarcity of subsequent commentary on his impassioned thesis about the spiritual crisis of modern man and the potential of depth psychology to contribute to its solution. (For one response in a psychoanalytic forum, see Gedo, 1972a).

Rieff (1966) paid respect to psychoanalysis as a "severe and chill anti-doctrine" that refuses to impose cultural change through moral coercion. In his view, it accomplishes a correction of our standard of conduct without moralizing or any other explicit "message"—in contrast to the inculcation of ideals advocated by Adler (see Stepansky, 1983, p. 279) or the role of the Jungian therapist as "a ritual elder, a wise man who understands the process of passage from the conventional world to that of the new self" (Homans, 1979, p. 207). Consequently, Rieff (1959) regards Freud as the prophet of the present, the first irreligious moralist, and the "saving critic" of liberal culture.

203

Philosophical meliorists, he pointed out, have always found it intolerable to recognize the relative intractability of human behavior and have therefore looked on Freud as a pessimist. Rieff effectively refuted this view, demonstrating that Freud's faith in the prudence and rationality of the ego can scarcely be regarded as a tragic portrait of man. Neither can the Freudian concept of the emergence of conscience from instinctual roots be classified as pessimistic (Roazen, 1968).

After a considerable hiatus, the role of psychoanalysis in making possible the development of a new vocabulary of moral deliberation has once again found an advocate in Richard Rorty (in press). In contrast to Rieff, Rorty supplied a reading of Freud as a pragmatist who delivered the *coup de grâce* to the hope of philosophers to justify a conception of man's "true self" as moral and rational. Where Rieff saw psychoanalysis as heir to the Stoic tradition of rationality and self-control, exemplified by Epictetus, Seneca, Montaigne, and Hobbes, Rorty believes that Freud's insights into the human depths have shown that the search for self-improvement through purification—the effort to transcend man's status as an animal in the direction of spirituality—is doomed to disappointment. Not that Rorty sees Freud as a pessimist in consequence; to the contrary, he acknowledges the therapeutic promise of psychoanalysis as an optimal approach to the alternative in the search for perfection, for self-creation through the expansion of freely chosen personal experience of maximal variety. Thus, in agreement with Rieff, Rorty underscores the fundamental hopefulness of the Freudian enterprise, its enhancement of human spontaneity and mitigation of constraints.

I do not intend here to begin by reconciling the divergent assessments of Freud's philosophical stance given by Rorty and Rieff. Suffice it to say that in his immense corpus of writings one may find plentiful support for both readings. Neither can I, in the space available here, substantiate my impression that Rorty's version is based mostly on the early Freud, whereas Rieff's reflects the relative disillusionment of Freud's old age, the sobriety born of the moderation of therapeutic ambitions. What I wish to emphasize is the tendency of both scholars to neglect the evolution of psychoanalysis as an empirical science, reflected both in changes within Freud's own thought and in the complex development of the discipline after the death of its founder. Rorty writes about "Freud and the vocabulary of moral deliberation"; as I have tried to show in these studies of psychoanalytic dissidence, the psychoanalytic method has continued to provide fresh empirical data that cannot be fitted into Freud's theoretical schemata (Gedo & Goldberg, 1973). Thus, Rorty's discussion of this topic calls for expansion in two directions: to encompass all of psychoanalysis and to consider its *alternative* vocabularies of moral deliberation.

The problem I want to highlight has, over and over again, bedeviled interdisciplinary efforts wedding psychoanalysis to the humanities. In reminding interested scholars that psychoanalytic propositions require empirical validation, I do not echo Adolf Grünbaum's (1984) demand for *proof* of these hypotheses. As Rorty has also noted (in press, fn. 18), scientific convictions are legitimated by their superiority to alternative explanations; but this superiority must refer to the power to predict and/or to alter events on the stage of actuality rather than to elaborate a conceptual system as such. Humanist scholars tend, often unconsciously, to assess Freud's oeuvre as if it consisted exclusively of a complex set of hermeneutic propositions—as if psychoanalysis could truly be judged by the standards applicable to moral philosophy.

To illustrate my point, let me cite Rorty's exposition of the Freudian conception of mind as a set of more or less coherent beliefs and desires, a set of such infinite potential variety that this limitless range of possibility belies the very notion of "human nature." In making this claim, Rorty highlights the dynamic point of view of Freud's metapsychology, and his choice is appropriate in so far as he is interested in the functioning of most adults "in normal life," as he puts it. In doing so, however, Rorty disregards an empirical finding of psychoanalysis that even Grünbaum might hesitate to challenge: under psychoanalytic scrutiny, scarcely anyone can be regarded as "normal." The infinite variety of life turns out to reflect the multiplicity of developmental possibilities, every one of which entails certain "pathological" disadvantages.

I would guess that Rorty prefers the early Freud because that corpus of writings fails to give proper weight either to a structural or to a developmental-genetic viewpoint. Freud introduced these added dimensions into his metapsychology not on aprioristic philosophical grounds, as if he had abandoned Aristotelian premises for Platonic ones, as Melanie Klein was to do, but because reliance on the theory of the Unconscious—the topographic model of mind—left him helpless to explicate a host of novel empirical findings in the *pathological* realm (see Gedo & Goldberg, 1973, Chapter 3). Discarded theories in psychoanalysis, unlike archaic styles in the arts, cannot legitimately be revived for scholarly purposes.

This problem of method is important enough for the scholar attempting interdisciplinary work to deserve further scrutiny through a detailed example. For this purpose, I should like to select Rorty's almost off-hand dismissal of Freud's redefinition of psychic conflict from the model of *Pcs.* vs. *Ucs.* to that of ego vs. id (Rorty, in press). For Rorty, this amounts to a reversion to the Platonic tradition of contrasting man's "higher part," or soul, with a lower, bodily part that is prelinguistic. Rorty declares, "But a witty unconscious is necessarily a linguistic unconscious." Shades of Jacques Lacan![1] In making this statement, Rorty confuses the manifest wit of certain dreams and parapraxes with their unconscious latent meanings.

The empirical findings of generations of clinicians certainly demonstrate that what is maximally meaningful in human life is not necessarily encoded in words, that the most affect-laden of our experiences are endlessly repeated through the vicissitudes of the body substrate. I have discussed these issues in detail elsewhere (Gedo, 1979, 1981b, 1984a) and will not repeat the arguments for this view here; suffice it to say that it ill behooves anyone to make cavalier judgments about these exceedingly complicated matters—judgments, moreover, that depend on empirical findings. But it should be noted that Rorty's view neglects not only recent analytic contributions stressing the import of the preverbal aspects of mental life but some of Freud's most seminal concepts as well, such as "actual neurosis" (1895b) and "repetition compulsion" (1920). In Freud's judgment, the Unconscious is not witty—it is unknowable!

As I attempted to show at some length in a volume I coedited with Pollock (1976), Freud's most revolutionary accomplishment may have been the reintegration into the scientific *Weltanschauung*, dominant in Western intellectual life since the Enlightenment, of the spiritual realm Descartes named the *res cogitans.* In challenging the prevailing scientific materialism of his predecessors by documenting the power of the Unconscious, Freud went as far to redress the Cartesian split between mind and matter as the epistemology of the early 20th cen-

---

[1]Lacan represents that tradition within French psychoanalysis which refuses to accept that the discipline is part of science and utterly disregards its empirical foundations. In his hands, psychoanalytic ideas dissolve into literary conceits and the psychoanalytic situation loses its therapeutic aim. Little wonder that the psychoanalytic establishment forced Lacan into an involuntary secession!

tury permitted. As he is reported to have said (Jung, 1963, pp. 150–151), his scientific theories, that of the libido in particular, were intended to safeguard psychoanalysis from engulfment by a "black tide of occultism." This remark reminds us of the anxiety Freud had to master to abandon the safe and respectable neurophysiological, materialist premises of his prepsychoanalytic work.

It has taken several generations to transcend Freud's positivist legacy, but contemporary theoreticians are finally accomplishing this task. For instance, Whitehead (1983) characterizes the development of psychoanalysis since the death of Freud by comparing its avant-garde manifestations to certain aspects of Hellenic thought preceding Plato. He has called the spirit of unselfconscious subjectivity, of anxiety-free merger with a sacred order, "the Asclepian vision of psychosomatic harmony"—and this is the essence of the analytic situation as it is often practiced today (cf. Gardner, 1983).

Rorty's reading of Freud is in the service of a most attractive intellectual enterprise, an attempt to provide a solid psychological basis—I am tempted to write, *pace* Rorty, a scientific estimate of "human nature"—for the ethics of the liberal tradition. In this regard, it is of some interest that Rieff (1959) called the work of Freud the most influential "retreat" of liberalism in the modern world on the basis of an entirely different (and, in my judgment, more nuanced) understanding of the psychoanalytic position. Where Rorty sees in Freud an exclusive emphasis on self-creation through promotion of the freedom to expand personal experience, Rieff correctly stressed that Freud gave equal weight to man's need for authority, to the importance of community, and to law guided by reason. The analytic goal of individual autonomy and self-fulfillment is counterbalanced by awareness of the need to submit to cultural restrictions. Intrapsychic conflict is inevitable in consequence of man's pervasive *aggressiveness* and the imperative necessity to fit into a social organization that requires control over it.

According to Rieff (1959), psychoanalysis is the critic of the passions as much as of the irrational conscience, and it is this position of neutrality among the agencies of the mind that potentially makes it into a tutor in prudence and compromise. Rieff also points out that although the only explicit aim of psychoanalysis as a treatment procedure is self-cognition, it is implicitly understood that this, in turn, will lead to self-control. In other words, the ultimate aim of psychoanalysis is the correction of our standard of conduct—albeit this is

accomplished without moralizing.[2] In fact, it is precisely because of
this implicit aim of Freud's work that Rieff calls him the prophet of
the present, the first irreligious moralist, and the saving *critic* of liberal culture.

But let me return to the starting point of my argument, the methodological problem of the humanist in dealing with psychoanalysis as
a body of scientific propositions. Rorty feels free to dismiss the import
of some of Freud's scientific conclusions simply because they were
prefigured in the work of certain philosophers, such as David Hume.
To believe, as he does, that a hypothesis derived by induction from
observations offers nothing new if it echoes prescientific notions
without empirical foundations utterly misunderstands the purpose
and evolution of scientific ideas. Incidentally, such a cavalier procedure goes far to justify Freud's mistrust of philosophers following
his year of apprenticeship with von Brentano. That psychoanalysis is
not a product of Pure Reason (as Rorty's reading seems to imply) is
amply demonstrated by the fate of Freud's metapsychological propositions, which have been almost universally discarded because of
their lack of congruence with the recent findings of cognate disciplines such as neurobiology and cognitive psychology.

Where does my own conception of contemporary psychoanalysis
lead us in considering the ethical questions posed by Rorty's work?
Does my assessment of Rorty's version of the discipline as antiquated
put me into disagreement with his principal conclusions? The answers to such questions are necessarily complex and in some ways
equivocal. Nonetheless, at the risk of oversimplification, let me state at
the outset that I believe psychoanalysis is well on the way to articulating many crucial aspects of "human nature," that some of the most
essential of these are developmental hypotheses about the very process of "self-creation" Rorty places at the center of his thesis, and that
the empirical findings of psychoanalytic clinicians belie Rorty's claim

---

[2]The claim continually made by psychoanalysts that the only legitimate aim of
their therapeutic enterprises is the universal goal of every scientific effort, the acquisition of knowledge, therefore amounts to the disavowal of an important aspect of their
motivations. In everyday clinical practice, psychoanalysts are constantly obliged to
curb their ambition as healers, their *furor therapeuticus*. This must be done because the
therapist's narcissistic needs in this area, echoing as they do those of the analysand's
parents to produce successful offspring, tend to push patients into unproductive negativism. Perhaps because these dangers are so well known, a tendency has arisen to
deny altogether that analysts are paid to cure people, however carefully they refrain
from promising prospective analysands that they will succeed in doing so.

that such self-creation takes place exclusively through the expansion of the realm of personal experience—just as frequently, it takes more conservative forms, even those of the self-purification Rorty regards as illusory and futile.

Another way of stating my objections to Rorty's position is to characterize his conclusions as *prescriptive* rather than more or less neutral vis-à-vis his subject matter. I do not mean to imply that there is anything wrong with a moral philosophy simply because it is strongly committed to a certain set of values. Elsewhere (Gedo, 1984a, chapter 6), I have gone so far as to state that value judgments cannot be eschewed even within the psychoanalytic situation. Yet I suspect that a moral philosophy that aspires to be psychoanalytically informed should, like the clinical analyst, strive to minimize the influence of the author's personal system of values (see Moraitis, 1985). In other words, the psychoanalyst cannot *condemn* efforts at self-purification as Rorty would have us do—it is the task of psychoanalytic ethics to *illuminate* the age-old human aspiration to achieve perfection by emulating the gods.

I have no question about the appropriateness of Rorty's view that "self-enlargement" (generally in the sense of material resources and cultural exposure) is the only possible road to perfecting oneself for the vast majority of educated persons in advanced, postindustrial societies. However, although the clientele of American psychoanalysts consists exclusively of people of this sort, a significant number of exceptions continue to crop up in my clinical practice. Moreover, the need to purify oneself also is important to the personal ambitions and ideals of many people who largely conform to Rorty's vision of modern man's "quest for self-enrichment." The human being is truly a creature of shreds and patches. In the social arena, we see the effects of these ascetic commitments in the surging concern of influential groups in human ecology, in widespread demands for national policies promoting the human rights of all peoples, in the growth of interest in oriental faiths devoted to self-abnegation, or, in a more comical vein, in the contemporary American cult of thinness and a healthy diet. (With Richard Rorty, I prefer good cheer and *fine champagne* cognac!)

As a clinician, I cannot say that those of my patients who belonged to the category of persons seeking perfection by way of Rorty's prescription for optimal self-expansion by turning into "rich aesthetes," appeared to be more successful in their quest than were those who followed in the footprints of the saints. I am certain that this finding is not a consequence of some idiosyncrasy of mine, for I have never sought sainthood, and it took me many years of struggle in the psychoanalytic trenches to stop looking upon efforts at self-purification as *ipso facto* pathological, à la Rorty. When people commit themselves to spirituality and more or less turn their backs on the world of their fellows, their chances of success in "self-creation" depend to the greatest extent on their capacity to tolerate their own *imperfections*. The same capacity to curb one's presumption is a prerequisite for success in being a rich aesthete. To put the matter metaphorically, as in modernist architecture, so in the quest for perfection, the sound doctrine of "less is more!" has to be applied with discretion. In our day, hardly anyone has the capacity to be a successful ascetic mystic, in the manner of St. Jerome or St. Simeon Stylites, but lesser efforts to curb one's aggression, lust, or greed may still yield surprising degrees of fulfillment. This should not cause any real astonishment: are we not all familiar with the supreme gratification of a successful fast, never to be equaled by the accomplishments of the gourmet? It seems to me that life is even more varied than Richard Rorty's Baroque vision of self-enrichment implies. On some occasions, man craves the austerity of the Mosque of Ib'n Tulun!

Such fluctuations in human preferences are barely beginning to gain the attention of psychoanalysts. Insofar as we encounter persons with, for instance, an addiction to pain (Valenstein, 1973), or to a more or less stable commitment to repetitive bouts of self-restriction (see case #3 in Gedo, 1979), we have to understand *those* specific patterns of self-maintenance as expressions of prelinguistic organismic necessities that define that person's psychobiological essence. It would be fatuous to regard the life of St. Francis or of Vincent van Gogh (cf. Gedo, 1983, chapters 7 & 8) as futile quests based on illusions: striving to be a rich aesthete is not the only way to live well, even in late 20th century America. Perhaps Rorty might label the assorted saints and prophets I have encountered in my consulting room as anachronisms, people born out of their natural habitat. I do not see it that way. Not only is there room for these rare spirits in the modern world; it *needs* them, and, in turn, it provides for them a more nurturant societal matrix than did traditional communities that demanded conformity to their existing belief systems.

It is true, of course, that psychoanalytic observation of individuals whose quest for perfection to an important degree takes the form of self-purification lends no support to the views of philosophers like Sartre, whose assumptions of the essence of human nature as "pure freedom" Rorty wishes to refute through his psychoanalytic arguments. Freud and his successors have found—can there be anyone left to challenge these empirical findings?—that the core of human existence is a daemonic need to repeat the subjective patterns apprehended at the dawn of consciousness. These compulsions are the inescapable parameters of "human nature," rather than the mental contents whose infinite variety Rorty rightly dismisses as a basis for defining man's essence. And it is the various developmental possibilities at man's disposal for gaining a measure of personal autonomy despite the continuous pressure of the compulsion to repeat that constitute the psychoanalytic "laws of human nature"— the concepts that bridge the world of mechanism and that of moral discourse.[3]

Lest my conclusion sound overly abstract, I should like to illustrate this point by outlining a pair of very brief examples from my clinical experience. The most striking illustration I can provide is the case of a clergyman who was committed to vows of poverty, chastity, and obedience and sought assistance because he found it too difficult to bear the resultant frustrations. These ethical commitments helped him to transcend the patterns of human relatedness he had learned from his parents—transactions impregnated with sadism and ruthless exploitativeness. He was successful in avoiding unacceptable behaviors of that kind through his adherence to a morality based on the need for purity. But even the occasional dream in which his tendency to abuse others found some expression filled this man, whose conscious ideal was martyrhood, with unbearable guilt. The pattern of sadomasochistic relationships antedated his earliest memories, of traumatic incidents of overstimulation by tickling at the hands of his siblings. The patient's mother was a chronic schizophrenic who often used violence to enforce her demands on family members.

After five years of analysis, the patient's moral commitments remained unchanged, but he had learned to avoid his previous pattern of rebellion and expiation by moderating his ambition to be a martyr, so that he no longer exceeded his own tolerance for frustration. He deeply appreciated the help rendered by his analysis precisely be-

---

[3]For one attempt to outline these laws, in skeletal fashion, see Gedo, 1979 (esp. chapters 11–13), 1984a (chapter 1), Gedo & Goldberg, 1973 (chapters 6 & 7); see also Gedo, 1981c.

cause it had made him into a better clergyman, not merely with regard to the specific moral issues already mentioned but also by diminishing his attitude of self-aggrandizement as a result of his moral successes. It is true that this process of self-purification was paralleled by a modest expansion of his interest in the secular world. In essence, however, he remained a man one might expect to have encountered in the 16th century.

Should this example strike the reader as too atypical, let me cite another instance of would-be sainthood, in which the patient's commitment to purity and altruism represented a primary identification with the beloved and idealized grandmother who had raised him for the first five years of his life. This man had adequate material resources and was passionately devoted to the arts—Richard Rorty will find no better exemplar for his model of modern man!—but he was equally insistent on avoiding fame or profit as rewards for his creative endeavors (cf. Gedo, 1983, chapter 6). A decade after termination of his analysis, he continues to hold to his austere morality, having made this choice into a practicable way of life by dissolving a marriage that interfered with it and abandoning a job where his standards clashed with the prevailing mores.

In his attempt to overthrow the moral authority of imperatives that transcend man's spontaneous childhood behavior, Richard Rorty is willing to renounce altogether an *ethical* point of view concerning human action. In his judgment, Freud's demonstration of mind-as-machine has destroyed the very basis of "moral philosophy": he implies that the problem of evil (or, if you will, of human destructiveness) is best tackled pragmatically, by providing people with more education, leisure and money (in press, fn. 33). There can be no argument with the desirability of such measures, although the psychoanalytic study of lives has found no connection between destructiveness on the one hand and poverty, ignorance, or the pressures of work on the other, so that material progress is scarcely likely to eliminate human aggression. As best we can judge, its occurrence is correlated instead with certain experiences of excessive frustration, most frequently at certain critical junctures in early childhood (see Parens, 1979). If these impressions should be borne out, Rorty's argument about the problem of evil will in fact be strengthened, for such a correlation would provide a causal connection between passively experienced events and later behaviors that we classify as destructive. In other words, these psychoanalytic findings would truly shift our focus from judging behaviors morally to explanations in terms of mental mechanisms.

Despite my agreement with Rorty on this score, I continue to believe, with Philip Rieff, that the fundamental aim of psychoanalysis is the moral improvement of mankind. In a pragmatic sense, we can best contribute to this effort by promoting more effective methods of childrearing that will minimize the incidence of those experiences that might increase the possibility of producing evil-doers. Is this not an imperative of human solidarity—a *moral* obligation? To be sure, there are too many people whose ethical standards are parochial, who are unable to empathize with anyone measurably different from themselves. Rorty is correct in asserting that the morality many of us advocate is *not* a universal attribute of human nature.

In line with my previous definition of the psychoanalytic view of human nature, I would counter Rorty's argument by pointing out that, in this regard, the universal attribute of humanity is the capability, given minimally favorable conditions during the relevant critical periods in the course of development, of internalizing a set of moral standards—to form a superego, as Freud (1923a) called this process. Persons who have failed to reach this desirable nodal point (Gedo and Goldberg, 1973) are utterly incapable of regulating their behavior in terms of ethical considerations, however sophisticated their cognitive understanding of moral distinctions may become. With such people, our own judgments must focus on pragmatic remedies before turning to ethical concerns. Othello's crime was not so much an act of immorality as it was a personal disaster, a collapse into incoherence. *Ecco il leone di Venezia!*, laughs Verdi's Iago.

Moral judgments become relevant in relation to persons who have an internalized morality, and we need moral philosophers to make comparative judgments about the desirability of *various* ethical standards. Is the Mafia code of *omertà* a moral substitute for the Judeo-Christian proscription of murder? Is Western indifference about the genocide of nonwhite populations as adequate a moral position as an attitude of universal human brotherhood? Are we ethically justified in condoning police brutality or vigilante actions against dangerous outlaws, or had we better insist that our personal safety should not be secured through extralegal means? These are not merely pragmatic questions but also moral ones—however they are answered, the response may or may not represent an *ethical* position. Psychoanalysis will have to take a role in evaluating competing systems of morality, the alternative vocabularies of moral deliberation disclosed by the scrutiny of individual lives.

Having illuminated a variety of moral systems, psychoanalysis cannot espouse a single ethical point of view. Yet Freud's discipline still aspires to provide a basis for the moral improvement of mankind. For, without being constitutive of *a* morality, psychoanalysis does supply data about the developmental preconditions of a moral sense, that is, preconditions pertaining to the potential for moral conduct. Whereas it cannot posit the *substance* of a moral code, psychoanalysis must theorize in recognition of the fact that moral decisions must be made.

Clay Whitehead (1983) has described psychoanalysis, in words he borrowed from Julian Huxley, as an attempt to lead people toward new patterns of thought, new organizations of awareness, by means of new patterns of cooperation among the participants. There is no reason to shrink from the conclusion that such an enterprise has spiritual dimensions—"the Asclepian spirit of psychosomatic harmony" Whitehead wishes to invoke. In other words, psychoanalysis as a therapy *is* a moral enterprise. In this sense, the Freudian discovery of mental functions as mechanisms in no way transcends the moral realm: every effort to teach or to learn to live life in harmony with the biological necessities of the individual's constitution is in itself an ethical imperative. Freud's morality demands total commitment to the need to overcome psychological deficits that may ultimately cause damage to others. The fact that some of these difficulties have their genesis in the preverbal era merely compels the conclusion that the attempt to repair them can never stop at the boundary of the realm encoded in words.

Whitehead proposes to name efforts to ameliorate such profound and archaic disorders "developmental psychoanalysis." I agree with his judgment that such an orientation is an outgrowth of the succession of dissident movements in psychoanalysis, for the defenders of analytic orthodoxy have been reluctant to tackle the archaic depths of human subjectivity. In 1985, we may be approaching consensus about these controversies: we may all espouse the view that the therapeutic effectiveness of psychoanalysis depends to a very large degree on our ability to describe, simultaneously from the subjective point of view of the analysand and from the consensually confirmable perspective of a scientific observer, the transactions that constitute treatment (see Gedo, 1984b)—thereby training analysands to apprehend aspects of their existence hitherto lacking symbolic representation.

Another way to state this is to emphasize that the curative agent in psychoanalysis is the patient's acquisition of previously missing psychological skills, a process whereby developmental deficits or distortions that lead to renewed conflict are remedied. This viewpoint has been brilliantly presented by Robert Gardner (1983), who showed that the main therapeutic benefit of a correct interpretation is the opportunity it provides the analysand to learn how to make valid interpretations for himself. In contrast, the value of the bit of self-knowledge imparted by the *content* of an interpretation is limited, for the need to interpret the unconscious meanings of human behavior is literally without end.

In Sigmund Freud's terms, the unflinching quest for personal knowledge constitutes the essence of moral deliberation.

References

Abraham, K., Ferenczi, S., Jones, E. & Simmel, E. (1919), *Psychoanalysis and the War Neuroses*. London: International Psycho-Analytic Press, 1921.

Abraham, R. (1982), Freud's mother conflict and the formulation of the oedipal father. *Psychoanal. Review*, 69:441–453.

Baron, S. & Pletsch, C., ed. (1985), *Introspection in Biography: The Biographer's Quest for Self-Awareness*. Hillsdale, NJ: The Analytic Press.

Basch, M. (1975a), Perception, consciousness, and Freud's "Project." *The Annual of Psychoanalysis*, 3:3–19. New York: International Universities Press.

_____ (1975b), Toward a theory that encompasses depression: A revision of existing causal hypotheses in psychoanalysis. In: *Depression and Human Existence*, ed. E. Anthony & T. Benedek. Boston: Little Brown, pp. 483–534.

_____ (1976a), The concept of affect: A re-examination, *J. Amer. Psychoanal. Assn.*, 24:759–777.

_____ (1976b), Psychoanalysis and communication science. *The Annual of Psychoanalysis*, 4:385–422. New York: International Universities Press.

_____ (1976c), Theory formation in Chapter VII: A critique. *J. Amer. Psychoanal. Assn.*, 24:61–100.

_____ (1977), Developmental psychology and explanatory theory in psychoanalysis. *The Annual of Psychoanalysis*, 5:229–263. New York: International Universities Press.

_____ (in press), "How Does Analysis Cure?": An appreciation. *Psychoanal. Inquiry*.

Bergin, A. & Lambert, M. (1978), The evaluation of therapeutic outcomes. In: *Handbook of Psychotherapy and Behavior Change*, 2nd ed., ed. S. Garfield and A. Bergin. New York: Wiley, pp. 139–189.

Bettelheim, B. (1983), *Freud and Man's Soul*. New York: Random House.

217

Billinsky, J. (1969), Jung and Freud (The end of a romance). *Andover Newton Quarterly*, 10:39–43.

Binion, R. (1968) *Frau Lou. Nietzsche's Wayward Pupil.* Princeton, NJ: Princeton University Press.

Bonaparte, M., Freud, A., & Kris, E., eds. (1954), *The Origins of Psychoanalysis.* New York: Basic Books.

Brenner, C. (1983), *The Mind in Conflict.* New York: International Universities Press.

Breuer, J. & Freud, S. (1895), *Studies in Hysteria. Standard Edition,* 2. London: Hogarth, 1955.

Brome, V. (1983), *Ernest Jones: A Biography.* New York: Norton.

Carotenuto, A. (1982), *A Secret Symmetry: Sabina Spielrein Between Jung and Freud.* New York: Pantheon.

Covello, A. (1984), Lettres de Freud: Du scénario de Jones au diagnostic sur Ferenczi. *Confrontation,* 12:63–78.

Crews, F. (1975), *Out of my System: Psychoanalysis, Ideology and Critical Method.* New York: Oxford University Press.

Décarie, T. (1973), *The Infant's Reaction to Strangers.* New York: International Universities Press.

deForest, I. (1954), *The Leaven of Love.* New York: Harper.

Dénes, Z. (1970), *Szivárvány.* Budapest: Gondolat.

Eissler, K. (1953), The effect of the structure of the ego on psychoanalytic technique. *J. Amer. Psychoanal. Assn.,* 1:104–143.

———— (1972), *Talent and Genius.* New York: Quadrangle.

Erle, J. (1979), An approach to the study of analyzability and analyses: The course of forty consecutive cases selected for supervised analysis. *Psychoanal. Quart.,* 48:198–228.

———— & Goldberg, D. (1984), Observations on assessment of analyzability by experienced analysts. *J. Amer. Psychoanal. Assn.,* 32:715–738.

Federn, P. (1933), Obituary, Sándor Ferenczi. *Internat. J. Psycho-Anal.,* 14:467–485.

———— (1952), *Ego Psychology and the Psychoses,* ed. E. Weiss. New York: Basic Books.

Ferenczi, S. (1908–1914), *Contributions to Psychoanalysis,* 2nd ed., retitled *Sex in Psychoanalysis.* New York: Basic Books, 1950.

———— (1908–1926), *Further Contributions to the Theory and Technique of Psychoanalysis,* 2nd ed. New York: Basic Books, 1952.

———— (1908–1933a), *Bausteine zur Psychoanalyse,* Vol. 1 & 2. Leipzig/Wien/Zürich: Internationaler Psychoanalytischer Verlag, 1927; Vols. 3 & 4. Bern: Hans Huber, 1939.

———— (1908–1933b), *Final Contributions to the Problems and Methods of Psychoanalysis.* New York: Basic Books, 1955.

———— (1924), *Thalassa: A Theory of Genitality.* Albany: Psychoanalytic Quarterly, 1938.

_____ (1927), Review of O. Rank's *Technique of Psychoanalysis*. *Int. J. Psycho-Anal.*, 8:93.

_____ & Hollós, I. (1922), *Psycho-Analysis and the Psychic Disorder of General Paresis*. New York & Washington: Nervous and Mental Disease Pub. Co.

_____ & Rank, O. (1924), *The Development of Psychoanalysis*. New York & Washington: Nervous and Mental Disease Pub. Co.

Firestein, S. (1978), *Termination in Psychoanalysis*. New York: International Universities Press.

Fraiberg, S. & Freedman, D. (1964), Studies in the ego development of the congenitally blind. *The Psychoanalytic Study of the Child*, 19:113–169. New York: International Universities Press.

Freedman, D. (1979), The sensory deprivations: An approach to the study of the emergence of affects and capacity for object relationships. *Bull. Menniger Clin.*, 43:29–68.

_____ (1981), The effect of sensory and other deficits in children on their experience of people. *J. Amer. Psychoanal. Assn.*, 29:831–867.

_____ (1982), Of instincts and instinctual drives: Some developmental considerations. *Psychoanal. Inquiry*, 2:153–167.

_____ (1984), The origins of motivation. In: *Psychoanalysis: The Vital Issues*, Vol. I, ed. J. Gedo & G. Pollock. New York: International Universities Press, pp. 17–38.

_____ & Brown, S. (1968), On the role of coenesthetic stimulation in the development of psychic structure. *Psychoanal. Quart.*, 37:412–438.

Freud, A. (1936), *The Ego and the Mechanisms of Defense*. New York: International Universities Press, 1946.

_____ (1965), *Normality and Pathology in Childhood*. New York: International Universities Press.

Freud, E., ed. (1970), *The Letters of Sigmund Freud and Arnold Zweig*. New York: Harcourt, Brace & World.

Freud, M. (1957), *Glory Reflected*. London: Hagus & Robertson.

Freud, S. (1892), Letter to Josef Breuer, *Standard Edition* 1:147–148. London: Hogarth, 1966.

_____ (1895a), Project for a scientific psychology. *Standard Edition*, 1:295–343. London: Hogarth, 1966.

_____ (1895b), On the grounds for detaching a particular syndrome from neurasthenia under the description 'Anxiety neurosis.' *Standard Edition*, 3:90–115. London: Hogarth, 1962.

_____ (1899), Screen Memories, *Standard Edition*, 3:303–322. London: Hogarth Press, 1962.

_____ (1900), *The Interpretation of Dreams. Standard Edition*, 4 & 5. London: Hogarth, 1953.

_____ (1908), Creative writers and day-dreaming. *Standard Edition*, 9:141–153. London: Hogarth, 1959.

_____ (1909), Analysis of a phobia in a five-year-old boy. *Standard Edition*, 10:5–149. London: Hogarth, 1955.

———— (1913), On beginning the treatment (further recommendations on the technique of psycho-analysis I). *Standard Edition*, 12:121–144. London: Hogarth, 1958.

———— (1914a), On narcissism: An introduction. *Standard Edition*, 14:73–102.

———— (1914b), On the history of the psycho-analytic movement. *Standard Edition*, 14:3–66. London: Hogarth, 1957.

———— (1917a), A difficulty in the path of psycho-analysis. *Standard Edition*, 17:137–144.

———— (1917b), Mourning and Melancholia, *Standard Edition*, 14:243–258. London: Hogarth, 1957.

———— (1920), Beyond the pleasure principle. *Standard Edition*, 18:7–61. London: Hogarth, 1955.

———— (1923a), *The ego and the id.* Standard Edition, 19:12–66. London: Hogarth, 1961.

———— (1923b), Dr. Sándor Ferenczi (On his 50th birthday). *Standard Edition*, 19:267–272.

———— (1925), An autobiographical study. *Standard Edition*, 20:3–74. London: Hogarth, 1959.

———— (1926), Inhibitions, symptoms and anxiety. *Standard Edition*, 20:77–178. London: Hogarth, 1959.

———— (1931), Female sexuality. *Standard Edition*, 21:225–246. London: Hogarth, 1961.

———— (1933), Sándor Ferenczi. *Standard Edition*, 22:226–232. London: Hogarth, 1964.

———— (1937a), Analysis terminable and interminable. *Standard Edition*, 23:216–253. London: Hogarth, 1964.

———— (1937b), Lou Andreas-Salomé. *Standard Edition*, 23:297–298. London: Hogarth, 1964.

———— (1939), Moses and monotheism. *Standard Edition*, 23:7–140. London: Hogarth, 1964.

———— (1969), Some early unpublished letters of Freud. *Internat. J. Psycho-Anal.*, 50:419–427.

Friedman, L. (1982), The humanistic trend in recent psychoanalytic theory. *Psychoanal. Quart.*, 51:353–371.

Gardner, R. (1983), *Self Inquiry.* Boston: Atlantic-Little Brown.

Gay, P. (1976), *Art and Act. On Causes in History—Manet, Gropius, Mondrian.* New York: Harper & Row.

———— (1978), *Freud, Jews, and Other Germans.* New York: Oxford University Press.

Gedo, J. (1967), The wise baby reconsidered. *Psychological Issues*, Monogr. 34/35. New York: International Universities Press, 1976, pp. 357–378.

———— (1968), Freud's self-analysis and his scientific ideas. *Psychological Issues*, Monogr. 34/35. New York: International Universities Press, 1976, pp. 286–306.

_____ (1972a), The dream of reason produces monsters. *J. Amer. Psychoanal. Assn.*, 20:199–223.

_____ (1972b), *Haute Cuisine. Contemporary Psychology*, 17:528–529.

_____ (1975a), To Heinz Kohut: On his 60th birthday. *The Annual of Psychoanalysis*, 3:313–322. New York: International Universities Press.

_____ (1975b), Forms of idealization in the analytic transference. *J. Amer. Psychoanal. Assn.*, 23:485–505.

_____ (1979), *Beyond Interpretation*. New York: International Universities Press.

_____ (1980), Reflections on some current controversies in psychoanalysis. *J. Amer. Psychoanal. Assn.*, 28:363–383.

_____ (1981a), A psychoanalyst reports at mid-career. *Amer. J. Psychiatry*, 136:646–649.

_____ (1981b), *Advances in Clinical Psychoanalysis*. New York: International Universities Press.

_____ (1981c), Measure for measure: A response. *Psychoanal. Inquiry*, 1:286–316.

_____ (1983), *Portraits of the Artist: Psychoanalysis of Creativity and Its Vicissitudes*. New York: Guilford.

_____ (1984a), *Psychoanalysis and Its Discontents*. New York: Guilford.

_____ (1984b), Discussion of Joseph Lichtenberg's "The empathic mode of perception and alternative vantage points for psychoanalytic work." In: *Empathy II*, ed. J. Lichtenberg, M. Bernstein, & D. Silver. Hillsdale, NJ: The Analytic Press, pp. 137–142.

_____ (in prep.), Intractable character pathology and childhood psychosis.

_____ & Goldberg, A. (1973), *Models of the Mind*. Chicago: University of Chicago Press.

_____ & Pollock, G. (1976), *Freud: The Fusion of Science and Humanism. Psychological Issues* Monogr. 34/35.

_____ & Wolf, E. (1970), The "Ich." letters. *Psychological Issues*, Monogr. 34/35, 1976, pp. 71–86.

_____ _____ (1973), Freud's Novelas Ejemplares. *Psychological Issues*, Monogr. 34/35, 1976, pp. 87–114.

_____ (1976), From the history of introspective psychology: The humanist strain. *Psychological Issues*, Monogr. 34/35, pp. 11–45.

Gill, M. (1976), Metapsychology is not psychology. *Psychological Issues*, Monogr. 36, pp. 71–105.

_____ (1983), Analysis of Transference, Vol. I. *Psychological Issues*, Monogr. 53. New York: International Universities Press.

_____ & Hoffman, I. (1983), Analysis of Transference, Vol. II. *Psychological Issues*, Monogr. 54. New York: International Universities Press.

_____ & Holzman, P., ed. (1976), Psychology Versus Metapsychology: Psychoanalytic Essays in Memory of George S. Klein. *Psychological Issues*, Monogr. 36. New York: International Universities Press.

Gitelson, M. (1964), On the identity crisis of American psychoanalysis. *J. Amer. Psychoanal. Assn.*, 12:451–476.

Goldberg, A., ed. (1978), *The Psychology of the Self: A Casebook.* New York: International Universities Press.

————, ed. (1980), *Advances in Self Psychology.* New York: International Universities Press.

Greenacre, P. (1971), *Emotional Growth,* 2 vols. New York: International Universities Press.

Groddeck, G. (1977), *The Meaning of Illness: Selected Psychoanalytic Writings.* New York: International Universities Press.

Grossman, W. (1976), Knightmare in armor: Reflections on Wilhelm Reich's contributions to psychoanalysis. *Psychiatry*, 39:376–385.

———— (1984), Freud and Horney: A study of psychoanalytic models via the analysis of a controversy. Unpublished manuscript.

Grünbaum, A. (1984), *The Foundations of Psychoanalysis.* Berkeley: University of California Press.

Grunberger, B. (1980), From the "active technique" to the "confusion of tongues." In: *Psychoanalysis in France,* S. Lebovici & D. Widlöcher. ed. New York: International Universities Press.

Gustafson, J. (1984), An integration of brief dynamic psychotherapy. *Amer. J. Psychiatry*, 141:935–944.

Hamilton, V. (1982), *Narcissus and Oedipus: The Children of Psychoanalysis.* London: Routledge & Kegan Paul.

Hartmann, H. (1939), *Ego Psychology and the Problem of Adaptation.* New York: International Universities Press, 1958.

———— (1956), The development of the ego concept in Freud's work. In: *Essays in Ego Psychology.* New York: International Universities Press, 1964, pp. 268–296.

———— (1964), *Essays on Ego Psychology.* New York: International Universities Press.

————, Kris, E., & Loewenstein, R. (1964), Papers on Psychoanalytic Psychology. *Psychological Issues,* Monogr. 14. New York: International Universities Press.

Heller, E. (1978), The dismantling of a marionette theater; or, Psychology and the misinterpretation of literature. *Critical Inquiry*, 4:417–432.

Holland, N. (1975), *Five Readers Reading.* New Haven: Yale University Press.

Holt, R. (1965), A review of some of Freud's biological assumptions and their influence on his theories. In: *Psychoanalysis and Current Biological Thought,* N. Greenfield & W. Lewis. ed. Madison: University of Wisconsin Press, 1967, pp. 93–124.

———— (1967a), Beyond vitalism and mechanism: Freud's concept of psychic energy. In: *Science and Psychoanalysis,* Vol. 11, J. Masserman. ed. New York: Grune & Stratton, pp. 1–41.

REFERENCES

_____ (1967b), The development of the primary process: A structural view. *Psychological Issues,* Monogr. 18/19. New York: International Universities Press, pp. 344–383.

_____ (1976), Drive or wish? A reconsideration of the psychoanalytic theory of motivation. *Psychological Issues* Monograph 36. New York: International Universities Press. Pp. 158–196.

Homans, P. (1979), *Jung in Context,* Chicago: University of Chicago Press.

Imber, R. (1984), Reflections on Kohut and Sullivan. *Contemp. Psychoanal.,* 20:363–380.

Isakower, O. (1938), A contribution to the patho-psychology of phenomena associated with falling asleep. *Internat. J. Psycho-Anal.,* 19:331–345.

Jones, E. (1933), Sandor Ferenczi, 1873–1933. *Internat. J. Psycho-Anal.,* 14:463–466.

_____ (1953/1955/1957), *The Life and Work of Sigmund Freud,* 3 volumes. New York: Basic Books.

Jung, C. (1963), *Memories, Dreams, Reflections.* Trans. R. Winston & C. Winston. New York: Vintage.

Kernberg, O. (1975), *Borderline Conditions and Pathological Narcissism.* New York: Jason Aronson.

Klein, G. (1968), The ego in psychoanalysis: A concept in search of identity. In: *Psychoanalytic Theory: An Exploration of Essentials.* New York: International Universities Press, 1976, pp. 121–160.

_____ (1976), *Psychoanalytic Theory: An Exploration of Essentials.* New York: International Universities Press.

Klein, M. (1923), Early analysis. *Writings,* 1:77–105. New York: Free Press, 1984.

_____ (1926), The psychological principles of early analysis. *Writings,* 1:128–138. New York: Free Press, 1984.

_____ (1927a), Symposium on child-analysis. *Writings,* 1:139–169. New York: Free Press, 1984.

_____ (1927b), Criminal tendencies in normal children. *Writings,* 1:170–185. New York: Free Press, 1984.

_____ (1928), Early stages of the Oedipus conflict. *Writings,* 1:186–198. New York: Free Press, 1984.

_____ (1929), Personification in the play of children. *Writings,* 1:199–209. New York: Free Press, 1984.

_____ (1931), A contribution to the theory of intellectual inhibition. *Writings,* 1:236–247. New York: Free Press, 1984.

_____ (1932), *The Psycho-Analysis of Children. Writings,* 2. New York: Free Press, 1984.

_____ (1933), The early development of conscience in the child. *Writings,* 1:248–257. New York: Free Press, 1984.

———— (1935), A contribution to the psychogenesis of manic-depressive states. *Writings*, 1:262–289. New York: Free Press, 1984.

———— (1936), Weaning. *Writings*, 1:290–305. New York: Free Press, 1984.

———— (1937), Love, guilt, and reparation. *Writings*, 1:306–343. New York: Free Press, 1984.

———— (1940), Mourning and its relation to manic-depressive states. *Writings*, 1:344–369. New York: Free Press, 1984.

———— (1945), The Oedipus complex in the light of early anxieties. *Writings*, 1:370–419. New York: Free Press, 1984.

———— (1946), Notes on some schizoid mechanisms. *Writings*, 3:1–24. New York: Free Press, 1984.

———— (1948), On the theory of anxiety and guilt. *Writings*, 3:25–42. New York: Free Press, 1984.

———— (1952a), On the origins of transference. *Writings*, 3:43–47. New York: Free Press, 1984.

———— (1952b), The mutual influences in the development of ego and id. *Writings*, 3:57–60. New York: Free Press, 1984.

———— (1952c), Some theoretical conclusions regarding the emotional life of the infant. *Writings*, 3:61–93. New York: Free Press, 1984.

———— (1952d), On observing the behavior of young infants. *Writings*, 3:94–121. New York: Free Press, 1984.

———— (1955a), The psycho-analytic play technique: Its history and significance. *Writings*, 3:122–140. New York: Free Press, 1984.

———— (1955b), On identification. *Writings*, 3:141–175. New York: Free Press, 1984.

———— (1957), Envy and gratitude. *Writings*, 3:176–235. New York: Free Press, 1984.

———— (1958), On the development of mental functioning. *Writings*, 3:236–247. New York: Free Press, 1984.

———— (1959), Our adult world and its roots in infancy. *Writings*, 3:247–263. New York: Free Press, 1984.

———— (1961), *Narrative of a Child Analysis*. *Writings*, 4. New York: Free Press, 1984.

Kohut, H. (1957), Observations on the psychological functions of music. In: *The Search for the Self*. New York: International Universities Press, 1978, pp. 233–253.

———— (1959), Introspection, empathy, and psychoanalysis: An examination of the relationship between mode of observation and theory. In: *The Search for the Self*. New York: International Universities Press, 1978, pp. 205–232.

———— (1966a), Forms and transformations of narcissism. In: *The Search for the Self*. New York: International Universities Press, 1978, pp. 427–460.

———— (1966b), "Termination of training analysis" by Luisa G. de Alvarez de Toledo, León Grinberg, and Marie Langer. In: *The Search for the Self*. New York: International Universities Press, 1978. Pp. 409–422.

_____ (1968), The psychoanalytic treatment of narcissistic personality disorders: Outline of a systematic approach. In: *The Search for the Self*. New York: International Universities Press, 1978, pp. 477–509.

_____ (1970), "The self: A contribution to its place in theory and technique" by D. C. Levin. In: *The Search for the Self*. New York: International Universities Press, 1978, pp. 577–588.

_____ (1971), *The Analysis of the Self*. New York: International Universities Press.

_____ (1972), Thoughts on narcissism and narcissistic rage. In: *The Search for the Self*. New York: International Universities Press, 1978, pp. 615–658.

_____ (1973a), The future of psychoanalysis. In: *The Search for the Self*. New York: International Universities Press, 1978, pp. 663–684.

_____ (1973b), Psychoanalysis is a troubled world. In: *The Search for the Self*. New York: International Universities Press, 1978, pp. 511–546.

_____ (1973c), The psychoanalyst in the community of scholars. In: *The Search for the Self*. New York: International Universities Press, 1978, pp. 685–724.

_____ (1976), Creativeness, charisma, group psychology. In: *The Search for the Self*. New York: International Universities Press, 1978, pp. 793–843.

_____ (1977), *The Restoration of the Self*. New York: International Universities Press.

_____ (1978a), Conclusion: The search for the analyst's self. In: *The Search for the Self*. New York: International Universities Press, pp. 931–938.

_____ (1978b), Remarks about the formation of the self. In: *The Search for the Self*. New York: International Universities Press, pp. 737–770.

_____ (1978c), Letters. In: *The Search for the Self*. New York: International Universities Press, pp. 851–929.

_____ (1978d), Narcissism as a resistance and as a driving force in psychoanalysis. In: *The Search for the Self*. New York: International Universities Press, pp. 547–561.

_____ (1978e), "On the adolescent process as a transformation of the self" by Ernest S. Wolf, John E. Gedo, and David M. Terman. In: *The Search for the Self*. New York: International Universities Press, pp. 659–662.

_____ (1978f), "Some comments on the origin of the influencing machine" by Louis Linn. In: *The Search for the Self*. New York: International Universities Press, pp. 259–261.

_____ (1978g), *The Search for the Self*, 2 vols, ed. P. Ornstein. New York: International Universities Press.

_____ (1978h), Psychoanalysis and the interpretation of literature: A correspondence with Erich Heller. *Critical Inquiry*, 4:433–450.

_____ (1979), The two analyses of Mr. Z. *Internat. J. Psycho-Anal.*, 60:3–18.

_____ (1980a), From a letter to one of the participants at the Chicago conference on the psychology of the self. In: *Advances in Self Psychology*, A. Goldberg. ed. New York: International Universities Press, pp. 449–456.

———— (1980b), From a letter to a colleague. In: *Advances in Self Psychology*, A. Goldberg. ed. New York: International Universities Press, pp. 456–469.

———— (1980c), Reflections on "Advances in Self Psychology." In: *Advances in Self Psychology*, A. Goldberg. ed. New York: International Universities Press, pp. 473–554.

———— (1982), Introspection, empathy, and the semi-circle of mental health. *Internat. J. Psycho-Anal.*, 63:395–407.

———— (1983), Selected problems of self psychological theory. In: *Reflections on Self Psychology*, J. Lichtenberg & S. Kaplan. ed. Hillsdale, NJ: The Analytic Press, pp. 387–416.

———— (1984), *How Does Analysis Cure?* Chicago: University of Chicago Press.

———— & Seitz, P. (1963), Concepts and theories of psychoanalysis. In: *The Search for the Self*. New York: International Universities Press, 1978, pp. 337–374.

———— & Wolf, E. (1978), The disorders of the self and their treatment: An outline. *Internat. J. Psycho-Anal.*, 59:413–426.

Leavy, S., ed. (1964), *The Freud Journal of Lou Andreas-Salomé*. New York: Basic Books.

Levin, D. (1970), The self: A contribution to its place in theory and technique. *Internat. J. Psycho-Anal.*, 50:41–51.

Lichtenberg, J. (1982), Frames of reference for viewing aggression. *Psychoanal. Inquiry*, 2:213–232.

———— (1983), *Psychoanalysis and Infant Research*. Hillsdale, NJ: The Analytic Press.

———— (1984), The empathic mode of perception and alternative vantage points for psychoanalytic work. In: *Empathy II*, J. Lichtenberg, M. Bornstein, & D. Silver. ed. Hillsdale, NJ: The Analytic Press, pp. 113–136.

Livingstone, A. (1985), *Salomé: Her Life and Work*. Mt. Kisco, NY: Moyer Bell.

Loch, W. (1971), Determinanten des Ichs. Beiträge David Rapaports zur psychoanalytischen Ich-Theorie. *Psyche*, 25:374–400.

Loewald, H. (1971), On motivation and instinct theory. *The Psychoanalytic Study of the Child*, 26:91–128. New York: Quadrangle.

———— (1978), Instinct theory, object relations and psychic-structure formation. *J. Amer. Psychoanal. Assn.*, 26:493–506.

Luke, D. & Reeves, N. (1978), Introduction. In: H. Kleist, *The Marquise of O and Other Stories*. Harmondsworth, England: Penguin.

Maass, J. (1983), *Kleist: A Biography*. New York: Farrar, Straus & Giroux.

Mahler, M., Pine, F., & Bergman, A. (1975), *The Psychological Birth of the Human Infant: Symbiosis and Individuation*. New York: Basic Books.

Masson, J. (1984), *The Assault on Truth: Freud's Suppression of the Seduction Theory*. New York: Farrar, Straus, & Giroux.

————, ed. (1985) *The Complete Letters of Sigmund Freud to Wilhelm Fliess*. Cambridge, MA: Harvard University Press.

McGuire, W., ed. (1974), *The Freud/Jung Letters*, trans. R. Manheim & R.F.C. Hull. Princeton: Princeton University Press.

Miller, P., ed. (1982), *An Abyss Deep Enough. Letters of Heinrich von Kleist, with a Selection of Essays and Anecdotes.* New York: Dutton.

Modell, A. (1983), The two contexts of the self. Presented to the 50th Anniversary Symposium, Boston Psychoanalytic Society & Institute, October 30.

Moraitis, G. (1985), The psychoanalyst's role in the biographer's quest for self-awareness. In: *Introspection in Biography*, S. Baron & C. Pletsch. ed. Hillsdale, NJ: The Analytic Press, pp. 319–354.

O'Shaughnessy, E. (1984), "Psychoanalysis and Infant Research" by Joseph D. Lichtenberg. *Internat. J. Psycho-Anal.*, 65:492–495.

Panel (1954), The widening scope of indications for psychoanalysis. L. Stone, reporter. *J. Amer. Psychoanal. Assn.*, 2:565–620.

―――― (1974), Advances in psychoanalytic technique. A. Freedman, reporter. *J. Phila. Assn. for Psychoanal.*, 1:44–54.

―――― (1984), The neutrality of the analyst in the analytic situation. R. Leider, reporter. *J. Amer. Psychoanal. Assn.*, 32:573–588.

Parens, H. (1979), *The Development of Aggression in Early Childhood.* New York: Jason Aronson.

Peters, H. (1962), *My Sister, My Spouse.* New York: Norton.

Pfeiffer, E., ed. (1972), *Sigmund Freud and Lou Andreas-Salomé Letters*, trans. W. & E. Robson-Scott. New York: Harcourt Brace Jovanovich.

Radó, S. (1933), Obituary, Sándor Ferenczi. *Psychoanal. Quart.*, 2:356–358.

Rapaport, D. (1942), *Emotions and Memory.* Menninger Clinic Monograph Series #2. Baltimore: Williams & Wilkins.

―――― (1951), *Organization and Pathology of Thought. Selected Sources.* New York: Columbia University Press.

―――― (1959), The Structure of Psychoanalytic Theory. A Systematizing Attempt. *Psychological Issues*, Monogr. 6 New York: International Universities Press.

―――― (1967), *The Collected Papers of David Rapaport.* ed. M. Gill. New York: Basic Books.

―――― (1974), *The History of the Concept of Association of Ideas.* New York: International Universities Press.

Reich, W. (1933). *Character Analysis.* New York: Orgone Institute Press, 1948.

Ricoeur, P. (1970), *Freud and Philosophy.* New Haven: Yale University Press.

Rieff, P. (1959), *Freud: The Mind of the Moralist.* New York: Viking.

―――― (1966), *The Triumph of the Therapeutic.* New York: Harper & Row.

Roazen, P. (1968), *Freud: Political and Social Thought.* New York: Knopf.

Robbins, M. (1983), Toward a new mind model for the primitive personalities. *Internat. J. Psycho-Anal.*, 64:127–148.

Rorty, R. (in press), Freud and the vocabulary of moral deliberation. In: *Psychiatry and the Humanities.* J. Smith. ed. Baltimore: The Johns Hopkins University Press.

Rosenblatt, A. & Thickstun, J. (1977), Modern Psychoanalytic Concepts in a General Psychology. *Psychological Issues,* Monogr. 42/43.

Rubinstein, B. (1965), Psychoanalytic theory and the mind-body problem. In: *Psychoanalysis and Current Biological Thought,* N. Greenfield & W. Lewis. ed. Madison: University of Wisconsin Press.

‾‾‾‾‾‾ (1967), Explanation and mere description: A metascientific examination of certain aspects of the psychoanalytic theory of motivation. *Psychological Issues,* Monogr. 18/19, pp. 20–77.

‾‾‾‾‾‾ (1974), On the role of classificatory processes in mental functioning: Aspects of a psychoanalytic theoretical model. *Psychoanalysis and Contemporary Science,* 3:101–185.

‾‾‾‾‾‾ (1976a), On the possibility of a strictly clinical psychoanalytic theory: An essay in the philosophy of psychoanalysis. *Psychological Issues,* Monogr. 36, pp. 229–264.

‾‾‾‾‾‾ (1976b), Hope, fear, wish, expectation and fantasy. *Psychoanalysis and Contemporary Science,* 5:3–60.

Sadow, L. (1984), Two modes of psychoanalytic thought. In: *Psychoanalysis: The Vital Issues,* Vol. I. ed. J. Gedo & G. Pollock. New York: International Universities Press, pp. 413–429.

Salomé, L. (1921), Narzissmus als Doppelrichtung. *Imago,* 7:361–386. Also (1962), trans. S. Leavy, *Psychoanal. Quart.,* 31:1–30.

Sander, L. (1983), To begin with—reflections on ontogeny. In: *Reflections on Self-Psychology.* ed. J. Lichtenberg & S. Kaplan. Hillsdale, NJ: Analytic Press.

Schaefer, M. (1975), Kleist's "About the puppet theater" and the narcissism of the artist. *Amer. Imago,* 32:366–388.

Schafer, R. (1968), *Aspects of Internalization.* New York: International Universities Press.

‾‾‾‾‾‾ (1976), *A New Language for Psychoanalysis.* New York: Yale University Press.

‾‾‾‾‾‾ (1978), *Language and Insight.* New Haven: Yale University Press.

Schlessinger, N., Gedo, J., Miller, J., Pollock, G., Sabshin, M., & Sadow, L. (1967), The scientific styles of Breuer and Freud and the origins of psychoanalysis. *Psychological Issues,* Monogr. 34/35, 1976, pp. 187–207.

‾‾‾‾‾‾ & Robbins, F. (1983), *A Developmental View of the Psychoanalytic Process.* New York: International Universities Press.

Schorske, C. (1980), *"Fin de Siècle" Vienna.* New York: Vintage.

Schur, M. (1972), *Freud: Living and Dying.* New York: International Universities Press.

Schwaber, E. (1981), Empathy: A mode of analytic listening. *Psychoanal. Inquiry,* 1:357–392.

‾‾‾‾‾‾ (1983), Psychoanalytic listening and psychic reality. *Internat. Rev. Psycho-Anal.,* 10:379–392.

Schwartz, F. (1973), Psychoanalytic research in attention and learning: Some findings and the question of clinical relevance. *The Annual of Psychoanalysis*, 1:119–215.

———— & Schiller, P. (1970), A psychoanalytic model of attention and learning. *Psychological Issues* Monogr. 23.

Segal, H. (1974), *Introduction to the Work of Melanie Klein*, 2nd ed. New York: Basic Books.

Silverman, D., Silverman, L. (1984), "Advances in Clinical Psychoanalysis," by John E. Gedo. *Rev. of Psychoanal. Books*, 2:321–341.

Skura, M. (1981), *The Literary Use of the Psychoanalytic Process*. New Haven: Yale University Press.

Spence, D. (1984), *Narrative Truth and Historical Truth*. New York: Norton.

Stepansky, P. (1983), *In Freud's Shadow: Adler in Context*. Hillsdale, NJ: The Analytic Press.

Stern, D. (1983), The early development of schemas of self and other, and of various experiences of "self with other." In: *Reflections on Self-Psychology*, ed. J. Lichtenberg & S. Kaplan. Hillsdale, NJ: The Analytic Press, pp. 49–84.

Sulloway, F. (1979), *Freud: Biologist of the Mind*. New York: Basic Books.

Swales, P. (1982a), Freud, Johann Weier, and the status of seduction: The role of the witch in the conception of fantasy. Privately printed.

———— (1982b), Freud, Minna Bernays, and the conquest of Rome. *New American Review*, 1:1–23.

———— (1982c), Freud, Fliess, and fratricide: The role of Fliess in Freud's conception of paranoia. Privately printed.

———— (1983a), Freud, Martha Bernays, and the language of flowers: Masturbation, cocaine, and the inflation of fantasy. Privately printed.

———— (1983b), Freud, cocaine, and sexual chemistry: The role of cocaine in Freud's conception of the libido. Privately printed.

———— (1983c), Freud, Krafft-Ebing, and the witches: The role of Krafft-Ebing in Freud's flight into fantasy. Privately printed.

Swanson, D. (1977), A critique of psychic energy as an explanatory concept. *J. Amer. Psychoanal. Assn.*, 25:603–633.

Terman, D. (1976), Distortions of the Oedipus complex in severe pathology: Some vicissitudes of self development and their relationship to the Oedipus complex. Presented to the American Psychoanalytic Association, December.

Tolpin, M. (1980), Discussion of "Psychoanalytic theories of the self: An integration" by Morton Shane and Estelle Shane. In: *Advances in Self Psychology*, ed. A. Goldberg. New York: International Universities Press, pp. 47–68.

Tomkins, S. (1980), Affects as the primary motivational system. In: *Feelings and Emotions*, M. Arnold. ed. New York: Academic Press, pp. 101–110.

Török, M. (1979), L'os de la fin. *Confrontation*, 1:163–186.

—— (1984), La correspondance Ferenczi-Freud. La vie de la lettre dans l'histoire de la psychanalyse. *Confrontation*, 12:79–100.

Valenstein, A. (1973), On attachment to painful feelings and the negative therapeutic reaction. *The Psychoanalytic Study of the Child*, 28:365–392.

Waelder, R. (1962), Psychoanalysis, scientific method, and philosophy. In: *Psychoanalysis: Observation, Theory, Application*. New York: International Universities Press, 1976, pp. 248–274.

Wallerstein, R. (1983), Psychoanalysis and psychotherapy. Relative roles reconsidered. Presented to the 50th Anniversary Symposium, Boston Psychoanalytic Society and Institute, October 29.

Weiss, J.M. (1985), A model of the mind as alive: Theoretical and clinical considerations. Presented to the San Francisco Psychoanalytic Society, April 8.

White, R. (1963), *Ego and Reality in Psychoanalytic Theory. Psychological Issues* Monogr. 11.

Whitehead, C. (1983), On the Asclepian spirit and the future of psychoanalysis. Presented to the American Psychoanalytic Association, December.

Winnicott, D. (1931–1956), *Collected Papers*. New York: Basic Books, 1958.

—— (1957–1963), *The Maturational Processes and the Facilitating Environment*. New York: International Universities Press.

—— (1964), Review of C. G. Jung, *Memories, Dreams, Reflections. Internat. J. Psycho-Anal.*, 45:450–455.

Wolf, E. (1976), Ambience and abstinence. *The Annual of Psychoanalysis*, 4:101–115. New York: International Universities Press.

Zelmanowitz, J. (1968), Review of *The Collected Papers of David Rapaport. Psychiatry*, 31:292–299.

Index

231